# FLOWERS OF THE WIND
## Papers on Ritual, Myth and Symbolism in California and the Southwest

Edited by

# Thomas C. Blackburn

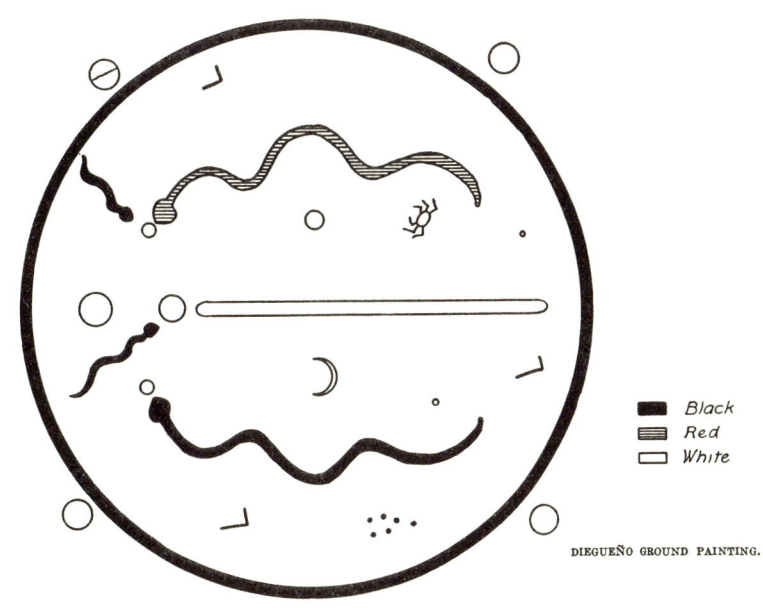

DIEGUEÑO GROUND PAINTING.

**BALLENA PRESS**
P.O. Box 1366
Socorro, New Mexico 87801

ISBN 0-87919-066-3

Copyright © 1977 by Ballena Press.

All rights reserved. No part of this book may be reproduced in any form or by any means without the prior written permission of the publisher, excepting brief quotes used in connection with reviews written specifically for inclusion in a magazine or newspaper.

Printed in the United States of America.
1st Printing.

# Contents

FOREWORD
    by *Lowell John Bean* . . . . . . . . . . . . 5

INTRODUCTION
    by *Thomas Blackburn* . . . . . . . . . . . . 7

THE ROLE OF SECRECY IN A PUEBLO SOCIETY
    by *Elizabeth Brandt* . . . . . . . . . . . . 11

BREATH IN SHAMANIC CURING
    by *Donald Bahr* . . . . . . . . . . . . . 29

HEART AND FECES: SYMBOLS OF MORTALITY
IN THE DYING GOD MYTH
    by *C. Patrick Morris* . . . . . . . . . . . 41

THE SUPERNATURAL WORLD OF THE KAWAIISU
    by *Maurice Zigmond* . . . . . . . . . . . . 59

BEHAVIORAL PATTERNS IN CHEMEHUEVI MYTHS
    by *Carobeth Laird* . . . . . . . . . . . . 97

NATIVE CALIFORNIA CONCEPTS OF THE AFTERLIFE
    by *Richard Applegate* . . . . . . . . . . . 105

WEALTH, WORK, AND WORLD VIEW IN NATIVE NORTHWEST CALIFORNIA:
SACRED SIGNIFICANCE AND PSYCHOANALYTIC SYMBOLISM
    by *John and Donna Bushnell* . . . . . . . . . 120

REFERENCES . . . . . . . . . . . . . . . . . 183

# Foreword

The publication of this volume of the Ballena Press Anthropological Papers marks the beginning of a new era in the history of the series, for Thomas Blackburn, an old friend and valued colleague, will henceforth join me as co-editor. It is particularly fitting that Dr. Blackburn's editorship should begin with a volume which he has personally and painstakingly assembled; it is also appropriate that the primary theme of the volume (the philosophical bases of hunting and gathering societies) is one to which he has himself recently contributed. The subject matter is one of particular importance to anthropologists, inasmuch as they are now beginning to seriously reassess much earlier "wisdom" concerning simpler stages of socio-cultural development. I believe this volume will serve as a significant catalyst for research in this field. It will do this not only because there has tended to be a dearth of research in the subject area, but also because the volume reflects theoretical and methodological points of view of a very far-reaching order. However, the reader should not expect an integrated or coordinated viewpoint throughout the volume--the several authors bring a variety of methods, insights, and theoretical stances to their analyses of the societies which they consider, and it is virtually certain that each reader will find a great deal with which to both agree and disagree. But that, of course, is a primary function of a work such as this, and I congratulate the various authors for a series of stimulating and thought-provoking papers. I also congratulate Dr. Blackburn for eliciting and producing this timely study--I look forward with great anticipation to our future collaboration in editing the Ballena Press Anthropological Papers.

Lowell John Bean<br>
CSU Hayward<br>
November 1976

# Introduction
## by
## Thomas C. Blackburn

In spite of the burgeoning interest in the hunting-gathering way of life that followed the publication of *Man the Hunter* in 1968, the greatest emphasis in recent anthropological research has been on the techno-economic systems of peoples who today occupy environments that by any standard must be considered marginal at best. It is somewhat ironic that in this respect California anthropology has been something of a microcosm of the very field that has tended to overlook it and its corrective data on complex nonagricultural societies in favorable environments. For a variety of reasons, many of them interrelated, a majority of contemporary anthropologists conducting research in California or adjacent areas such as the Great Basin have employed, either explicitly or implicitly, some form of ecological perspective, model, or paradigm. It is evident that such approaches have been exceptionally productive; they have furnished new theoretical insights, stimulated the development of completely new bodies of data, and provided an integrative framework for a growing number of scholars with diverse (but often parallel) interests and disciplinary backgrounds (Bean and King 1974; Bean and Blackburn 1976:5-10). However, it might also be suggested that the virtual dominance of theory by the ecological perspective could perhaps be considered something of a mixed blessing; other, equally valid approaches and problems may occasionally have been overlooked or neglected in the rush to exploit what has become a rather popular paradigm. Such an omission might very well result after a time in a gradual, inadvertent reintroduction of bias into what is more and more frequently being referred to as the "new persepctive" in Californianist studies. That such a development would be unfortunate is readily apparent--how best to correct the situation, however, is less obvious, although the encouragement and exploration of alternative research interests, strategies, and models would seem to be a logical beginning.

In April 1976, a symposium on "Mythology, Ritual, and World View in Native California and the Greater Southwest" was organized for the annual meeting of the Southwestern Anthropological Association in San Francisco, prompted by two major factors: (1) a growing realization that present information on the ideological aspects of cultures with relatively simple technologies is seldom either current or entirely satisfactory from the standpoint of contemporary anthropological theory; and (2) a genuine interest in stimulating the kind of alternate approach referred to earlier. The response of the scholarly community to the call for papers was gratifying--there seemed to be a great deal of interest in symbolic and cognitive behavior among the anthropologists who were initially contacted, even when they were unable to participate directly in the symposium, while those who did participate approached the topic from diverse points of view and with quite varied concerns in mind that rather accurately reflect the present state of the art. Some might argue that such a lack of methodological or theoretical uniformity detracts from the value of the present volume, the core of which is comprised primarily of revised and expanded versions of the papers initially presented in San Francisco, since a frequent criticism leveled at works that represent the proceedings of particular symposia is the absence of unifying themes or common perspectives. But in the present case, at least, such an argument would, I believe, somewhat miss the point--*Flowers of the Wind* neither claims nor attempts to be either the delineation of a coherent paradigm or an exploration of its implications. It does, however, offer fresh data and new syntheses or interpretations of old data, and outlines areas of study that might profitably be explored at greater length elsewhere. In addition, certain conclusions that may play a significant role in future research on the topic of ritual, myth, and symbolism in western North America are at least implicitly suggested, even if not explicitly stated.

In one way or another, most of the papers in this volume are concerned with analyzing or explaining some facet of behavior in terms of various existential or normative postulates, emic categories, or cognitive structures--in other words, in terms of some aspect of what is generally referred to as *Weltanschauung* or world view. This is both understandable and predictable in light of the current debate between the materialists and the idealists over etic as opposed to emic models-- it might very well be that the only logical alternative to the ecological paradigm with equivalent explanatory potential would be a paradigm based on some refinement of the concept of world view. This conclusion is certainly implicit in a great deal of contemporary research other than that reported upon here (e.g., Blackburn 1975; Bean 1975)--it is also, of course, an important element in a time-honored tradition that would include Benedict's 'configurationalism', Opler's concept of 'themes', and Kearney's recent work on world view in general. (Parenthetically, it is ironic that two of the finest examples of the ecological perspective--White's *Luiseño Social Organization* [1963] and Bean's *Mukat's People* [1972]--are also excellent arguments for the usefulness of world view concepts!) Thus at least a portion of the resurgence of interest in symbolic behavior that I commented upon earlier could be seen as resulting from a common perception of many anthropologists that the tentative outlines of a new, cognitive paradigm may be beginning to emerge from the concerted efforts of scholars in such diverse fields, for example, as anthropology, psychology, linguistics, physiology, or philosophy. Hopefully, the present volume will encourage others to examine their own data in terms of such a general schema.

Another conclusion (and, in fact, a corrolary of the first) that seems implicit in the papers presented here involves the complex issue of interrelationships between societies in different cultural regions of western North America. One of the unexpected but serendipitous results of the symposium was the appearance of several papers that indirectly touched upon the old but unresolved problem of cultural similarities between California and the Southwest, a problem usually discussed primarily in terms of historical factors. Bean, for example, recently observed in a new introduction to William Duncan Strong's classic *Aboriginal Society in Southern California* [1929] that "repeatedly, [Strong] discusses southwestern influences, offering hints of the harvest awaiting researchers who will explore the relationships of southern California culture to southwestern cultural traditions. Needless to say, the impact of southwestern influence on southern California is scarcely appreciated, and because of deemphasis on diffusionist studies in recent years represents an almost totally neglected field of study" (1972:xvi). But again it may very well be that the most significant similarities (and differences?) lie not in the area of social structure but in *Weltanschauung*. I have commented elsewhere (Blackburn 1975) on the often remarkable similarities in values, basic assumptions, symbolic themes, and other elements of world view that frequently characterize quite widely separated societies in California and the Greater Southwest, and Bean (1975) has made a comparable observation in a discussion of native concepts of causality. Certainly the papers presented here clearly reinforce this suggestion by abstracting some of the underlying uniformities in points of view, social strategies, ritual forms, and symbolic expressions from the bewildering array of diverse and seemingly discrepant ethnographic details recorded by anthropologists over the years about various native societies. Perhaps the next step should be to recognize the fact that we may be dealing with complex permutations of elements within common cognitive sets that appear to have a wide geographic distribution and considerable time depth, and explore in detail the precise nature of both the similarities and the differences in world view that exist between societies in this part of the world in order to develop an explanatory paradigm that would offer a truly viable alternative to the ecological perspective.

    I would like to take this opportunity to thank the various people who have helped to make this book a reality. My co-editor, Lowell Bean, first suggested a conference on world views and then provided necessary advice and encouragement (some of it rather forcefully expressed) when I occasionally faltered. Michael Kearney generously provided unpublished materials on several occasions, and was a discussant at the SWAA symposium in San Francisco. Harry Lawton brought Dr. Zigmond's paper on the Kawaiisu to my attention initially, and suggested its inclusion here. Pat Harrell, as on so many other occasions, labored diligently over a variety of recalcitrant and sometimes oddly edited manuscripts with her customary sangfroid. I am most grateful to all of these friends. But most of all I wish to extend my heartfelt appreciation to the several scholars whose work this truly is--Richard Applegate, Donald Bahr, Elizabeth Brandt, John and Donna Bushnell, Carobeth Laird, Patrick Morris, and Maurice Zigmond. They have given us all an added perspective on a fascinating but complex aspect of the human condition.

# The Role of Secrecy in a Pueblo Society
## by
## Elizabeth Brandt

The central problem confronting any Pueblo scholar is secrecy. Pueblo society presents two fronts, a complex secular organization, and a religious grounding of like complexity. The first aspect can be understood, but the second is always shrouded by secrecy; yet both are essential to a complete understanding of Pueblo society. Anthropologists such as Bloom, Parsons, Scholes, Dozier, and Spicer have attributed secrecy to the pressures of external contact, but I believe that this emphasis is mistaken and has obscured the real issue which is *internal* secrecy. *External* secrecy directed toward outsiders is merely a special case of a much larger process. The genesis of secrecy lies in the nature of religious societies, their ritual and political functions, and the fact that all esoteric and much secular knowledge is communicated through speech in the Pueblos.

This paper explores the sociology of knowledge of the Pueblos in a preliminary way, and the structure and function of the societies insofar as it is known, using Taos Pueblo as a case study in secrecy. The details of organization will differ from village to village, but I am confident that the general model presented here is applicable to all the Pueblos.[1]

---

[1] This paper is a preliminary exploration of the nature of information transmission and non-transmission in Pueblo societies. It ties into the literature on secret societies and has a number of aspects that will be elaborated in later papers. The initial idea which stimulated this paper was a remark by my colleague, Donald Bahr, on the nature of oral cultures. I am grateful to George L. Trager, M. E. Smith, William Leap, Jay Miller, Amy Zaharlick, and James Bodine without whose willingness to share data and ideas this paper would not have been possible. I would also like to thank those who read earlier drafts of this paper and by whose criticism I have benefitted: M. E. Smith, Alfonso Ortiz, Melvin Firestone, and Joseph Gross. I am solely responsible for any misinterpretations in the data and the opinions expressed do not necessarily represent the views of these individuals. I also wish to thank individuals at Taos who were willing to explore the whys rather than the whats of secrecy. Data were collected in 1967 while I was at Ft. Burgwin Research Center and during summer 1975 and 1976. This research was funded in part by a grant

The classical view of Pueblo secrecy began early and has been commented on by many authors (Bloom 1931; Scholes 1942; Parsons 1939; Spicer 1962; Dozier 1961). Dozier (1961:94-97) is the most articulate statement of this historical theory. Secrecy is attributed to the program of forced culture change in political structure and religious belief and practices imposed by the Spanish conquest. The forced Christianization of the Pueblos and incidents of kiva destruction and mask burning, the whipping and imprisonment of religious leaders, and witchcraft trials for practice of native religion caused the Pueblos to adopt an attitude of outward compliance with Christian belief while religious ceremonies went underground and secrecy became important (Spicer 1962). Both Dozier and Spicer attribute the continued maintenance of religious secrecy to unfavorable publicity about Pueblo beliefs and acts by the church and the Indian Service under the Religious Crimes Code in the 1920s. Taos Pueblo was investigated at this time for breach of the Code and was able to argue successfully for First Amendment Rights in the courts. This interpretation has protected the politico-religious nature of tribal government ever since. Dozier states:

> The unsuccessful attempts of recent ethnologists to break the Pueblo iron curtain appear to demonstrate that these Indians still believe that the release of ceremonial knowledge will be used against them. They, therefore, guard tenaciously their native ceremonial system from all outsiders, offering only the Spanish-Catholic and some less sacred aspects of the native system to public scrutiny (1961:97).

While the historical explanation is logical and certainly useful in explaining slight shifts in the degree of openness of the Pueblos to outsiders, it diverts us from more general questions about the sociology of knowledge in the Pueblos. It is a case of misplaced emphasis which obscures the real issue of how knowledge is used and transmitted in Pueblo society.

For secrecy, selective transmission of information is the key point—what you tell and to whom you tell it. Access to knowledge and proper use of knowledge are primary concerns of Pueblo people. Rather than seeing secrecy as a bar to understanding Pueblo societies, we should see it as a striking phenomenon, one deserving of investigation in its own right. The classical explanation ascribes only one function to secrecy, the maintenance of traditional religion in a hostile context. It also implies that secrecy is a phenomenon practiced only against outsiders, which is definitely not the case. This paper will show that secrecy is a dynamic rather than a static phenomenon, a tactic that serves a variety of functions.

SECRECY

Pueblo people make a conceptual distinction between insiders and outsiders. In its broadest sense, the term "outsiders" refers to

---

from the Research Board of Arizona State University and the American Philosophical Society.

Anglos, Spanish-Americans, and Indians of other tribes who exist outside of the symbolic and spatial limits of a Pueblo village. It distinguishes those who are not integrated into the social networks within a village. The term may also be used in a narrower sense to distinguish the social roles and statuses of individuals based on their participation in village information networks. Thus, an individual may be an insider with respect to his own kiva group, but an outsider to others. An individual married into the community may be an insider in all respects except religious participation. The distinction is thus a flexible one which can be used to include or exclude any individual from social participation in any activity or context. This conceptual distinction creates a web of social boundaries that cross-cut a village and extend outside of it.

Inhibition of information flow across any of these boundaries is secrecy. Anthropologists, including Dozier, have misinterpreted the process of information flow. They have tended to use the imagery of a wall, an "iron curtain," or a similar physical or spatial boundary which demarcates the limits of information flow from within a Pueblo community to the outside. The outsider also accepts this distinction and focuses on the external boundary, rather than seeing that this boundary is not the only one, but merely one of many. If a spatial analogy is needed at all, a more appropriate one would be the multi-level architectural massing of individual living units at a pueblo such as Taos. The boundaries are not rigid, though they may be relatively permanent for any one individual given his status or social role. The outsider's view of himself as locked out of information channels by a wall of secrecy can be called external secrecy. As I have discussed briefly here and continue to elaborate in this paper, this view is incorrect. There is also a sense in which this view implies a homogeneity of knowledge within a community, a serious error.

I have used the term internal security to contrast with external secrecy. Free access to all information does not occur within a community. There are outsiders within the village for certain kinds of information. Though I will continue to use the terms internal and external secrecy, they must be understood as two superficial aspects of a single process, inhibition of information flow across any boundary. The relationships between internal and external secrecy may be unclear at this point, but will be explained much more fully later in the paper. Briefly though, internal secrecy is primary; external secrecy is maintained to prevent information from going back into pueblo communities from the outside where it might have disruptive effects if the wrong individuals possessed it. There can be little control over outsiders, but there is a high degree of control over insiders and information can be channeled and controlled in very precise ways.[2] It is also true, though, that external

---

[2] I believe internal secrecy is a prime factor in Pueblo factionalism, though of course it also owes much to the changing demography of the Pueblos, increased education, and outside employment. At Taos, the leaders have reacted to the threat of the outside world by increasing internal secrecy, and this has created a bitter factional dispute of almost ten years' duration. The role of secrecy in factionalism is explored in

secrecy is a powerful boundary-maintenance mechanism.

Knowledge or information is power in both a spiritual and a secular sense and the use of power must be controlled. Power is here defined as the ability to influence the behavior of others. The asserted belief in supernatural power and supernatural sanctions is a powerful determinant of behavior for some individuals. Information as power is also discussed more fully in a later section.

The social boundaries are permeable to some kinds of information flow, but not to others. Certain kinds of information are declared secret, particularly information concerning religious matters, and there is a high degree of concern over "the secrets." The content of a secret is variable to some extent and what is secret is defined by religious leaders, not left up to individual choice of community members. For the most part, "the secrets" consist of esoteric information underlying the meaning and symbolism of a ritual or part of a ritual, the ritual paraphenalia used, the sequencing and timing of ritual, and the figures responsible for conduct of ceremonials and their activities.

There is a relationship between the kinds of knowledge and the ability to communicate it that is non-arbitrary. It may be profitable to explore different categories of religious knowledge and determine how they relate to secrecy. While the categories are Western, I believe they are adequate cross-culturally, although they are not exhaustive or comprehensive. The five categories are: (1) mystical; (2) theological; (3) liturgical; (4) dogma or catechism[3]; and (5) participatory. Each kind of knowledge has some restriction on transmission and media of transmission by its very nature and thus is "secret" automatically. This is especially true of level 1, mystical knowledge, which is private, ineffable and non-verbal. To communicate this kind of knowledge is to destroy it. It is always secret.

Level 2, theological knowledge, is a kind of deep knowledge that penetrates below the surface levels of three through five and may result in new information, interpretations, or innovations. It is the source of new information in a relatively closed system. Prophets would draw on this kind of knowledge. It is frequently the result of a long process of familiarity, experience, and meditation on the part of the knower. It may be communicated in narrative form or in visual or gestural symbols, but it is difficult to communicate without a long period of training on the part of the information recipients. It may be either public or private and may not be communicated at all. In some senses it is also secret by nature, except to those who are willing to expend the time and effort it takes to acquire this knowledge. It may be acquired individually or by a formal learning process.

---

a forthcoming paper. (See also Smith 1969; 1974.)

[3]I have used the nominal form of dogma to avoid the unpleasant associations of the adjectival form.

Level 3, the liturgical level, deals with knowledge about behavior; in a sense, knowledge of the participatory technology of a ritual. This kind of knowledge is unlikely to be transmitted to any but initiates in any formal sense. It can be transmitted by narrative, but some information must be acquired by viewing and participating in ritual and ritual preparation. Because of this, it is possible for an outsider to gain some liturgical knowledge by witnessing ceremonies, though knowledge thus gained may be fragmentary or trivial.[4] When communicated formally it involves memorization of a large corpus of material and frequently involves gestures as well. It deals with how, when, and why rituals are performed and may also deal with the overt symbolism present in performances.

Knowledge of the dogma or the catechism, level 4, is essentially a superficial form of knowledge in contrast to the preceding levels. It typically involves a rote form of learning and represents the officially "received" view on religion, both asserted beliefs and practices. It is always public, not private knowledge, and may be communicated in highly structured narrative forms, such as myths or prayers, to initiates. It is always explanatory material about behavior and belief. It is typically taught to initiates as the first stage of their religious education. It is restricted to initiates and is not generally public knowledge, although it is much less secret than the preceding levels. Some outsiders may be in possession of some catechismic knowledge without being considered to have violated secrecy.

Level 5, or participatory knowledge, is essentially a miscellaneous ad hoc category. Participants in ritual may be a very diverse group in terms of the knowledge they control. They may receive explicit instructions on their roles and perform them but never go beyond this level to understand any others. In many cases they are prohibited from asking any questions that do not pertain to their roles. In this category I am also including spectators to public ceremonies, many of whom will be total outsiders. They possess little or no knowledge about what they witness, but are under some restrictions if they attempt to find out more about it. By analogy, we might think of an individual attending a mass in Latin, knowing no Latin, who participates by watching what others do, but has no deeper understanding of what it all might mean.

All of these levels are present in Pueblo religion. There may be other levels and some of these levels may overlap as they are not intended to be mutually exclusive, but it is important to consider them as a background for understanding secrecy. We must realize something of the nature of knowledge in general and realize the diversity of knowledge among individuals. From this background, cultural mechanisms which

---

[4]This explains some of the opposition to data gathering devices which provide more complete retrieval of information (see also point seven on p.   ). Taos Pueblo attempted to suppress Parsons' *Taos Pueblo* (1936) when it first appeared as it "gave away the secrets." Parsons' *Isleta Paintings* (1962), much of Leslie White's work and Ortiz's (1969) are also considered to contain secrets.

disseminate and control knowledge can be understood.

There are a number of strategies for practicing secrecy. Outsiders are barred from the village for specific rituals, and the private performance of ceremonies in ritual spaces such as kivas, society houses and shrines prevents outsiders from witnessing them. Other strategies are prohibition against photographs, drawings, and tape recordings at otherwise open ceremonies and villages. Another strategy is the well-known Pueblo propensity to construct false and misleading information for the benefit of the curious. Another is polished evasion of questions. Trager and Leap (1968) found a pattern in speaking which they called "the purist tendency." Loanwords from Spanish and English are purged in the presence of outsiders who might understand them. Elaborate circumlocutions are employed in the native language to convey information without using a term which might be understood. Some of these circumlocutions have become well-known idiomatic expressions in the native languages. At the beginning of an encounter with native speakers of an Indian language, if there is an outsider present who understands some of it, the other parties will be warned to watch their speech.

The presence of ritual speech in religious contexts which contains archaic words, borrowing from other languages, and a different semantic system with non-ordinary referents also preserves secrecy. There are also special styles of speaking, such as the speech of the Black Eyes, the Chiffoneti clown group at Taos, and "talking backwards" which serve to exclude the curious. Simple use of the native language in religious and political contexts serves effectively to exclude outsiders. It is quite frequent for leaders to use the native language with an interpreter when engaged in political meetings with Anglos and Hispanos even when the leader speaks English or Spanish. This is an important dramatic speech act which serves to distance the hearers and enhance the status of the Indian leader. In many communities, though not at Taos, use of the native language in religion and politics serves to exclude the younger members of the community who do not speak the language.

SOME CONSEQUENCES OF SECRECY

It has been demonstrated earlier that there are certain forms of knowledge which are secret due to inherent restrictions and that there is diversity among individuals in the kinds of knowledge they possess. This creates some internal secrecy and also has consequences for external secrecy. Individuals cannot transmit information that they do not possess, either within the community or outside of it. Internal secrecy in the sense of deliberate exclusion of individuals from witnessing ceremonies, asking about them or participating ensures that relatively few individuals in a community will actually be in possession of secret information. The majority of the people in the community simply do not know secret information, or if they do know may be in possession of a very small amount.

A major consequence of internal secrecy is the establishment of status hierarchies based upon access to knowledge which is communicated only in oral form. Pueblo communities contain a number of small-group cultures which store, retrieve, and transmit different kinds of information (McFeat 1974). For the Pueblos as a whole, the important small-group cultures we are concerned with in this paper are dual organizations, clans, societies, and kiva groups. There is relatively little overlap or information leakage between the groups. Since Pueblo governing systems are linked in important ways with these small-group cultures, the establishment of status hierarchies based on secret information in the possession of one group rather than another can have important political consequences.

Possession of religious knowledge and participation in religious works are prerequisites to full participation in the political system. While most individuals know the theory of their governing system and can observe its overt acts, many are excluded from significant roles and have little real conception of what actually occurs. The inability of individuals to obtain certain kinds of information makes any challenge to internal governing risky and generally doomed to failure. Internal secrecy thus slows innovation in Pueblo communities and provides a stabilizing influence, though at times this is seen as oppressive and unresponsive by those without full participation.

The focus for secrecy is internal, not external. The society can bring a full range of sanctions into play against a community member, but can do little against a non-resident. Thus, if you can control the information sources within a community, you can also control information going to the outside. Religious knowledge is necessary for political power within the community. If this knowledge can be restricted to a very small group, they can control the community. External secrecy primarily prevents back contamination, keeping information that could threaten the established leadership hierarchies from coming back into the community. Secrecy is also maintained within the community on a great many political matters.

This last point requires some amplification. I do not mean to imply that secrecy is a relatively new phenomenon or that there are not legitimate secrets and non-political reasons for keeping them. One reason often adduced for secrecy by Pueblo leaders is that religious ceremonies lose their power if they are known by the wrong people. This is certainly an attitude commonly encountered in many parts of the world.

Non-religious secrecy has received little attention from anthropologists because of the tremendous interest in Pueblo religion and the texture and complexity of Pueblo ceremonialism. While some secrecy surely existed in the past as a way of integrating culturally diverse groups, it has expanded from its original contexts within the historic period.

Archaeological evidence, historic documents, and Pueblo tradition all confirm that Pueblo villages were internally diverse communities that periodically received groups of immigrants from other areas. These migrating groups must have brought their own traditions and religious beliefs with them. Secrecy about religion would enable the community to achieve a measure of religious freedom for its members and minimize conflict over ceremonial practices. Differing groups could be accommodated and the pueblo might gain ceremonial specialists it did not originally possess. With the advent of Spanish colonization, secrecy took on new dimensions as Dozier theorized and the Pueblos added another religion. In the twentieth century yet another vector of secrecy came into play.

Secrecy now becomes a conscious political strategy adopted to maintain political autonomy and freedom in a hostile world, but in a different sense than envisioned by Dozier. Beginning in the 1920s and 1930s, a cloak of secrecy is thrown over a great many things that were formerly open.[5] This new use of secrecy is especially pronounced at Taos. I believe that it correlates with two events: (1) the advent of extensive tourism in the pueblos; and (2) the discovery by Pueblo leaders that the U.S. Constitution protects freedom of religion. The first event made it difficult to control information due to the sheer numbers of nosey tourists poking around. The latter enabled Pueblo leaders to throw a cloak of obscurity over any internal matter and to gain a greater degree of internal control and freedom by claiming outside interference in traditional religion; at Taos, the refrain for any denial of information on anything is that it is part of the religion. A political proposal may be justified or denied by an appeal to religion. If pressed for a reason, tribal leadership may assert that the reason is part of the religion and therefore secret.

The foregoing discussion does not mean to suggest that there are not legitimate reasons for secrecy and legitimate secrets, only that leadership has learned to use secrecy in a new manner for explicitly political purposes. It also does not imply that secrecy is not broken upon some occasions. In some cases violations are inadvertent or the result of sophisticated digging by outsiders. In the majority of cases when secrecy is broken, however, it is done for a specific political purpose by those in possession of the secrets and is a deliberate strategy; e.g., in the Taos case for the necessity of winning support and understanding in their attempts to win back the Blue Lake area.[6] Secrecy is thus a dynamic complex of behaviors which serves a variety of functions, and those functions have changed through time.

In the next section of this paper, I will examine the ceremonial and political organization of Taos in some detail to show how information is controlled and political power allocated within the community. The following points provide the structural socio-cultural groundwork for the process of the secrecy dynamic:

---

[5] I am indebted to M. E. Smith for pointing this out to me.

[6] It is also possible for other individuals to break secrecy if they have strong kin and/or political support.

(1) The existence of cross-cutting religious societies or groups which have secular political functions as well is the most important factor in Taos social organization and possibly in other villages as well. While dual organization is also an important organizational principle in some villages, especially the Tewa (Ortiz 1969), there is no evidence for its importance at Taos.

(2) As a consequence of these societies, the specialization of their functions, and the differential training involved, no one individual in any village serves as a repository for *all* ceremonial and religious knowledge (this would be true in dual organization as well). This is a controversial assumption as some Pueblo scholars have placed the *cacique* in this position, but a careful review of the evidence, both ethnographic and linguistic, shows little support for this view.[7] The *cacique* may coordinate activities and perform an integrative role, but I do not believe he possesses all the knowledge relevant to each group. My own fieldwork at Taos and Sandia also supports this view.

(3) Categories and levels of being such as those described by Ortiz (1969) are a universal in Pueblo society. Ranked status categories are based on access to ritual knowledge and exist in every village.[8]

---

[7] The current *cacique* at Taos is not considered the legitimate heir to the position. In addition, he is incapacitated by age and blindness. In recent testimony in U.S. District Court he was criticized by some community members for misrepresentation of his position and power.

[8] I have quoted Parsons' (1939:112) footnotes in their entirety for their clarity. She gives important terms for these categories.

> Keres *sishti*, which denotes any person not actually engaged in ceremonial work or any common person without ceremonial or governmental affiliation. Santo Domingo (Acoma: White 4:167, White 7), or anyone who knows all about the kachina (San Felipe; White 3:27). Compare Laguna and Cochiti, *shuts*, *shurdze* (Dumarest, 198). The kachina dance cult is everywhere that of the "poor man," or commoner. Distinctive terms or references are applied or made by Hopi of Second Mesa to chiefs, neophytes, or members merely, *pavunshinum*, small mound caused by corn just starting to come up out of the ground (Nequatewa, 103; Stephen 4: glossary) and to non-members or commoners.

> In the quote [sic] given above, I am following the Hopi distinction between belonging and to a ceremony (or society with ceremony) and belonging to a dance group (or society without ceremony). Dance groups or societies are large in all the towns, since they are generally inclusive of all the males. Kiva memberships are similarly inclusive, and of course, moiety membership. The memberships of the clown societies at Cochiti and Jemez are strikingly large, showing moiety influence.

See also term used by Tewa in Ortiz (1969:17), 'Dry Food People' *whe towa* and *nayi wha towa*, 'Dust Dragging People'.

These categories also serve to define the extent of political participation in many Pueblo communities, especially Taos. There is some evidence at Taos that they may represent incipient social classes and research is continuing on this topic (Brandt 1975). Interestingly, Parsons states:

> In Zuni definition, poor people are people without ceremonial property or connection, belonging in no rain or curing society--people who are not valuable. In this sense the poor of Zuni are about half the population. The proportion of poor would be very much larger in the East, but I doubt if the distinction would be made at all there; the society membership lists are too small[9] (1939:112).

(4) Religious societies and their leaders are socially ranked with respect to one another. There is differential access to knowledge within and between the societies. Rewards for participation in the secular sense are primarily political and, in the last decade or two, economic.

(5) Processes of society recruitment and training within a society lead to extreme variations in the nature and amount of knowledge that individuals possess. This makes it possible to control information in very explicit ways and to ensure a high degree of conformity.

(6) Oral transmission of religious information provides a high degree of control over information impossible with any other system of data storage and retrieval. This is a crucial factor in the maintenance of the religious and political systems of Pueblo communities. As such it explains much of the opposition of Pueblo communities to any relatively permanent forms of data storage such as writing, recordings, and photographs. Systems without the rapid fading characteristic would allow unqualified and potentially unsocialized individuals access to the deepest and most central concepts of Pueblo life without the cautionary experiences and explanations of those more knowledgeable. This would be true whether they were insiders or outsiders. We might liken this to the control Anglo society attempts to exercise over classified material.

---

[9]The distinction *is* made between categories of people even in the eastern Pueblos. Normally this is translated in English as the "Made" or "Cooked" people as opposed to everyone else. At Taos it is the *łułiną*, 'Old (People)' as opposed to *'it'oysemayana*, 'the New People'. Among the Keresans we find the terms *shurdze* or *sishti* applied to individuals without ceremonial affiliation (Parsons 1939:112). Ortiz (1969: 17) gives *patowa* as the term for Made People. Another suggestive term for the 'Cooked People' is *nałent'óynema* as recorded by Trager in Parsons (1940:6). *Nałen* was not translated, but *t'óynema* is 'people'. The number of people in the 'Made' category at Taos is approximately 50. This agrees with Ortiz's (1969:82) figure for the Tewa of 52, though of this maximum number not all participate. At Taos only 36 individuals are active society leaders and council members (Brandt 1976).

(7) Since the society leadership is, in effect, coterminous with the technical secular political organization, it is able to exercise a variety of both religious and secular sanctions against potential or actual violators of secrecy. At the same time such leaders are also able to violate secrecy if political considerations warrant it without fear of reprisal other than gossip and factionalism.

Supporting data for the points mentioned above are discussed in the following section.

## TAOS CEREMONIAL ORGANIZATION

### Dual Organization

Taos possesses a dual organization with membership inclusive for all individuals in the named segments. Membership in these groups is the basic common denominator for the community, but the two groups seem to have little structural importance at the explicit level. Ortiz's (1965:389) useful distinction between moieties and dual organizations can be applied to Taos. The groups are not exogamous, have no connections with residence or political organization. Although Taos has six functioning kivas, three on each side of the village, their location does not seem to reflect dual organization. It is possible that the details of dual organization at Taos are secret.

### Cross-Cutting Societies

Within each kiva are two societies, each with its own leadership.[10] The true nature of the kiva societies is still somewhat unclear. Some societies have overlapping membership in two kivas, such as the Big Hail people, who are found in both Big-Earring Kiva and in Water Kiva (Parsons 1936:74). Other societies are restricted to one kiva. Some of these societies do not formally initiate members. A category of membership is reserved for those who sing but do not dance. The uninitiated membership is larger than the initiated membership. Each society gains members by dedication, trespass, and trapping. The most common way is by dedication, either by a personal vow or being promised by one's parents. Dedication may occur shortly after birth, but formal society initiation will take place later when the child is 10-12 years of age. Trespass occurs, usually, when a male individual is in a position to witness some secret ritual, touches a taboo society member or ritual object, or encounters an individual on ritual business (Parsons 1939:113). Trapping is rare and occurs only when a society is in need of a replacement and an individual must be coerced. In trespass, an individual becomes contaminated by power and must join the society to deal with the burden. It also serves to prevent an individual from divulging privileged information.

---

[10] At Taos, a kiva is a semi-subterranean chamber used as a meeting place for some societies. Additional societies exist, some using kivas, others society houses.

Each society is responsible for certain ritual activities and must inform the next group of its part if it is a cyclic or joint ritual. Authority over a ceremony and its participants is limited to the society directly concerned. An individual may not interfere with another society's rites.

While most individuals know the kiva and kiva society affiliation of most adult males, they do not have access to or knowledge of the specific details of internal group organization, nor knowledge of ceremonies held within other kivas. A rigid etiquette governs a man's participation in his kiva work. A Taos informant stated:

> I've talked to a lot of people up at Taos, and got a lot of friends and that kind, but we *never* do talk about that kind of thing, about what clan or society they belong to. They don't talk about themselves either. And I guess, that's where the questions comes in, as secrecy things.[11]

> Well, naturally, they don't want you to know what society they belong to. Naturally, you don't ask either. If you did, well, what is it to you? Just the way the answer comes out, you know. So I'm always afraid to ask, unless they come up and tell me. Unless you watch 'em and see where they go, like you watch an individual, like your close friend, and still you don't know which group he belong to, and he might tell you, "All right, I got to go tend to my society." When he tell you that, well you might follow him, watch him, see which kiva he goes into. That's one way of finding out (Brandt 1975).

If an individual wishes to know about a particular society, he must join to find out. An individual does not ask questions. If he does, he will be firmly put off or asked to join. If he persists, he may lose face or risk expulsion from the community. Once in a society an individual may not divulge his information to outsiders without fear of sanctions. Non-initiates or short-term initiates are also put off. As one short-term member stated:

> Well, all you do is just cooperate. Just follow the leader and forget the rest. That's the way it works, I mean the secrets that they keep. I mean I'll never go any farther than, "You do what I say and then forget it." Then you respect them, so you have to forget it. Do just what they ask you to do, that's all (Brandt 1975).

## Initiation

In addition to inclusive dual organization membership and general kiva membership, males may also belong to one or more societies in the kivas. There are two categories of membership, long-term and short-term, or easy-term, reflecting the differing degrees of training and knowledge that individuals receive. Initiation is a two-stage process beginning with registration or dedication at age 6 or earlier and formal incorporation at age 8-12.

---

[11]The Taos use the term clan to refer to societies and kiva groups. There is no notion of unilineal descent at Taos.

Fully trained or long-term initiates undergo an 18-month iniation period, beginning in February and coming out at the time of the annual Blue Lake pilgrimage the following August (Parsons 1936; Bodine: personal communication). Short-term initiates receive only a 6-month training period. At any one time, there are two groups in training. The kiva societies rotate initiation over a long period. Kiva leaders are drawn from the long-term group.

Short-term members are not fully trained and have little access to secret knowledge. Their training and the ritual prohibitions on their private lives are less strenuous. Their access to knowledge is on a "need-to-know" basis necessary for the performance of their duties, which consist of running errands, procuring supplies, and singing. They are individuals who have earned rights in the community by performance of community duties, but who have refused full initiation, were away when it normally would have happened, or who have come from other villages but have shown their willingness to participate and reside at Taos. They are called in English the "in-between" or "middle-people" by the Taos; there is no term in Taos for this category. Adult individuals are sometimes recruited into this category to serve the community politically if they have special skills or information the community needs (Brandt 1975). Essentially, short-term individuals are lay assistants (Parsons 1939).

Women also belong to the dual divisions and have in addition to their own societies (which are very few in number) a type of auxiliary kiva affiliation normally derived from their father's membership and changing to their husband's kiva upon marriage. Women prepare food, grind corn, repair and plaster kivas, but at least at the formal or technical level do not have access to esoteric information except as it is relevant for their duties. Women do not actually hold kiva membership, though they do perform functions for the kiva societies.

There are three groups present in Taos society, each with differential access to esoteric knowledge. One group, *'it'oysemayana*, 'The New People', consists of women and uninitiated adult males who have moiety affiliation and may have general kiva membership. The second group, the "Middle People," consists of short-term initiates who have somewhat greater access to knowledge than the first group. The third group are the 'Old People', *łułiną*, who are fully initiated and often kiva leaders or society leaders.

The New People are poor ceremonially and may be poor in other respects as well. They are disenfranchised and may lack kin support which would enable them to obtain favorable grazing permits and access to land. They are unable to hold political office and rarely have friends in high places. The "Middle People" are in a somewhat better position, but may not hold major offices. They are also ceremonially poor. The *łułiną* are leaders and produce leaders. They allocate land, water, and permits. Certain families tend to develop power bases in kiva societies and some individuals may sometimes misuse their access to Federal funds.

## Kiva Leadership

Each society has a leader and an assistant leader.[12] Leadership is lifelong. Some special training is given to leaders, assistants, and potential leaders at the time of initiation, and this continues most of an individual's lifetime. This long period of training is necessary to commit to heart the details of the ceremonies and the language that accompanies them. As positions become vacant and an individual is judged competent, he may move into a position of leadership. There is apparently a line of succession for leaders and assistants and occasionally a younger man is chosen in preference to an older one in the line, but my data are very incomplete in this area.

Leaders, by virtue of their positions in the religious hierarchy, are also automatically members of the Pueblo Council and thus receive political training by kiva society participation. It is also possible to become a council member by holding major office, such as Governor or War Captain. A survey of current council membership (Brandt 1976) indicated, however, that the majority of members had attained major office after they became leaders or assistants. If we count kiva leaders and their assistants, and society leaders and their assistants, we arrive at a figure of 36 individuals, which coincides exactly with the current active membership of the council, assuming long-term and short-term leaders and their assistants for each society.[13] This may surely be a coincidence as there are other members eligible for the council who do not actively participate and it includes 3 individuals who are not leaders and assistants. In any case, it demonstrates the interlocking nature of the secular and the ceremonial systems. Since basic governing positions in the pueblo are chosen from this group, it follows that the secular governing officials will also be religious leaders at some level. The positions in the political and religious systems thus have the same occupants.

The levels of leadership and the reservoir of trained people provide a continuity of religious knowledge, a necessity in a society relying on oral transmission. If only one or two individuals possessed the knowledge, it would be easy to lose precious cultural information at the death of a leader. In fact, this has happened in other villages and

---

[12]My earlier data and that of Smith (personal communication) indicate that Taos uses the general Tanoan body analogy for leadership (e.g., a head and a right-hand and left-hand assistant). Parsons did not find this and my data from 1976 contradict my earlier data. At the request of some Taos, this statement reflects the more recent position, but is still controversial.

[13]If the data for two assistants are used as in footnote 12, the figure becomes 48 which correlates well with an approximate figure of 50 individuals in a village who are 'Made' people. If the lower figure is used, we could include leaders of other societies not considered as kiva societies. The exact number of these groups is unknown (see also footnote 9).

probably also at Taos. The long period of apprenticeship serves not only for technical mastery of a leader's duties, but is a powerful force in molding proper attitudes and respect. It allows the existing leadership a high degree of control over attitudes and behavior of members and provides a political leadership that is firmly grounded in religious principles. It denies major political participation to those who do not have the proper religious training and bars them from access to religious knowledge. In other words, religious training is a prerequisite for secular office-holding at the senior level. Non-traditionalists cannot gain technical or formal power, and secrecy prevents them from learning the underpinnings of certain political acts because religious reasons are frequently given as their rationale.

## Political Organization and Process

While Taos accepted the provisions of the Indian Reorganization Act, it has never been fully implemented. (For details of the governing system, see Smith 1969; 1970.) Only fully initiated members can fill any of the major governmental roles such as Governor or War Captain or their first lieutenants. Short-term initiates and even non-initiates can fill appointive positions in the secular government such as secretary, interpreter, or sheriff, or be on the staff of the governor, but they cannot hold any major office. Since only approximately 50 people are fully initiated, the pool of potential officials is very small when compared with the total resident population of over 1400. This pool also remains relatively constant over time. With the exception of the appointive positions, government is a closed system with the łułiną choosing one another for major positions again and again. The same individuals occupy positions of authority and power in both the religious system and the political system. They also use their esoteric knowledge to direct the course of the village. As one informant put it:

> What you call our self form of government, it's all based on a religious ground. So those that doesn't belong to the kiva religion or society, we have no right to hold office. We can be appointed to help the Old People in terms of interpreting what the non-Indians, you know, want to do . . . or we can be selected as one of the ten staff officers, but we--like myself, I can't be a Governor up there, 'cause I was never initiated into the clan. So that makes the Old People carry on all the government to themselves, and they can appoint whoever they want. And then in another way, they have more advantage, appointing themselves, even if they have to appoint their own nephews or brother and sister (Brandt 1975).

The Old People also use their knowledge of the "secrets" to prohibit undesirable behavior. For years, certain Taos have asked that the village have electricity.[14] The Old People prohibited electricity

---

[14] Since, electricity has been allowed on the west side of the village outside the walls. Members of the People's Committee, an internal faction, recently lost a suit in Federal District Court against the Council to force electricity on the east side of the village. The Council claimed that the east side was sacred ground and would be harmed by the introduction of electricity.

(inside the walls) in the village proper on religious grounds, but would not explain to the rest of the population the details of the reason because it was secret. One Taos says:

> We have been restricted all along--like electricity. Nobody up to this time tell us as to why it was restricted or against the religion. Course, that's a most sacred thing and they won't tell us (Brandt 1975).

Rights in the community are inherited bilaterally. For an individual to hold rights in the community, he must participate in the kiva religion and should have undergone at least short-term initiation. A current factional dispute at Taos concerns the whole question of tribal enrollment and community rights and duties. Some of the New People, *'it'oysemayana*, have formed a political group, the People's Committee, to fight for their rights in the Federal Courts and are suing the tribal government, the Old People, under the Civil Rights Act. They want an end to what they see as abuses in tribal government; they want certain rights for themselves and their children as tribal members--rights to which they are denied access; and they want a democratic form of government. They have approached the tribal government on many occasions with their grievances, but as much of this group consists of women who have married out or married in, males who have married in, and non-Taos men who are not initiated, the group has little hope of success. In 1975, one of their members who was initiated became Governor and for the New People this was seen as a sign of success. However, he was quickly co-opted and lost or denied his affiliative ties with the *'it'oysemayana*:

> Well now, in term of talking about the Old People is not the age of a person at the pueblo. Alright, we have a young governor, now . . . and he's been initiated into the clan. Alright, when that young man get into the, become one of the officers, he became one of the Old People. That's why I say the Old People, they are so influence. So automatically, within his knowledge in himself, he feel that civilization is alright, but the same time he have to deny the civilization to make the Old People happy or satisfied. So he got to do what the Old People according to the functions of their government. So the Old People, they don't talk about age. They talk about the things that function (Brandt 1975).

> You can't do as you please when you are initiated, cause you have to do just what your society tells you to do. . . . I was told when we were fighting this paved road up to the Pueblo and the electricity and what have you, we bring in, try to bring in the modern type of things, better living conditions in their home and that's one of the things I was told, that the signs say, well, that's not allow here. It's against the religion. And everything was against the religion (Brandt 1975).

The Old People have a firm grip upon the society through control of the secular political system which their access to knowledge gives them. Through secrecy they can invoke dire but unnamed supernatural sanctions on the rest of the population. They can ban anything they wish without the necessity for explanation by invoking secrecy. The łułiną are the judicial system within the village and the legitimate agents of social control with the power to fine, imprison, whip, or expel anyone who threatens their authority. The tribal government is also backed by the support of the Federal government. The secrets can only be revealed if one of the łułiną chooses to reveal them. Secrecy is thus an internal political tool of great utility.

## SUMMARY

Secrecy is a complex of behaviors and a dynamic process which has changed through time. Pueblo leaders control information by limiting access to information to a small number of individuals who must be socialized into the proper uses of information through a lengthy and complex process of group recruitment and training. Since information is transmitted primarily by oral means, their degree of control is high. The opposition of Pueblo leaders to permanent sources of data storage such as writing, filming, or recording becomes quite clear on two levels. The religious objection that this sacred information should not be known by those who are not properly socialized into its uses and who do not have proper respect for it is also true at the secular political level. The religious knowledge possessed by the Old People is a source of natural power as Pueblo religion deals with the forces of the universe and nature generally, and as leaders they are required to fulfill their duties, responsibilities, and rights to the community to keep these forces in balance. Their authority (the technical rights of their status and role) stems from their sacred knowledge; their power (the informal extensions of their authority) from their co-terminous positions in the political and religious systems. By limiting access to the religious system, they limit access to the political system. Their power and authority are reinforced by the complexity of these systems. In both the religious and political sense, New People are too rash, too unbalanced, and too dependent upon others to exercise power and authority. In the view of the Old People, they do not have the knowledge or the social maturity to weigh all considerations before making decisions. A long period of training provides the seasoning necessary to make decisions that are in harmony with nature and the universe and a Pueblo's special relation to the forces there. On the political side, a young man must learn balance on the person-to-person level and respect his culture's ways.

Religious leaders are the only ones who possess the secrets, and in order to retain their internal control over the community, the secrets must not be exposed. External secrecy is an attempt to prevent the spread of information to the outside world; from the internal perspective, however, it functions more importantly to keep such information from coming back into the community and effecting a radical shift in internal organization. Outsiders who gain information cannot be controlled effectively and may spread information into the wrong hands. I believe external secrecy has proved adaptive for the maintenance of a power elite.

Traditional leadership at Taos has been criticized extensively by the People's Committee. One of the first activities of this group was to have Parsons' *Taos Pueblo* (1936) read to them and to request its reprinting so that every disenfranchised individual could own a copy. This gave members some understanding and access to the secrets so necessary for a secular political challenge to Pueblo leadership. In a very real sense, knowledge is power and Parsons spoke the truth when she said:

> Our ways would lose their power if they were known. People have learned about the ways of other pueblos and those pueblos have lost their ways (Parsons 1939:433).

I believe it could be demonstrated that secrets would not be given away unless the traditional religious organization had begun to disintegrate. After this process got underway, we would expect that the political system would show serious changes and realignments, and that a village would accept writing and other forms of data storage.

Secrecy as the source of power and authority also explains a fact that surprises many investigators. When a factional split becomes so intense as to cause village fission, it is the conservatives who leave, taking their information with them.[15] They have the ability and the techniques to reconstitute a complete new village, but those who are left behind are in the same position as an American community might be if all the utilities were abandoned and the trained personnel were gone as well as all the religious and political leadership. The fear of this happening is sometimes enough to effect a reconciliation of sorts. Today, of course, it is difficult to found a new village, given the reservation system, but secular villages do exist and leaders do walk out, abandoning their people until they find the right "path" again.

Secrecy is intimately tied up with political factionalism and the stresses and strains of continued existence in the modern world, but I believe I have demonstrated that the process is of a different nature than that envisioned by Dozier. While I have stated that I believe secrecy of the sort we currently see is a relatively recent phenomenon, I also believe that institutionalized secrecy was present even in precontact times and was necessary to preserve the coherent social organization that we know was present. It is debatable whether there was a need to maintain an external form of secrecy, but if my argument is correct, there *must* have been a necessity for internal secrecy. I hypothesize that in this same aboriginal period (from, say, at least Pueblo II on) the number of initiated members and societies was larger and/or that there was greater overall involvement in the political organization. Many of these themes will be explored elsewhere. At the present time, socio-ceremonial and political organization differs from village to village, but I believe that an examination of the data would show secrecy functioning in a similar way in each one.

---

[15]M. E. Smith enlightened me on this point and is responsible for many suggestions that I have incorporated in this paper.

# Breath in Shamanic Curing
# by
# Donald Bahr

INTRODUCTION

North American Indian curing is generally termed "shamanic." If we ask why, a number of answers are usually given: because the curers use personal spirit helpers, because they transcend ordinary reality, because they suck out sickness with their mouths, etc. It is difficult to coordinate these answers with each other. Our concept of shamanic curing on this continent is spongy.

I have the scholar's faith that the sponginess is due more to the state of our observations than to the reality observed. The present paper thus presupposes the existence of a structured continental culture of native curing and takes steps so that we may see it better. Our starting place is the act of sucking, the most observable of the traits listed above. Also, it is perhaps the most widely reported datum on shamanic curing in the ethnographies, so much so that "sucking shaman" is used almost interchangeably with "shaman."

As California is the center of gravity of the papers in this volume, we will first note the relation between sucking and shamanism in a short summary statement by Kroeber (1953). For reasons given below, I have divided the statement into three parts; Kroeber wrote it as a single paragraph. Except for that division, the statement is copied verbatim:

(1) The shamanistic practices of most California groups are fairly uniform and similar to those obtaining among the North American Indians generically.
(2) The primary function of the California shaman is the curing of disease.
(3) The latter is almost always considered due to the presence in the body of some foreign or hostile object, rarely to an abstraction or injury of the soul. The Mojave are the only tribe for whom there is a definite record that shamans recovered souls, although the attitude of other southern Californians is such that the belief may well have prevailed among them also. Over most of California, the shaman's business is the removal of the disease object, and this in the great majority of cases is carried out by sucking. Singing, dancing, and smoking tobacco, with or without the accompaniment of

genuine trance conditions, are the usual diagnostic means. Manipulation of the body, brushing it, and blowing of breath, saliva, or tobacco smoke are sometimes resorted to in the extraction of the disease object (1953:851).

Let us consider this statement as a text and take it, as I ask others to be taken later, as testimony from the larger culture of which Kroeber was a part. It is the culture of American anthropologists here; later it will be the culture of Indian shamans. The first sentence says that California shamanism is of a piece with North America in general: a piece internally for shamanic practices in California tend towards uniformity, and of a piece externally because the California practices are similar to the rest of North America. In his first sentence Kroeber has expressed the point of view of this paper. The second sentence underwrites this paper's concentration on curing rather than some other shamanic function. The sponginess which we seek to rectify is in the final multisentence passage. In this passage just one practice stands out as something *shared* by the tribes in question: sucking. A number of other items are mentioned, essentially as free variables. This, then, is what the exposition started in sentence (1) comes down to: North American shamanism exists; California is a piece of it; it is largely concerned with curing; and sucking is its clearest common denominator. It is the unstructured relation between sucking and the other shamanic items included under (3) that I term spongy. The present paper attempts to bind a number of these items to the act and concept of sucking through studying a particular case.

The case is the Pimans (Pima and Pagago) of southern Arizona; i.e., a Southwestern rather than a California people. If the Piman case articulates many of the items written into Kroeber's synopsis of California shamanism, the cause of continental ethnology will have been served. Viewed in this light, our choice of cases is not unfortunate because it is outside California, but because it is not from farther away. A New England tribe would have served the purpose better. The Pimans were chosen because I know them well and because of what they oppose the act of sucking to.

The additional items of Kroeber's list will be brought under control via the act and concept of blowing. By our formula, blowing is to sucking as breathing out is to breathing in. The one is the natural counterpart of the other *except that* different local varieties of shamanism may stress one, the other, or both acts.

It is asserted that shamanism in general is concerned with *breath*. This is not necessarily its only concern and this concern is obviously not the monopoly of shamanism. Sucking, however, from all that we know, is peculiarly identified with our subject matter, so we will not go wrong in building outwards from that act. Accordingly, sucking is the stressed form of breathing in, the counterpart of which is, of course, the act of exhaling, which, in stressed form, is blowing.

We will note that the stressed acts of sucking and blowing lend themselves to different ends. The act of sucking is by nature directed at something within a patient's body. The body, tangible and close at hand, constitutes the spatial frame of reference for this act. The act of blowing, in contrast, may be directed at something far beyond the body, namely spirits. The ability of blowing to go both onto the body and out to the spirits is felt to be crucial.

We concentrate on the Pimans in this paper because they use both stressed acts but their theory and practice of curing have more to do with blowing than with sucking. Sucking is done but the act of blowing is decisive in effecting a cure. This runs counter to the general tendency in the ethnographic literature, so such a case should be viewed with interest.

Our data come from didactic texts collected in Piman on the theory of curing, and from "real world" observations on how their cures are performed. It is felt that the logic behind sucking and blowing is as much a logic of experience as of theoretical reason, so reference must be made to behavioral as well as textual materials. The ideas presented here, especially on the native theoretical side, are discussed more fully in a booklength study on Piman medicine (Bahr, Gregorio, Lopez and Alvarez 1974). They are essentially the ideas of one shaman, Gregorio, whose texts are the basis of the book. The behavioral side has for the most part been recorded since the completion of that book.

PIMAN TECHNICAL TERMS

The easiest way to see the centrality of blowing in Piman medicine is by examining the tribe's technical medical vocabulary.[1] The Piman word for "cure" is *wûsosig*, meaning literally 'the blowing'. The word for "curer" is *s-wûsos ó'odham*, meaning literally 'blower man'. Both words are

---

[1]This discussion of Piman medical vocabulary is testimony to the importance of working in the native language. Two quite good studies of Piman curing were made prior to mine, one by Russell on the Pima (1908) and one by Underhill on the Papago (1946). Both were conducted with English as the contact language and both ignored blowing. (The studies were good in recording the names and symptoms of many kinds of sickness, and in giving careful translations of many curing songs.) I attribute their shortcomings on blowing, first to the fact that English was used to collect information on native doctrines and second to the probable fact that neither Russell nor Underhill saw actual cures.
On the first point, it is simply but bluntly true that one cannot talk in Piman about curing without making constant use of words derived from *wûsot*, 'to blow'. It is also true that the word "blow" has no respectable place in the English discourse on sickness. Bilingual Pimans know this and they expunge the word from their speech in English on sickness. On the second point it is noted that cures are private affairs among the Pimans and therefore difficult for outsiders to witness. It need only be added that Piman cures are complex enough, and Pimans have proved reticent enough in describing them in the abstract, that there is no substitute for actually seeing cures.

built on the verb *wúsot*, 'to blow', a word which, incidentally, only designates *animate* blowing. (There is another word for "wind"--*héwel*--and in Piman, unlike English, one does not say that the wind "blows," presumably because it is not seen as being produced by any creature's puffing.)

These "cures" are only half of the typical sequence in treating a sickness. Prior to the 'blowing' another kind of person does another kind of treatment primarily for diagnostic purposes. The event is called *kúlañmada* or *dúajida*, the first being a "short" form of the latter. The first word literally means 'the application of medicine' and the second literally means 'the vitalization'. The person who does them is called *kúlañ o'odham* or *má:kai*, two synonymous words for 'shaman'. The first literally means 'medicine man' (and is clearly a loan translation)[2] while the second is unanalyzable and undoubtedly is a more ancient word.

The effective relation between *kúlañmada/dúajida* and *wúsosig* is as diagnosis to cure, notwithstanding that *kúlañmada/dúajida* "means" curing in an etymological sense. I will not try to explain how this linguistic situation came about, but will only state a few further facts about the differences between the two types of events in native theory. The act of blowing figures in both *kúlañmada/dúajida* and *wúsosig*, but the purpose of blowing is to 'illuminate' sickness in the first case and to 'do away with it' in the *wúsosig*. Sucking is done only in the *kúlañmada/dúajida*. It is the prerogative of shamans. The 'blower man', being in effect "lay" ritual curers, do not suck. What is sucked by the shamans is more like *information* on the nature of the sickness than the sickness itself, which is why the typical *kúlañmada/dúajida* must be followed by a curative 'blowing' by the lay ritualists in order to do away with the sickness.

To sum up, blowing by lay ritualists is the expected way to cure sickness, while blowing and sucking by shamans are the expected ways to 'illuminate' and diagnose a sickness.

## THE PATIENT'S BODY AND THE LANDSCAPE OF THE SPIRITS

The kinds of affliction that we are concerned with are the so-called 'staying sicknesses' which are the central concern of traditional Piman medicine. These sicknesses are said to be caused by the 'strengths' and 'ways' of 'dangerous objects'. Dangerous objects are comprised of

---

[2]*Kúlañ* is from the Spanish verb *curar*, 'to cure'. Piman *kúlañ* is used only as a noun for some reason, meaning 'medicine'. The verb form built from this word is *kúlañmad*, 'to apply medicine', the *-mad* being a verbalizing suffix. *Kúlañmada*, 'the application of medicine', is a noun built from the verbal form *kúlañmad*. *O'odham*, the other term in the Piman loan translation from "medicine man," simply means 'man' or 'Indian'.

about thirty distinct kinds of things, such as Coyote, Ghost, Devil, Dog, and Jimson Weed. Each dangerous object has a 'way', the violation of which results in the arrival of an unwanted 'strength' in the patient's body. Every act in a *kúlañmada/dúajida* or a *wúsosig* is aimed directly or indirectly at these strengths, which correspond to the foreign or hostile objects mentioned by Kroeber.

Certain actions are aimed at strengths directly; for example, the act of sucking is intended to remove just enough of a strength to permit its diagnosis. Other actions, for example singing (a feature of *dúajida* and *wúsosig*, but not of *kúlañmada*), are actually aimed at spirits, but their purpose is to enlist the spirits' aid in dealing with strengths. The spirits addressed in songs are not in the patient's body, but are understood to be far away from the house where the singing takes place. We call this distant place the landscape of the spirits. In Piman it is called 'the dark', meaning the darkness of night. *Dúajidas* are always performed at night, *wúsosigs* ideally are supposed to be, and *kúlañmadas*, which make no appeal to spirits, tend to be done in the daytime. The landscape of the spirits, in short, unlike the spiritual realm addressed in Christian rituals, is accessible only at night.

Blowing is the one act in Piman medicine which is *meant* to go both places, both onto the patient and away past him into the landscape of the spirits. Singing normally registers on the patient, but it is not specifically meant to. It is directed at the spirits. There is no theoretical necessity for the patient to hear the songs. He may be asleep or he may be an infant too young to understand the words of the songs.

Sucking of course *cannot* have an effect on distant spirits. The only way for sucking to engage spirits is if the latter are conceived as present in the patient's body; i.e., if some form of "possession" is postulated. This, by and large, is not the Piman concept. It could be but it isn't, so far as it known, just as songs could be viewed as therapeutic to the patient hearing them, but are not.

It remains to show how blowing articulates both realms, that of the body and that of the landscape of the spirits.

BLOWING

The essential behavioral fact about blowing is that it is the softest as well as the longest range method for humans to touch each other. Blown breath is felt on the skin as the breath collides against the body. One can blow farther than the arm can reach. Smell, sight, and sound of course are effective at greater distances between humans than blown breath, but they are not tactile. So blowing belongs to the sense of touch, and it is the "long distance toucher." All this I take to be "universal" or "archetypal" about blowing. It is true for us, but we don't use it. It is true for Pimans and they do. Further behavioral or "phenomenal" facts about breath, which will be discussed later, are that it is colorless and odorless, and is associated with life.

We have noted that blowing occurs in *kúlañmada/dúajida* and in *wúsosig*. We will discuss its role in the two long night-time forms, *dúajida* and *wúsosig*, ignoring the *kúlañmada* as a short form in which spirits do not enter.

The *dúajida* and *wúsosig* follow a similar scenario of periods of singing punctuated at intervals by blowing. There are typically four periods of four songs each in a *dúajida* or *wúsosig*. The singing is done from a seated position about four feet from the patient. In this position the patient is just about at the threshhold of blowing's tactile sensibility. The singers, whether shamans or lay curers, blow from this position at the conclusion of each of the four songs within a "period" of singing. The expressed purpose of this blowing is to propel the words of the song *past* the patient out into the night toward spirits. In other words, the patient is not the theoretical target of blowing from the seated position. If he feels it, it makes no difference except to remind him that most of it is going past.

The songs of the *dúajida* are theoretically aimed at spirit helpers to gain their help in making a diagnosis. The songs of a ritual cure (*wúsosig*) are aimed at a spirit representative of the 'way' which has been diagnosed as causing the sickness in question. Upon hearing the songs, the latter spirit is expected to lift the 'strength' that it controls from the patient's body.

After each period of singing, the singer (whether shaman or ritual curer) arises from his chair, approaches the patient (lying on a bed), and blows on him or her from a distance of about 16 inches. In a *dúajida* the purpose of this blowing is to illuminate the strengths in the patient. The shaman also fans the patient with eagle feathers and 'shines' him with a quartz crystal for the same purpose.

In a *wúsosig* the purpose of blowing is to transmit sublime bits of a fetish representing the dangerous object onto the patient's body. The fetish is held in the hand (analogous to the shaman's divining tools) in such a way that the curer's breath goes past it.

In both rituals, then, breath is used to cover the short distance between the blower and the patient. While the shaman or lay curer *could* touch the patient from this range, he blows instead. This is as close as the ritual curer gets to the patient while the shaman also *sucks* him to remove strengths.

A further observation may now be made: while the shaman and ritual curer both blow, sing, and hold an object in the hand, they do so with different rationales. The shaman's *breath* is said to have the power to illuminate, which is due to the nature of his own heart (called 'breathing thing' in Piman). This power is crucial in a diagnosis but not in a ritual cure. The ritual curer neither has this power nor needs it. The shaman's *songs* are said to attract his personal spirit helpers, while the curers' songs are learned and used by the general public as prayers. The spirits that are sung to are public rather than personal figures. The shaman uses a hand-held feather *tool* to aid his charismatic breath (corresponding to Kroeber's act of "brushing"), while the reverse relation obtains between breath, tool, and power in a ritual cure: it is the tool as 'fetish' rather than the breath which is said to have power. Blowing by the ritual curer serves only to transmit this power physically onto the patient.

Finally we note the function of tobacco smoke in the system. Used by a shaman, it is rationalized in the same way as the crystal or feather tool: to aid his charismatic breath in identifying strengths in the patient's body. If a shaman is strong enough, it is said, he doesn't need tobacco and neither does he need the other tools. They only *augment* his own essential charisma. According to my information, smoking is not a regular part of the *wúsosig* ritual cures. It is done in "rest periods" for relaxation after a cycle of singing and blowing has been completed and before the next cycle begins. It is not itself a ritual act. In behavioral terms, this means that the smoke is not carefully *blown* in any particular direction. It is simply gotten rid of through the mouth or nose.

The Pimans seem peculiar in their use of smoke, for it is commonly used through North America as a means of praying or, in other words, of establishing sensory contact with distant spirits. This use has not been noted from the Pimans. Mr. Gregorio did not mention it in his texts and it was not observed in the two *dúajidas* and twenty-odd ritual cures that I have witnessed.

We can see in principle why smoking would lend itself to long distance communication. It imparts both color and odor to blown breath with the effect of greatly extending the range of breath's sensibility. If one assumes that where smoke goes, breath is also present, the value of tobacco as a long distance breath tracer is evident. In other words, the "logical" reason to smoke should be to shift the theater of action from the patient to the landscape of the spirits. Why the Piman record does not testify overtly to this logic I cannot say. I would like to thank Thomas Blackburn for providing J. P. Harrington's unpublished notes on a similar case involving the Chumash of California. There, too, the emphasis is on blowing smoke over things close at hand--tobacco pipes (to bless them for future use), rattlesnakes, and sick people--with no mention of distant spirits. This suggests that the Pimans are not alone, and that more and better records are needed on the "targeting" of blown smoke.

Stressed and Unstressed

Both forms of blowing, from the seated and "approach" position, are strong acts. They register clearly on a tape recorder, while the ordinary breathing of everybody present does not register. It is the converse with the shaman's sucking. When he sucks, it is heard as a loud series of implosive whooOII's. When he breathes out, however, nothing is heard. One cannot watch one of these cures without being impressed by the extent to which they are orchestrated around sucking and blowing--

particularly the latter. They are literally methods of cure based on breath.

Review

The key to the system is the two positions, seated and "approach," and the oscillation between spirits and the patient as the ritual moves from one position to the other. The catalogue of ritual acts can be divided among those done from the seated position, those done from the approach position, and the one act--blowing--which is done from both.

| <u>Seated</u> | <u>Both</u> | <u>Approach</u> |
|---|---|---|
| Singing | | |
| Shaking | | |
| | Blowing | |
| | | Looking |
| | | Fanning |
| | | Pressing |
| | | Sucking |

Tools of one sort or another are used for most of the actions. Shaking is done with a rattle (by shamans and ritual curers) or divining plume (shaman only). Fanning is done with a divining plume or, in some ritual cures, with a feather fetish representing the dangerous object. Pressing is done with an effigy figurine (fetish). The list could be extended to include still other acts done in *dúajidas* or *wúsosigs*, but these are the main acts. Extending the list would not change the form.

As blowing is the one act that goes both places, tobacco smoke has a special status among "tools." It is a substance extrinsic to the shaman's breath but it completely merges with it. As such, the use of tobacco is indicative not only of the importance of blowing in general (for whatever it is used, blowing is implicated as a ritual technique), but of the mix obtaining in a particular culture between spiritual and bodily targets for blowing. As was noted above, the Pimans seem peculiar for their emphasis on short distance blowing with smoke.

BREATH AND LIFE

We have discussed this system of curing by breath as a record of behavior and native rationales. It must be admitted that the record adds up to a mystery. The mystery is what actually causes an improvement in the patient's condition. As I see it, the system is by nature purposefully ambiguous and extremely bold.

The boldness is the starting assumption that one person's breath can save another person's life. If we do not grant this assumption (i.e., grant that it is believed), we are discussing a peoples' dramas ("fictions," "symbolisms") rather than their cures. There is every indication that the events are meant to be taken as cures.

We have seen that breathing has two "halves," of which I propose that breathing out is in fact the more important, as an archetypal *imparting* of life.[3] The curious thing about sucking is that it does not remove the patient's breath, which would be deadly, but removes a bit of his sickness, which is seen as beneficial.

If that is the essential or archetypal scheme, it is overlain with an elaborate cargo of other acts and rationales that complicate and mystify the relation between the breathing shaman and his patient. This is the ambiguity, which I attempt to catalogue below. To say that it is intentional is simply to recognize it as present in one form or another in every recorded shamanic system.

Chief among the buffers in the Piman system is the landscape of the spirits and all acts directed towards its inhabitants. Between the shaman's breathing and the cessation of the sickness there are in the first place the shaman's spirit helpers who receive ultimate credit for his diagnosis. Secondly, because the Pimans divide the curing process between two events, there are the spirits of the 'way', who are blown and sung to by ritual curers, and who hold ultimate responsibility for the patient's recovery.

We call these spirits buffers because they are not viewed as extensions of the humans involved in the healing process, but as independent third parties. As such they are different from the spirits in soul loss and soul rescue theories of sickness and cure, such as Kroeber mentioned for the Mojave. The critical theater of operations in the latter kind of curing is the landscape of the spirits and not the patient's body, but the methodology of these cures is very bold. The shaman's own soul (or spirit) goes "in trance" to rescue the patient's soul. No buffering third party spirit intervenes. The question about such cures, which I am not prepared to discuss, is whether there is in fact no action via blowing or sucking before, during, or after the trance rescue journey. In the ideal type of soul rescue there would be none. Consistent with our claim of blowing as the basic shamanic act, however, there would *be* none in the ideal case because something *like* the breath of each has been sent or abducted elsewhere. In a sense, the entire case has been breathed into another realm.

---

[3]No Piman is on record as having said, "Blowing imparts life." I say that it is implicit in their and (all?) other shamanic systems because (1) blowing on the patient is done in such systems, and (2) breath in a vague sense is associated with life (e.g., when one stops breathing, one is dead). I am aware that the concept of "buffering," developed below, explains away cases where blown breath is said to do something other than impart life. Buffering says in effect that the idea has been suppressed. I do not believe that this could be proved, but would simply call for further research into the prevalence of (1) and (2) in the ethnographic record. If (1) and (2) are solid, the case is made as well as it can be.

Another means of qualifying the role of the shaman's breath is the entire large subject of medications; i.e., tangible substances introduced into the patient's body from a source extrinsic to the shaman's own nature. We have noted a form of this in the Piman use of fetishes. To the extent that these are attributed power, they qualify the shamanic process. Smoke is such a substance to the degree that it and not the shaman's breath is held responsible for a bodily change. Piman shamans use other substances as well. There are herbs that some shamans bite, mix with their saliva, and put into the body as an alternative to sucking out strength. When this is done, the act in a *dúajida* which we call "sucking" actually becomes a third and most intimate position for both aspects of breathing: with his lips against the patient's skin the shaman kisses him and may "breathe" a medication in as well as draw a strength out.

Logically the heading of medications includes all substances such as pills, teas, injections, liquid "spirits," etc. Pimans lump them all under the noun *kúlañ*, 'medicine', and assign them a remarkably small role in their essentially breathed system of treatment.

A final variable is the extent to which the patient is implicated in his own recovery or, in other words, the extent to which he is felt to be helplessly sick. If the bulk of the curing process is felt to be a function of the patient's own regenerative forces, then all of the abovementioned factors, including the shaman's breath, pale into insignificance. If the reverse is true, the medical system perforce must weigh the other factors more heavily. Shamanic cures are usually depicted as being quite bold and heroic, but much depends on the weighting of these other factors.

It is plain that the total medical culture of a tribe is no less complex in principle than medicine among ourselves. One may even say it is more complex under shamanism because this mode or "layer" of thought[4] insists on curative breathing on top of, or prior to, the more familiar methods of prayer and medication.


CONCLUSION

This paper's narrow goal was to see blowing as the counterpart to the often-reported shamanic act of sucking. We started with a specimen text by Kroeber and turned to the Pimans to see how many of the items listed by Kroeber structure around the paired acts of sucking and blowing.

---

[4]When I use the word "layer" in reference to shamanic curing, I do not mean that there was an evolutionary sequence in which shamanic breathing existed alone for a million years, then prayer was invented and then medications. Perhaps all three methods are equally old. On the other hand it would seem clear that in the last 7000 years the other two methods have expanded tremendously at shamanism's expense. There is an evolution from the primitive in that sense.

More speculatively, I have suggested that sucking and blowing are shamanism's original contribution to curing:

(1) In the minimum case, shamanism requires just two parties, a patient and a practitioner. The practitioner uses one or both of the two stressed forms of breathing. The purpose of sucking must be to remove something and that of blowing, to put something in. If we accept the general equation of life and breath, the meaning of blowing would seem to be to impart life.

(2) The process of curing is always more elaborate than that.[5] The next logical step up is to include spirits in the equation, a step which must be through the blowing rather than the sucking half of breathing. There are two modes of spiritualized shamanism, bold and modest. The bold form posits soul loss and soul rescue; the modest form opts for spirit helpers who are distinguished from the shaman's own soul or spirit.

(3) A notable point about shamanism is its disinterest in addressing the patient verbally as part of the cure. Speech (or song or chant) enters the picture primarily as prayer addressed to spirits. "Raw breath" is what is primarily addressed towards the patient, not words. This fact sets shamanic curing apart from psychoanalysis and other highly verbal forms of psychotherapy. Shamanism is an oral form of curing in which speech is theoretically downplayed.

(4) Shamanism is also relatively uninterested in medications in the sense of swallowable (or otherwise physically ingested) substances. Those that are used are primarily transmitted through the practitioner's mouth, from what we have termed the breathing system's maximal degree of approach, the kiss.[6]


## AFTERWARDS: THE *WÍLANTA*

It will be instructive now to test the shamanic model against a form of Piman ritual cure derived from Christianity. It is called *wílanta*, from the Spanish *vela*, 'household prayer vigil'. We are interested in *wílantas* performed for the sick, and will simply note that the same ritual form is used as well for wakes over the dead and to honor household saints on their feastday when nobody in the family is sick.

The typical Piman house has just one room. The household altar

---

[5]The Piman *kúlañmada* actually consists of just those two acts, although the blowing is normally accompanied with tobacco smoke. *Kúlañmadas*, however, are viewed as insufficient to deal with severe sicknesses.

[6]Kiss may be an unfortunate term for this act, as it has connotations in English which should not be transferred onto our subject matter. Granting that kissing is an intimate act everywhere, we are interested in its use for curing among people who may lack the custom of kissing for love or affection. Perhaps the two practices are in negative correlation.

and the family's beds are thus in close proximity. The *dúajida*s and *wúsosig*s discussed earlier are performed in the house but directed towards the patient's bed. Prayer vigils are performed facing the altar. Vigils resemble the shamanic events in that they consist for the most part of songs. As in a *dúajida* or *wúsosig*, the songs are divided into periods; e.g., four periods of four songs each. The singers in each type of event are specialists called in for just that purpose: a single shaman (always male to my knowledge) for a *dúajida*, one or more ritual curers for a *wúsosig* (always male again), and normally several old women for a prayer vigil. The songs of a *wílanta* are Spanish hymns.

There the similarity ends. There is no sucking or blowing in a prayer vigil. At the end of the rite, the patient comes to the altar and inhales from the same holy object that the singers had addressed their songs to.

Our point is that the system of breathing fundamental to shamanism has no place in this ritual, which is purely and simply a prayer session. The *wílanta* is interesting because, being done by the Pimans, it has a strong external resemblance to their shamanic curing. We can say, for example, that the *wílanta* songs are addressed to indoor representatives of the landscape of the spirits. From the point of view of the *dúajida* and *wúsosig*, these representatives have displaced the patient from the center of the stage. With the patient off-center, the system of breathing is also absent. The one bit of ritual breathing in the cure, the patient's inhalation, is in a context entirely different from shamanism. The patient does it rather than the curer. It is more akin to taking a medicine than to shamanic sucking.

# Heart and Feces: Symbols of Mortality in the Dying God Myth
## by
## C. Patrick Morris

INTRODUCTION

Included in E. W. Gifford's collection of ethnographic data on the Yavapai cultures of northwestern Arizona are several freely translated texts of the Dying God story, a myth prominent among Southern California Shoshoneans and other Yumans. The Dying God myth, including those of the Yavapai and other Upland Yumans, tells of the death and cremation of a god whose heart is stolen and eaten by Coyote. Kroeber (1925:790) and others (Strong 1929; DuBois 1908; Gifford 1933; and Devereux 1961) have stated that the theme of the Dying God myth is mortality, "probably the dominant and most poignantly felt motive of every mythology in Southern California" (Kroeber 1925:790). Devereux (1961: 287) finds that the Mohave Dying God myth "contains, in a condensed form, allusions to practically every form of death, suicide, and funeral practice" recognized by the Mohave. Kroeber further notes that while "all of the Californians make much of the origin of death, the Yuman and Southern Californian Shoshonean tales appear to think less of the impending end of the great god himself than of the fate of humanity as typified by him" (Kroeber 1925:790).

Despite the recognized importance of the Dying God story little has been published about the significance of specific elements in the myth and how such elements convey the theme of mortality. In this paper we want to examine recurring elements in 10 Upland Yuman Dying God myth variants to appraise their meaning in this important and widely told myth-drama.

The ten Upland Yuman myths analyzed include: one Western Yavapai variant (Gifford 1933:402-412): two Southeastern Yavapai variants (Gifford 1932:243-246); two Northeastern Yavapai variants (Gifford 1933: 349-364); three Havasupai variants, two published by Smithson and Euler (1964:32-35, 49-56), and one by Cushing (1965:72-75); and two Walapai variants (Kroeber 1935:12-36, 249-250).[1] In addition, several Southern

---

[1]Walapai 1 is found in Kroeber (1935:12-36) and Walapai 2 in

California variants and other Yuman variants were consulted to expand patterns only partially developed in the Upland Yuman materials. Gifford's Western Yavapai text is the focus for the analysis and the interpretations drawn here.

A brief summary of the plot of the Western Yavapai variant will present the reader with the essentials of the story. Additional details will be introduced when needed.

Western Yavapai Plot Outline

In the beginning people lived in the Underworld. Older Brother[2] creates the moon. Younger Brother creates the more radiant sun which nearly smothers the people before Older Brother adjusts the roof of the world. Older Brother becomes sexually interested in his two daughters and he touches their sexual parts. He goes to a stream to defecate, and his angered daughters, who are now frogs, catch his feces and eat them. Older Brother becomes ill, but before he dies he advises the people to cremate him. They send Coyote away so he won't eat the corpse. While he is gone the cremation begins. However, Coyote sees the smoke and returns in time to jump over the protective rings of people surrounding the corpse, steal the heart, and eat it. Before Older Brother dies he explains the yearly calendar.

After this the people have no food and decide to migrate. A fir tree and grape vine are planted which the people climb to the Upperworld. Younger Brother sees water rising from the Underworld. A flood caused by the two frog-daughters drowns mankind. Only a girl placed in a hollow log survives.

The Upland Yuman variants are listed by episode in Figure 1. The letters along the left margin are keyed to the plot outline of the Western Yavapai variant. The numbers in the body of the figure refer to the sequence of episodes in each variant. The chart shows which episodes are found in each variant and their order.

From Figure 1 we can see the similarities in the variants. Seven variants include the illness and death of the Dying God. The three variants without the death (NE 1, SE 1, and Hav 1)[3] seem to be short

---

Kroeber (1935:249-250). The Northeastern Yavapai variant 1 is in Gifford (1933:349-364) and variant 2 in Gifford (1933:353 fn). Southeastern Yavapai variant 1 is in Gifford (1932:243-245) and variant 2 in Gifford (1932:245-246).

[2]The character Dying God has a different name in each of the variants. The Western Yavapai call him Older Brother. To avoid confusion the term Dying God will be used throughout.

[3]NE 1, SE 1 and Hav 1 are abbreviations for the Upland Yuman variants used when they are cited in the text.

Figure 1

Comparison of Upland Yuman Variants by Episode

| EPISODES | | VARIANTS | | | | | | | | | |
|---|---|---|---|---|---|---|---|---|---|---|---|
| | Description | W Yav | NE (1) | NE (2) | SE (1) | SE (2) | Hav (1) | Hav (3) | Hav (4) | Wal (1) | Wal (2) |
| A) | People Live in Underworld | 1 | 1 | 1 | 1 | | 1 | | 1 | 1 | |
| B) | Creation of Sun and Moon | 2 | | | | | 4 | | | | |
| $C_1$)* | Older Brother's Incest | 3 | | | | | | | | | |
| $C_2$)* | Older Brother Becomes Ill | 4 | 3 | | | 1 | | 3 | 4 | 5 | 1 |
| $D_1$)* | Cremation | 5 | 7 | | | 3 | | 5 | 6 | 6 | 4 |
| $D_2$)* | Heart Stolen | 6 | 10 | | | 4 | | 6 | 7 | | 5 |
| $E_1$)* | Calendar | 7 | 5 | | | 5 | | | 8 | | |
| $E_2$)* | Teaching About Plants | 8 | 6 | | | 2 | | 4 | | 8 | |
| F) | Migration to Upperworld | 9 | 2 | 2 | 2 | | 2 | | 3 | | |
| G) | Flood and Escape of Girl | 10 | 11 | 3 | 3 | | 5 | | | | |
| H) | Building a Shade | | 4 | | | | | 2 | | | |
| I) | Coyote Denies Immortality | | 8 | | | | | | | 7 | 2 |
| J) | Coyote Makes Snow | | 9 | | | | | | | | |
| K) | Woman Becomes a Frog | | | | | | | 3 | | | |
| L) | Snake Holds Sing | | | | | | | 1 | | | |
| M) | Earth Covered with Water | | | | | | | | | 2 | 2 |
| N) | Fly Starts Fire | | | | | | | | | 5 | 3 |
| P) | People Made from Cane | | | | | | | | | 3 | |
| Q) | Frog Killed | | | | | | | | | 5 | 4 |
| R) | People Divided | | | | | | | | | 9 | |
| S) | What Is Given | | | | | | | | | 10 | |

*$C_1$ and $C_2$ are one Episode in W Yav, as are $D_1$ and $D_2$, and $E_1$ and $E_2$.

introductions to another story assigned by Gifford to Cycle Two (Gifford 1933:347).[4] They have been retained here because they include the migration and worldwide flood caused by Frogs which is part of the overall story of the Dying God.

The analysis consisted of isolating episodes in each variant that made direct reference to death. These episodes were then examined to determine if they had elements that recurred and suggested some design or pattern. We found that those episodes which referred to death also made reference to some form of fire or water. Using this rather slender pattern we decided to explore all references to forms of fire and water in each variant and to seek other similar or contrastive elements to expand the pattern. This procedure was followed throughout, building patterns based on similarities and contrasts that recurred in the episodes. In addition to fire and water we found two important characters, Coyote and Frog(s), and two unique foods, feces and heart, to constitute a pattern that proved to be essential to understanding the mortality theme of the Dying God myth. It was discovered that for the Upland Yumans the Dying God's heart symbolized maize and the more general topic of plant food and its relationship to cultural development.

The episodes that describe events which threaten or result in death were: (1) the creation or introduction of the sun; (2) the bewitchment of the Dying God; (3) the Dying God's cremation; and (4) the world flood. In these episodes there were two general expressions of mortality: collective mortality involving mankind, and individual mortality involving the Dying God. We begin by discussing collective mortality.

## COLLECTIVE MORTALITY

Our analysis of collective mortality focuses on two episodes: (1) the creation of the sun and (2) the world flood. The creation of the sun occurs in three Upland Yuman variants (WYav, Hav 1 and Hav 4). Havasupai 1 and the Western Yavapai variants are discussed first. Havasupai 4 is presented separately as a special case of the association of sun and mortality.

### Creation of the Sun

In both the Western Yavapai and Havasupai 1 variants mankind is threatened because the Dying God and his younger brother have failed to control their celestial creations, the sun and moon. In the Western Yavapai variant the sky is too close and the sun[5] "nearly smothers the

---

[4]According to one informant the Yavapai Dying God variants are the first in a larger, four cycle origin or creation epic similar in organization to other mythologies in the Southwest (Gifford 1933:347).

[5]The cane used by Older Brother, a *dikeru* (WYav:S.23), is described in the ethnography as a "hook of ash wood used to adjust hot

people" (WYav:S.21).[6] In Havasupai 1 it is the excessive motion of the sun that threatens mankind with starvation because there is not enough light to hunt (Hav 1:S.46).

Besides these two Upland Yuman variants, several Southern California variants make direct reference to the power of the sun and its impact on mankind. The Luiseño say, "When Sun was born he gave tremendous light which struck the people into unconsciousness or caused them to roll upon the ground in agony" (DuBois 1906:52); Sun "gave so much light and heat that he nearly killed all the people" (DuBois 1908:132). The Cahuilla say that after the Dying God created the sun it "was too hot to hold and slipped away from him," leaving the world in darkness (Hooper 1920:319). In addition, the neighboring Diegueño note that the Dying God "made the moon . . . , but finding that the moon was not bright enough, he made the sun to light the world" (DuBois 1907:236). Similar associations are made by the Mohave (Kroeber 1972:7) and the Maricopa (Spier 1933:238). The variants argue that the sun's power must be controlled or the resulting chaos will precipitate worldwide suffering and death.

One Upland Yuman variant (Hav 4) expresses the sun-mortality relationship in causal terms. In Havasupai 4 "bright lights" are discovered when the people emerge from the Underworld. Soon after the emergence a "Cacique [Dying God] is overcome by the bright lights and angry waters and dies" (Hav 4:S.4). Here the sun in the form of "bright lights" is not seen as a threat to mankind but instead joins with "angry waters" to kill the first man.

When we compare the other variants with Havasupai 4 we see a pattern that outlines the association of water and forms of fire/light to contrastive forms of mortality, collective and individual.

In Havasupai 1, the Western Yavapai and the California variants, mankind is only threatened by the Dying God's errors. No one dies, but it is clear that the behavior of the God(s) has cosmic significance. Misjudgements by the Creators are a source of danger to mankind. In contrast, Havasupai 4 sees a direct relationship between "bright lights" and the first death of man. Threats to mankind are omitted and the story begins with the use of water and light/fire to kill the Dying God.

Like mirror inversions the Western Yavapai and Havasupai 1 variants are contrastive expressions of the theme occurring in Havasupai 4. In the Havasupai 4 variant sun/light and water are used to kill an individual. In the other variants the contrastive elements sun/fire and water

---

stones in the mescal pit" (Gifford 1936:279). This seems an appropriate tool to adjust "hot objects" such as a moon and sun.

[6]This expression (WYav:S.6) is the format used for citing specific sentences within each variant; it means sentence 6 of the Western Yavapai variant.

threaten mankind. The Havasupai 4 variant suggests that we need to examine all the flood episodes to determine their relationship to the theme of mortality.

World Flood

Seven of the Upland Yuman variants end the Dying God story with a world wide flood.[7] In these terminal floods the water rises from the Underworld and everyone drowns except one girl who is placed in a log. She later repopulates the second world which is included in Cycle Two of the Yavapai creation epic (Gifford 1933).

All the terminal floods are specifically said to be caused by frog-witches: two daughters of the Dying God who became frogs (WYav); the loss of Hanyiko's (frog's) heart (NE1); a large frog (NE2); a large frog (SE1); and a scorned woman who becomes a frog (Hav 1).

Like the sun, floods are related to collective mortality. The exception is Havasupai 4, noted earlier, where the flood and lights occur at the beginning and kill only the Dying God. As with the near catastrophes precipitated by the Dying God's creation of celestial bodies, the terminal floods are acts of revenge by Frogs who earlier had bewitched and killed the first man. In both instances it is the misdeeds of the Dying God that result in the eventual destruction of mankind.

Of the other four Upland Yuman Dying God stories, two contain no floods (Wal 2 and Hav 3). The remaining two variants (Hav 4 and Wal 1) begin the story with the world flooded. In Walapai 1 the initial flood is not related to the death of mankind or to the death of the Dying God. Instead the flood recedes through a hole in the earth, leaving the world with little water. Thereafter, the God brothers set about creating mankind. In this version water in a less cataclysmic form, a river, is later associated with the abode of frogs who kill the Dying God.

In Havasupai 4, where the flood occurs early in the myth, the flood is not caused by a frog but by a surrogate, "angry waters." Like its contrastive use of the sun described earlier, Havasupai 4 makes a contrastive use of floods. The "angry waters" of the flood combine with the "bright lights" of the sun to kill the Dying God. Here the two contrastive elements are transformed into a lethal instrument. The pattern appears to be that the initial floods are related to individual mortality, whereas the terminal floods involve collective mortality, the death of mankind.[8]

---

[7]Hav 3 and Wal 2 do not have any floods. SE2 has been combined with SE1, so the lack of a flood is not considered.

[8]In Cycle Two fire and water are a source of life. They combine to impregnate the sole survivor of the world flood, thus insuring the repopulation of the world.

This contrast of initial and terminal floods is made explicit in Walapai 1 and Havasupai 4 by the description of the increasingly dry environment following the initial flood. "Now the earth became so dry that our forefathers had but little to drink" (Hav 4:S.22). These two variants begin with the world flooded, but end with the world dry. A similar pattern is given in Maricopa variants of the Dying God (Spier 1933:352).

In contrast to the Yavapai variants with the terminal flood, neither Walapai 1 nor Havasupai 4 includes a second creation cycle. The phenomenon of terminal floods appears to function as a transitional episode which permits the integration of the Dying God cycle with the succeeding creation story. Generally the floods, whether they are used to begin or end a cycle, function as "terminators," curtains which open or conclude the worlds in which they occur. No variant includes both the initial and terminal floods.

Figure 2 diagrams the contrastive uses made of forms of fire and water to present the theme of individual and collective mortality.

Figure 2

Contrastive Uses of Fire and Water

Expressing the Theme of Mortality

(WYav and Hav 1 *vs* Hav 4)

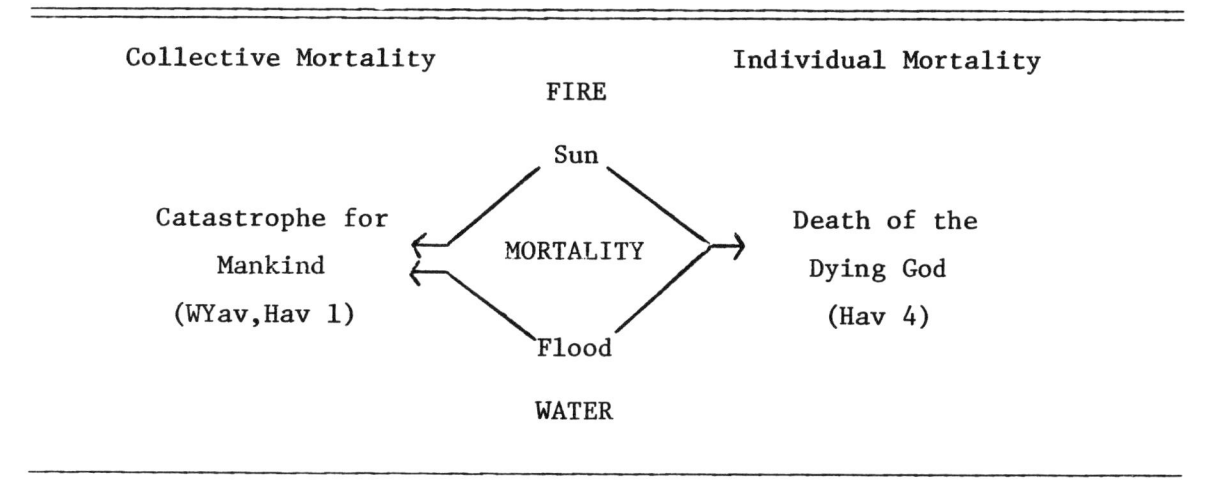

---

| Collective Mortality | | Individual Mortality |
|---|---|---|
| | FIRE | |
| | Sun | |
| Catastrophe for Mankind (WYav, Hav 1) | ← MORTALITY → | Death of the Dying God (Hav 4) |
| | Flood | |
| | WATER | |

---

We can see that individual mortality always proceeds collective mortality and the Dying God's death initiates a process that is culminated by the world flood and the death of mankind. In the variants, water in the form of a flood and fire/light in the form of the sun are involved in the origin of mortality.

## INDIVIDUAL MORTALITY

The second expression of mortality presented in the myths is individual mortality. Here we are concerned with one individual, a god, whose fate is intimately associated with the fate of mankind.

By way of introduction to the discussion of individual mortality, we have listed the contrastive elements associated with the events surrounding the bewitchment and cremation of the Dying God. These are presented in Figure 3. The sentences in Figure 3 are a summary of the Western Yavapai description of the bewitchment and cremation episodes which also agree with Kroeber's general outline of the Dying God story (Kroeber 1925:790).

Figure 3

Contrastive Elements Found in the Bewitchment

and Cremation of the Dying God

| BEWITCHMENT | | CREMATION |
|---|---|---|
| Older Brother defecates into a stream and his feces are eaten by Frogs | Death of the Dying God | Older Brother is cremated on a pyre and his heart is stolen and eaten by Coyote |

In our analysis we examine how the elements in the bewitchment episode are transformed into those found in the cremation episode. Our interpretation of this transformation process rests on demonstrating the appropriateness of these elements for a discourse on mortality. We first discuss the elements within each column and then demonstrate how they are related to each other in the myths and in the ethnographies. We begin with the characters of Frogs.

### Frogs

In addition to the Frogs' cataclysmic use of water to flood the world, Frogs are also associated with less cataclysmic forms of water. The Frogs, who make the Dying God sick, are associated with various forms of water: creek (WYav), pond (Hav 1), or river (Wal 1).

In every Upland Yuman variant where a cause is mentioned for the Dying God's illness, frogs are implicated, except in Havasupai 4 where "bright lights and angry waters" are used (Hav 4:S.4). Here we can infer that the anger of the frogs is expressed by reference to their associated element, water.

This association of frogs and water is given special significance by both the Upland Yuman and many of the California tribes. Among the Northeastern Yavapai it was "taboo to kill a frog because heavy rains would follow" (Gifford 1936:318). Spier states that the Havasupai associate the "rasping sound created by rubbing a notched stick on one laid flat on an inverted basket with the frog and the production of rain" (Spier 1928:288). Spier also cites a mythical precedent for this water-frog association: "Pulling a frog to pieces causes a flood" (Spier 1928:288).[9] Spier goes on to mention that the Northern Shoshoneans, Maidu, Southern Utes and Luiseño also associate frogs with rain, or fog and thunder (Spier 1928:291). The Mohave state this association directly: "He [Frog] knows the water, for he lives in it" (Kroeber 1963: 59).

After establishing the association between frogs, water and mortality we returned to see if the contrastive element sun was similarly associated with some character. We found that the element fire and the character Coyote seemed to recur together in several variants. We shall now examine Coyote and fire to see how this relates to the pattern of water and frogs and the death of the Dying God.

Coyote

In the Western Yavapai variant the people must cremate the Dying God, as it is from the ashes of his heart that a "marvelous" plant will sprout. This plant is immortal and will ripen year round.[10] Knowing that Coyote is a scavenger and will eat anything, the people decided that to cremate the Dying God and retain his heart they must divert Coyote's uncontrollable appetite. This fear is stated by the Dying God prior to his death in several variants (SE2:S.8; Hav 3:S.60). The ethnographies make similar mention that cremation occurs because the people fear that coyotes will eat the corpse if it is buried (Gifford 1932:235).

To complete the cremation before the diverted Coyote returns, the people speed up the burning by turning the body on the coals.[11]

---

[9]Spier did not publish this Havasupai myth. However, Gifford, who examined Spier's material, concluded that the Havasupai origin myths "virtually duplicate" the Northeastern and Western Yavapai material (Gifford 1933:348).

[10]The association of fire and planting is clear from ethnographic evidence: "A new field is cleared of brush by grubbing and burning it" (Spier 1928:101).

[11]Spier notes the cultural practice, "the corpse is poked with a pole to make it burn faster" (Spier 1928:297).

However, Coyote returns before the body is completely burned. At first he is blocked from getting to the corpse by a ring of people (WYav) or a fence built around the pyre (Wal 1). However, Coyote jumps over these obstacles, steals the heart, runs off and eats it.

The Dying God's heart is eaten by Coyote in all the variants of the Dying God story, except Walapai 1.[12] In the other Walapai version (Wal 2), the heart is stolen but the myth does not specifically say that it is eaten. However, the people do lose the heart as Coyote buries it.

From the preceding discussion we can see that two "parts" of the Dying God, feces and heart, are viewed as food by Frogs and Coyote, the two characters associated with the contrastive elements, water and fire. We now need to determine if the "floods" of these two characters are contrastive or similar in their relationship to the theme of mortality.

We begin by discussing feces and Frogs.

## Feces and Frogs

Among the Upland Yuman variants the eating of feces occurs only in the Western Yavapai variant, although in each case where a cause is given for the illness Frogs are involved. Other Yuman and Shoshonean versions of the Dying God myth were examined. These results are given in Figure 4.

From Figure 4 we can see that the Yuman, Mohave, Serrano, Cahuilla and possibly the Maricopa and Kamia variants indicate that the Frog-witches ate feces. In the Luiseño variants frogs bewitch the Dying God, although the method used is not described. It would appear that the Western Yavapai's use of feces to bewitch is part of a more widespread pattern of witchcraft.

A relationship between feces and witchcraft is given by the Mohave. The Mohave believe that a person who has been bewitched and is about to be cremated presents a difficult situation for the witch. A bewitched person is said to rise to a sitting position when cremated, thus indicating that the person's death was not "natural." Also, *the heart* (emphasis added) of a person who is killed by a witch tries "to escape from the funeral pit in the form of an owl that is like a person, *ipa:*" (Devereux 1961:391).[13] This *ipa:* can be caught by the witch and *taken to a river and drowned* (emphasis added), or the *ipa:* can be caught

---

[12] In Walapai 1 the body is buried. The heart is neither stolen nor eaten.

[13] Gifford (1933:308) notes this connection of owl and soul among the Cocopa.

Figure 4

Causes of Dying God's Illness

| Variant | Who Gets Sick | Cause of Illness | Source |
|---------|---------------|------------------|--------|
| WYav | Older Brother | Daughters become frogs & eat his feces | Gifford 1933:402 |
| NE 1 | Leader Hanyiko (frog) | Shaman daughters (frogs) make him ill | Gifford 1933:349 |
| SE 2 | Chief | Not given | Gifford 1932:245 |
| Hav 3 | Chief | Not given | Smithson & Euler 1964:92 |
| Hav 4 | Cacique. leader | Bright lights & angry waters | Cushing 1965:72 |
| Wal 1 | Older Brother | Squashes excrement out of a frog | Kroeber 1935:3 |
| Wal 2 | Matavila (Younger Brother) | Not given | Kroeber 1935:249 |
| Mohave | Matevilye | His daughter (frog) ate his excrement | Kroeber 1972:7 |
| Yuma | Kwikumat | His daughter (frog) ate his feces | Harrington 1908:337 |
| Maricopa | Cipas | Bull frog swallows water after Cipas went swimming | Spier 1933:349 |
| Diegueño | Tuchaipai | Frog exudes poison he swallows it | DuBois 1901:185 |
| Kamia | Pukumat | Daughter (frog) put piece of his hair in mud ball, another frog ate it | Gifford 1931:76-77 |
| Luiseño | Ouiot | Attacked by woman with a back like a frog | DuBois 1906:55 |
| Luiseño | Wyiot | Killed by 2 people, one named frog | Kroeber 1906:311 |
| Luiseño | Wiot | Bewitched by a frog medicine man | Davis 1921:106-7 |
| Serrano | Kukitate | Frog ate his excrement | Benedict 1926:1-3 |

by a real owl and taken to its nest. Once the *ipa:* lives in the nest he becomes an owl and goes around saying "ku:t, ku:t, which is the last syllable of *naku:tk*, father" (Devereux 1961:391). Bewitched persons are said to become relatives of the witch. Thus, the *ipa:* is identifying the person who bewitched it.

Only in cases of bewitchment does the heart burn slowly, giving time for the "soul" (heart) to escape and expose the murderer witch. Like the Mohave victim described by Devereux, the Dying God is bewitched by relatives (Frog-daughters who ate his feces) and consequently his body burns slowly. His heart is the last to burn and Coyote has the opportunity to steal and eat it.

The association between the eating of potent foods, bewitchment and cremation is found among the Maricopa. Spier (1933:289) recorded this puzzling phrase: "The bewitcher might swallow a morsel of coal from a cremation pyre and those who bewitch this way *dream of Frog*" (emphasis added). This becomes clear given the system of associations just outlined. Like Coyote, the Maricopa bewitcher eats from a cremation fire, as Frog eats human feces from the river. Special "foods" taken from fire and water are lethal. The cannibalistic attacks on the Dying God by creatures associated with mutually exclusive natural phenomena, fire and water, result in mortality. Immortal life is terminated by the improper utilization of "potent" foods.

We now want to determine if Coyote's cannibalistic appetite has any additional meaning for mankind.

## Coyote, Heart and Plants

From the ethnographies we know that the heart is considered a symbol of fertility and immortality by the Upland Yumans. The hearts of bears are eaten by men to protect their children from illness (Gifford 1936:319), although it is dangerous for the child himself to eat the heart (Kroeber 1935:74). For men and women, eating the hearts of certain animals could affect fertility (Kroeber 1935:75) and hunting prowess (Kroeber 1935:73). The heart is also seen as the "soul" and one word is used for both (Spier 1928:275).

The fertility meaning of the heart is expressed clearly in the Western Yavapai variant. Just before his death, the Dying God promises that if the people will put earth over the ashes of his heart a special plant(s) will grow. Similar statements are made in several other variants. These have been listed in Figure 5 along with the promised plants.

From Figure 5 we can see that with the loss of the heart, the promised immortal maize does not grow. However, various other "mortal" plants do grow. Because of the variability in the amount of heart consumed and the plants promised we decided to see if there was a corrolation. The results are listed in Figure 6.

From Figure 6 we can see that, with one possible exception,

Figure 5

Comparison of What the Dying God Promises
and What Actually Grows from His Heart

| Variant | What the Dying God Promised | What Actually Grows |
|---------|------------------------------|---------------------|
| WYav | Maize, pumpkins & beans | One tall stalk of maize with long ears, 1 small ear |
| NE 1 | Maize that produces many-fold | Sprout of maize with many big ears |
| SE 2 | Marvelous maize, produces at all seasons | Maize does not ripen year round |
| Hav 3 | Corn plant | Corn plant with roasting ears, long ones for Hav., short ones for Mohave |
| Hav 4 | --- | Corn plant with six ears of various colors |
| Wal 1 | A plant | Corn, pumpkins, watermelons and beans. Sow and harvest for years. |

(NE 1), the loss of the Dying God's heart results in a reduction in the amount of maize available to each Upland Yuman group. This reduction is expressed in two ways: (1) reduction in time, so that maize is available only during certain seasons, and (2) reduction in size, several groups getting only small ears while their neighbors get large, long ears.

Each form of reduction, either in seasons or size, explains why the Upland Yumans continue to rely on wild foods. When the Dying God's heart is lost and the availability of maize is reduced to only certain seasons, the Upland Yumans must search for wild foods during the remainder of the year. When the ears given to the Upland Yumans are smaller than those given to their neighbors, the harvest is insufficient and the Upland Yumans must spend part of the year in search of wild foods.

The Western Yavapai variant describes accurately the comparative importance of maize to their economy and that of their neighbors. The Hopi and Navajo get long ears. In contrast to their farming neighbors, the Western Yavapai are given the poorest corn, both in size (smallest) and in number (one), reflecting their limited use of cultigens (Gifford 1936).

Figure 6

Consumption of Heart and its Effect
in Cycle One, Pai Variants

| Variant | Amount of Heart Eaten | What Grows from Heart | Harvest | Remarks |
|---|---|---|---|---|
| WYav | Whole, unburned | One tall stalk of maize with long ears and one small ear | People out of food in underworld | Long ears given to Muka (Navajo & Hopi); WYav got poorest |
| NE 1 | Whole, unburned | Green sprout of maize, with many big ears | Maize grew, harvested for years | Maize grew from ashes where heart had rested |
| SE 2 | Whole, unburned | | Maize not ripen year round | |
| Hav 3 | Whole, unburned | Maize grew with roasting ears on stalk | | Short roasting ears for Mohave, long ears for Havasupai |
| Hav 4 | Part of heart eaten, rest is buried unburned | Corn plant grew with six colored ears (yellow, white, red variegated, black, and blue) | Spend half year cultivating & half gathering. (Didn't know how they were going to live on small portion given) | Maize grew where heart was buried; Havasupai got only little red ears of corn |
| Wal 1 | Body buried [Heart not stolen or eaten] | Corn, pumpkins, beans, watermelon | Sow and harvest for years | |
| Wal 2 | Small part of unburned heart is stolen, not eaten | Not mentioned | Not mentioned | |

The Southeastern Yavapai utilize maize the least of any Upland Yuman group (Gifford 1932:214). In the Southeastern variant no plant grows after the loss of the Dying God's heart. With the loss of the heart maize is no longer immortal and, therefore, will "not ripen year round" (SE 2:S.20). Maize is reduced from a year-round resource to one available only part of the year.

In Havasupai 3 the result of Coyote's deed is the growth of short-eared maize given to the Mohave. According to this variant "the Mohave will never get long-eared corn" (Hav 3:S.82). In fact, the Havasupai have both long-eared and short-eared corn (Spier 1928:103). However, the Havasupai say that short-eared corn was obtained from the Mohave and the long-eared corn from the Hopi (Spier 1928:103). Short-eared corn is of little importance to the Havasupai, who rely on the "better long-eared maize as do people to the east" (Hav 3:S.84). Consequently, the loss of the Dying God's heart explains to the Havasupai why the Mohave have short-eared corn and eastern people have the more desirable long-eared corn.

The Havasupai 4 variant collected by Cushing (1965) presents most clearly the thesis that the Dying God's heart reflects the relationship of the availability of maize to the yearly calendar. According to this variant Coyote eats part of the heart and buries the rest. Maize grows from the buried heart and is distributed to various neighboring groups. However, the Havasupai receive "only a small red ear" (Hav 4: S.15).[14] This meager portion is viewed as insufficient to support the Havasupai year-round. Instead, the Havasupai must spend the other half of the year hunting and gathering:

> But, alas! The Coyote ate a part of the heart
> of the great cacique; hence, only during summer
> do we live in the home of the Mother of the Waters,
> and plant as she told us; but in winter we have to
> follow the deer and our father, the Coyote, and
> live only as he does, in houses of grass and
> bark (Hav 4:S.30).

In this variant the loss of the Dying God's heart results in a reduction in time (limited to half the year) and in amount of harvest (small red ears).

From our analysis of the Dying God's heart we see that a single symbol is used by neighboring groups to express alternative views related to a common theme. In addition, the Havasupai 1 and 4 variants provide an illustration of how a symbol (the Dying God's heart) shared by a group can be used to make alternative statements in variants within the group (Hav 1 and 4).

Havasupai 1 explains, for the Havasupai, how they received long-eared corn like the eastern tribes (Hopi), while their western neighbors, the Mohave, received only small, red-eared corn. In Havasupai 4 an alternative use is made of the Dying God's heart. In this variant we are told that half of the Dying God's heart was eaten and this is the reason why the Havasupai only plant and eat corn half the year. The remaining half of the year they must spend on the plateau hunting deer "like Coyote."[15] A possible similar pattern is suggested by Walapai 1 and 2.

In one Walapai variant (Wal 1), the harvest is expressed in strong terms, in variety of plants (maize, squash, pumpkins, and melons), and in duration (many years). This is the same myth in which no attempt is made to steal the heart. The dead leader is burned and then buried. It is from his burned body that the bountiful harvest grows. Thus, no reduction occurs in amount or time of harvest. In a separate Walapai story (Wal 2) the familiar scene of Coyote stealing the heart is given

---

[14]Spier states that "teyadjipa [corn] with kernels mostly red with a little white . . . [is] accredited to the culture heroes" (Spier 1928:103).

[15]It is interesting to note that Spier probably sought information on the relations of Havasupai to the Mohave, while Cushing (Hav 4) came to Havasu from Zuni where he had been living. It is tempting to see the reason for the different variants as the raconteur's response to differences in his audience.

but no consequences to the harvest are offered.

The Northeastern Yavapai variant is the only exception to the thesis that the Dying God's heart has a bearing on the economic fortunes of the group.

In the Northeastern variant Coyote steals and eats the whole heart of the Dying God with no apparent effect on the availability or quality of maize obtained. The Northeastern Yavapai variant states that maize grew from the earth where the Dying God's heart has rested and that a harvest of "many big ears" (NE 1:S.116) follows. We have no explanation for this single exception, except to note that in the Northeastern variant the year-round availability of maize is lost when Coyote "turned white cornmeal that blanketed the mountains into snow" (NE 1: S.132). Coyote is also said to have "caused the first death" (NE 1: S.132).

The importance of maize to the economy of the Upland Yumans has generally been expressed in terms of amount of maize harvested, or by similar gross economic indicators. However, such information does not indicate the relative importance of maize from the point of view of the Upland Yumans themselves. When the harvest is diminished in amount or is restricted to one season, the people are required to spend a greater part of the year gathering wild foods. The heart of the Dying God is used by several Upland Yuman groups to express the availability and use of maize and its effect on the yearly food cycle.

We can now turn to a discussion of wild foods and their relationship to the death of the Dying God.

## Wild Plants

Even though cultivated foods are mentioned as being abundant in many of the myths, there comes a time when the people are out of food and must rely on wild plant foods. The only wild plant foods discussed in the cycle are those introduced and eaten after the loss of the Dying God's heart. These wild plants are either found in the Upperworld when the people migrate or are presented in a calendar by the Dying God just before his death.

Several variants specifically note that the reason for migrating from the Underworld is lack of food. In the Western Yavapai variant they are "out of food" (WYav:S.71); in the Northeastern they are motivated to migrate because they "found plenty of food" in the Upperworld (NE 2:S.10). The migration to find wild food is undertaken presumably because all domesticated plants are absent.

The other Yumans and California Shoshoneans also give significance to the loss of the Dying God's heart. The Gila Yumans see the loss of the heart as the reason they are "scattered and have to move to hunt wild foods, berries and game" (Spier 1933:352). Both the Mohave and Yuma say that "now everybody dies" (Harrington 1908:339; Kroeber 1972:6).

The Southern Diegueño say that they "lost knowledge of the arts of life" (Spier 1928:330). Among the Shoshoneans of Southern California, the theft of the Dying God's heart is said to explain why the Cahuilla "no longer prospered" (Seiler 1968:58), and why the Luiseño "must begin to kill and eat food," whereas before this they lived on clay (DuBois 1906: 57).

These variants use the Dying God's heart to articulate their own view of mortality and its relationship to the yearly food cycle.

The relationship between mortality and the death of the God is expressed eloquently by the Luiseño. They say, "In the last month he died, and death came to the world" (DuBois 1906:56).

In conclusion we can see that the theme of mortality exemplified by the death of the Dying God is not restricted to mankind. Rather the events surrounding his bewitchment, death and cremation demonstrate that life is closely associated with food, in particular plant foods. The fate of the Dying God is intimately related to the origin of plant mortality. Because of the death of the Dying God mankind does not escape nature but through death becomes a part of it.

# The Supernatural World of the Kawaiisu
# by
# Maurice Zigmond

The most obvious characteristic of the supernatural world of the Kawaiisu is its complexity, which stands in striking contrast to the "simplicity" of the mundane world. Situated on and around the southern end of the Sierra Nevada mountains in south-central California, the tribe is marginal to both the Great Basin and California culture areas and would probably have been susceptible to the opprobrious nineteenth century term, "Diggers." Yet, if its material culture could be described as "primitive," ideas about the realm of the unseen were intricate and, in a sense, sophisticated. For the Kawaiisu the invisible domain is filled with identifiable beings and anonymous non-beings, with people who are half spirits,

---

[1] This paper is based upon my fieldwork among the Kawaiisu extending from 1936 to 1974 (with a thirty-year gap between 1940 and 1970), but it also includes data gathered by the late Theodore D. McCown in 1929 and the late Stephen C. Cappannari in 1947-1949. Cappannari and I had agreed to publish our materials together, but other interests took him away from the field of anthropology. I had never met McCown though I knew of the existence of his notes. As far as I am aware, he never attempted to put them in publishable form. It seemed to me, therefore, that this study on the Supernatural World of the Kawaiisu provided an opportunity for at least some of the work of these two men to appear in print. I had long had copies of Cappannari's notes and his widow Lael sent me all the material she could find among his papers. Copies of McCown's notes reached me in March 1976, after the first draft of this paper had been completed. I then undertook to revise the manuscript in those sections where McCown's data were relevant. This gave rise to a problem of proper "credit." Whereas I had not always distinguished between the contribution of Cappannari and my own, I was careful to insert McCown's name wherever his material was added. Thus Cappannari's name does not appear as often as it deserves. Perhaps the inequity can be somewhat overcome by associating each of us with our most important informants, all now dead: Emma Williams assisted all of us. John Nichols assisted McCown and me. McCown was assisted exclusively by Bob Rabbit, Santos Phillips, Charlie Haslem, and Rafael Girado; Cappannari by Marie Girado and Sadie Williams; I by John Marcus, Setimo Girado, Sam Willie, and Henry Weldon. Living informants are indicated by their initials.

with mythical giant creatures and great sky images, with "men" and "animals" who are localized in association with natural formations, with dreams, visions, omens, and signs. There is a land of the dead known to have been visited by a few living individuals, and a netherworld which is apparently the abode of the spirits of animals--at least of some animals--and visited by a man seeking a cure. Depending upon one's definition, there are apparently four types of shamanism--and a questionable fifth.

In recording this maze of supernatural phenomena over a period of years, one ought not be surprised to find the data both inconsistent and contradictory. By their very nature happenings governed by extraterrestrial forces cannot be portrayed in clear and precise terms. To those involved, however, the situation presents no problem. Since anything may occur in the unseen world which surrounds us, an attempt at logical explanation is irrelevant. Experiences attributable to extra-human influences can only be described; they need not be explained or understood.

## TUUWARUUGIDɨ

Even a cursory inquiry into the nature of that other world gives the unmistakable impression that the prevailing mood is one of evil foreboding. With rare exceptions, the "signs" point to disaster and death, and they are so numerous that it can probably be said that any unusual sight or sound may be interpreted as conveying a portentous message. The word "unusual" as used here would include the flight at night of a bird normally expected to be seen during the day. The general term for such intimations of doom is *tuuwaruugidɨ*--a word which has thus far not yielded to linguistic analysis. It is to be understood that a *tuuwaruugidɨ* is an announcement of impending doom and not a key to prevention. Furthermore, the omen is not likely to specify the individual victim. The immediate reaction is not "What can I do to prevent it?" but "Who will be, or has been, the victim?" (The disaster may already have struck, but news of it may not yet have reached all parties concerned.) In a few situations counteraction may be possible. If it can be determined that the sign--especially in dreams--has been sent by a witch (a bewitching shaman) who can be identified, a powerful curing shaman may be able to nullify its evil intent. But for the most part the *tuuwaruugidɨ* is not responsive to human interference.

No exhaustive list of *tuuwaruugidɨ* can be compiled since most "unusual" phenomena are unpredictable. The following items were recorded in the course of fieldwork among the Kawaiisu and were embedded in ethnographic and mythological reports. Some of these will be considered at some length later.

Seeing a ring around the moon

Seeing a crescent moon standing on end (in this position the moon is called *nɨwɨnookarɨdɨ*, 'person-carrying')

Seeing a falling star which starts high and falls to the horizon

Counting the stars but counting short (cf. the story about the counting of bedrock mortar holes under Localized Supernatural Beings)

Seeing an eagle drop dead

Seeing strange behavior in animals--like a dog talking

Seeing a sudden gathering of animals, birds, or flies

Seeing a large fish in a creek where only small fish are expected

Seeing localized beings (animals or people)

Seeing a drop of blood in the house

Seeing a rattlesnake in the house (the plant which cures rattlesnake bites is never kept in the house for it also attracts rattlesnakes)

Seeing the "laughing" bird (species unknown) in the house

Seeing a person known to be elsewhere

Seeing an unknown person who has put in a sudden and unexplained appearance

Seeing a limb of a seemingly healthy tree break off (if an old tree, an elderly person will die; if a young tree, a young person)

Seeing White Coyote, the Great Snake, the Man-carrying Bird, or the Giant Locust

Seeing the Rock Baby or hearing his cry

Hearing unidentified knocking or walking around the house

Hearing a coyote howling near the house on successive nights

Hearing talking, calling, or whistling from an unknown source

Hearing an owl hooting in flight or quails calling after dark

Dreaming of the death of someone living

Dreaming of grizzly bear, rattlesnake, coyote, the Rock Baby, or the Giant Locust

Looking at the mountain with the "rattlesnake's tooth" rock formation in the spring

Cutting your hair (but you may shave yourself)


## DREAMS AND VISIONS

A central element in the supernatural structure of the Kawaiisu is the vision, whether it comes in the form of a dream or an hallucination. It may present itself at a time of consciousness or of unconsciousness; but its message, whether constructive or destructive, is never dismissed as meaningless. Artificially-induced dreams are called for in a variety of situations, and a number of ways of seeking them are known and practiced. The goal may be to live long, to avoid illness, to find a cure, to annul the dire effects of a vision which has come to one's self, or to someone else about one's self. Because visions may be sources of power, good luck, or information, they are deliberately sought even though there is always the possibility that they will presage disaster. The desire to gain beneficial visions leads people to undertake one of several accepted procedures. These include the drinking of an infusion of jimsonweed root (*Datura wrightii*), the eating of tobacco (*Nicotiana bigelovii*), the swallowing of live red ants in balls of eagledown, walking nude through a growth of nettles (*Urtica holosericea*)--all these regimens also have therapeutic value (see my forthcoming *Kawaiisu Ethnobotany*)--and talking to the mountains or to the darkness, usually alone on a mountain height and at night. The resultant revelation may call for further action or counteraction.

The meaning of some of the dreams is self-evident. When Emma Williams was a small girl, a woman who had taken the jimsonweed drink (toloache) related that in her hallucinatory vision she had seen Emma dead. This demanded a prompt response. Emma had to undergo toloache. Thereby she not only escaped harm, she lived to a ripe old age. But the messages of many dream-situations are more subtle. While these may have been an integral part of traditional knowledge, the data at hand do not provide a comprehensive analysis of dream interpretation. However, specific instances were cited from time to time, and from these it is clear that the revelation may be either benevolent or malevolent.

Dreaming of deer is a favorable omen. If a hunter dreams of killing deer, he will have successful hunting. Should a young man dream of deer singing, he will become a *huviagadɨ* (curing shaman, see below). If a hunter has a vision of women, he will see female deer the next day. Dreaming of rolling rocks is a good-luck sign for the hunter. Seeing one's self winning a fight brings good luck. Dreaming of clear water or of snow foretells good health, and an ill person having such a vision is assured of recovery. It is a good sign to dream of being in the mountains especially where there is timber. A dream of fish makes one a tireless swimmer (although such a consequence was cited, it should be noted that Kawaiisu territory offered little opportunity for swimming).

There are, of course, visions which have negative implications. It is unlucky to dream of fire for this means fever is coming. Falling off a cliff indicates that one may soon die. If you are beaten in a dream-fight, you will be sick and helpless. If you picture someone you know crying, disaster will befall one of his relatives. If you recognize someone drowning, he will die or is in some danger. Dreaming of sexual intercourse is a warning that you will be subject to sickness and weakness. In this situation it is advisable to refrain from intercourse for a time. As will be discussed in a later section, dreams involving Coyote and his children have sexual connotations. The hapless dreamer who is ravished by Coyote's sons or daughters will be left exhausted. But dream-contact with Coyote may be dangerous in other ways. Unless some counteraction is taken, he or members of his family may push you over a precipice or into water or fire. The death of Steban Miranda's wife (Tübatulabal) was attributed to Coyote's sons. She had dreamed of them but neglected to take the protective step of "talking to the dark." A day or two later, while getting water near a dam, she fell into the water and drowned.

Dreaded are those dreams recognized as having been sent by a *pohagadɨ* (bewitching shaman, see below). The sight of such creatures as the rattlesnake, the grizzly bear, the coyote, the *ʔuwanʔazi* (the Rock Baby, q.v.), and the *haakapainizi* (the Giant Locust, q.v.) may well prove that a *pohagadɨ* is using his baneful power against you. Counteraction is called for; several neutralizing steps are suggested. The dreamer can go to the mountains and tell the evil power not to bother him. A *huviagadɨ* may be able to reveal the identity of the witch, but a rash accusation without the corroboration of a *huviagadɨ* may prompt the witch to increase his pernicious activities. The latter, however, may be unaware of his destructive abilities and, when confronted by a curing shaman, may agree to desist. An informant told of a situation in which the victim and her relatives alternately threatened and bribed an alleged *pohagadɨ* in an effort to persuade her to stop causing pain and suffering in the form of arthritis. In extreme cases the witch might be put to death.

A potential consequence of the dreams sent by a *pohagadɨ* is that, if they persist, the dreamer might himself become a *pohagadɨ*. As soon as parents are aware that their child is having such dreams, they do what they can to alter his dream-pattern, since a witch's life is fraught with danger. (James Scobie, non-Indian rancher, told of five murders of Indians accused of witchcraft in the area.) Solitary vigils in the mountains are deemed effective counter-measures. A *pohagadɨ*, however, might instruct his children in his art. One element in this training is to toughen the skin by walking nude through a stand of nettles. Marie relates that, when she was a child, she encountered a young girl who said to her, "Let's walk through the nettles and see who is tougher." Marie would not come near, but the girl took off her clothes and walked through. The latter grew up to be a witch. Her father was also a *pohagadɨ*. She is said to have killed her first two husbands through witchcraft.

An elderly informant pointed out that, once a witch reaches adulthood, there is no way of removing his evil potentialities.

Though not altogether consistent with the dream data thus far presented, the following information was recorded by McCown from Bob Rabbit (1929): "Dreams of fighting always mean good luck in hunting. Bad luck results from dreaming of snakes, of 'devils' and of women. In the latter case it means no success in love and bad hunting. In order to counteract this, one scatters a little tugub [beads--see 'Prayers' and Offerings] and washes [?]."

## THE ʔɨNɨPI

Of the beings in the supernatural realm, the best known and most commonly experienced is the *ʔɨnɨpi* which, because of its diversified activities, is variously conceived of as "spirit," "ghost," and "devil."

No clear picture of the ʔɨnɨpi emerges from the several descriptions. He may be visible or invisible. If visible, he may look like a human being and be mistaken for one unless he gives himself away by performing superhuman feats like suddenly disappearing, flying off, or being impervious to bullets. Or he may have horns (though this idea may be a Christian borrowing), or appear as a skeleton--"all bones, no skin and red eyes." Once an ʔɨnɨpi was found sleeping in a bunkhouse. He wore black clothes and had fingernails so long that they protruded through the cracks in the wall. One informant thought an ʔɨnɨpi is like a bat--blind in the daytime but with vision at night. Bob Rabbit told McCown, "Devils may come as wood-rats and you can tell because they tap their tails." While there must be myriads of ʔɨnɨpi, they seem never to be spoken of in the plural, and apparently never act in concert.

Every human being--and probably every animal--has its own indestructible ʔɨnɨpi. Though the essence of one's life, it may wander off when one is asleep and leaves the body permanently when one is dead. When an individual is destined to die--whether through "natural" or malevolent causes or through accident--his ʔɨnɨpi may act as if he is already dead, not only forsaking the body but betraying to the living the foreordained demise. At death, however, the ʔɨnɨpi is reluctant to leave familiar haunts and is not likely to depart for a few days. Maybe he had cached money and he comes by to see it. As an informant explained, "It's just like your wanting to see your car again" (at the moment it was parked out of sight). McCown was told that "the ʔɨnɨpi of a dead man would come and take acorns and pinyons from trees where he had got these things in life. For a period of two or three years there was no food for the Indians." (The implication seems to be that the ʔɨnɨpi cleaned the trees bare.)

At the time of burial someone might enjoin the ʔɨnɨpi to go off to its new abode and not do injury to the survivors. As the mourners leave the place of interment, they are careful not to look back lest they catch sight of the ghost--an experience that would of itself be an evil omen. (In the tale *Coyote Marries His Daughter*, Coyote warns his family not to look back after igniting his pyre. He has other motives, but his wife understands well the danger of seeing his ʔɨnɨpi.) Ultimately the ʔɨnɨpi must take the path that leads across the desert eastward to the other world. When you walk through the desert and feel a sudden gust of hot wind "like from a fire," it is the ʔɨnɨpi passing by.

The ʔɨnɨpi is not always malevolent. He may be expected to behave very much as his living embodiment did. If the latter liked to tease, his ʔɨnɨpi may continue to do so. Once when a sudden breeze rustled the pages of my notebook so that I lost my place, an informant remarked, "It is the ʔɨnɨpi." But if you have been unkind to a person, his ʔɨnɨpi may come to frighten you. CG recalled an incident of her youth. Her young brothers were often mean to their grandmother. She would say to them, "I'll fix you when I die." Not long after her death, the boys and their sister were gathered around the fireplace. Suddenly they heard someone hitting the outer wall of the house with a cane. The old lady had always carried a cane. Then there was a sound like "Hm hmm" (said to be characteristic of old women). The boys were terrified, but their sister, who had been kind to her grandmother, was not disturbed. She knew her grandmother did not intend to frighten her.

The ʔɨnɨpi is most likely to make his presence known just before or just after death. Therefore evidence that he is around is usually taken to mean that someone is about to die or has already died but the tidings have not yet spread around. The victim may or may not be immediately recognized, but news of the actual demise will provide clear proof of the identity of the ʔɨnɨpi. If two people die at about the same time, relatives and friends would be sufficiently familiar with the habits of the deceased to realize whose ʔɨnɨpi is prowling about.

At least three people testified to the presence of the ʔɨnɨpi of Henry Willie, who was killed in an automobile accident. A few days after he was buried, his father was in the outhouse of his home. He heard sounds coming from a nearby shed where phonograph records and animal traps were kept. The records were being thrown about and the traps moved "as if someone wanted to put them out." A relative who had apparently come for the funeral was looking for the father. She found him visibly upset as he walked toward his house. He warned her not to go near the shed—Henry's ʔɨnɨpi was there.

Setimo Girado was staying at a friend's house not far away. One night he heard someone walking outside. It was a man's step. Next morning he asked if anyone had walked around that night. No one had. He went out and looked for tracks, but there were none. "Someone is going to die," he said. At first he thought it was the ʔɨnɨpi of Jim Manuel of whose death he was already aware. Two days later he learned of the death of Henry Willie who had lived with his family in a neighboring house. Then the identity of the ʔɨnɨpi was clear.

Five days after Henry died, his brother Raymond, who had a home of his own, heard noise coming from his car as if the car were being started. He looked around, but saw no one. He walked away, heard the sound again, but still there was no one to be seen. Then Raymond returned to his house where he fell "dead" for two or three hours. He woke up, but didn't feel well for two days. When asked why he had "died," he told about the car. His mother knew it was Henry's ʔɨnɨpi and commented that maybe it had touched Raymond. (This case was not isolated. Once a man came home in a stupor. His eyes rolled up, and he was "dead," but he was breathing "a very little bit." When he woke up three or four hours later, he was asked, "Why were you dead?" Then he remembered that he had seen the ʔɨnɨpi.)

When Francis (Frank) Phillips was in a Bakersfield hospital, Setimo was frightened several times. Once, when Setimo was home in bed, he heard someone coughing, clearing his throat, and spitting by the side of the house, but he couldn't see anyone. At another time he heard talking outside. He thought it was Ed Williams (a neighbor) and called out "Ed! Ed!" The ʔɨnɨpi answered, "Frank." Later Setimo told John Nichols that he knew Phillips was dead and would be buried in the Indian cemetery above his place. The body was kept overnight at Loraine (a few miles away) and brought to the cemetery the following day.

The impending death of Virginia Ball, Setimo's daughter, was indicated by signs extending over a winter season. Once Setimo heard whistling and other noises while he slept. It sounded as if dishes and utensils were being moved about. A frying-pan fell to the floor. Virginia used to cook there. Setimo heard a woman talking outside in the orchard. That is where he often chatted with Virginia. Two weeks before she died, Willie Leon was trying to sleep in a car near Loraine. He had a cover over him. Someone tugged at the cover as if to pull it off. Willie looked up quickly but didn't see anything. He hadn't known that Virginia was sick. She died later, "but that was her ʔinɨpi."

Emma Williams was picking beans at Harry McKay's (near the Piute Rancheria) when she heard a human cry. It came from somewhere near Setimo's place where Refugia Williams lived years before. Emma thought the sound came from Setimo and she was frightened. Two women were passing in their car on the way to tell Maude McKay of Refugia's death. Shortly after, Maude came out to tell Emma the news.

The ʔinɨpi of Marie Girado's uncle appeared the night he was buried. At the burial, Setimo (Marie's husband) blew across the palm of his hand and told the ʔinɨpi to go away. As it did so, it was heard to whistle. That night there was a knock at the door of one of the Girado daughters. She heard the ʔinɨpi say (in Kawaiisu), "Let me in!"

The ʔinɨpi of a non-Indian behaves the same way as that of a Kawaiisu. Jim Scobie, non-Indian rancher, well-known and liked by his Indian neighbors, died in a brush fire (though he apparently had a heart attack as he attempted to escape the fire). About two weeks before, three Kawaiisu women were camping out and gathering pinyons. They heard Jim coming along the trail whistling about dusk, but they couldn't see anyone. Joe Williams, who had been working at a house under construction not far away, was walking up to them on the trail. He heard two people riding horses and talking, but there was nothing to be seen. When he reached the place from which the sounds had come, "his bones nearly fell off" from fright. Nothing was there. "Jim was already ʔinɨpi."

An ʔinɨpi may be in the control of a bewitching shaman (*pohagadɨ*) and may be sent on destructive missions. The *pohagadɨ* can order it to push a man off a cliff or cause a car to crash. But whirlwinds are governed by an ʔinɨpi who is to be found at its center. One must therefore avoid whirlwinds for, in the midst of one, the ʔinɨpi may enter a person through the mouth. In this situation no counteraction is possible. Henry Weldon recalled an experience with a whirlwind which came after him as he was driving his car. It lifted the car slightly as it passed, then turned around and came back. Henry was frightened and yelled at the whirlwind in Kawaiisu (which he rarely used). The whirlwind turned away and did not return.

Not all the appearances of the ʔinɨpi can be understood as being a premonition or conveying a message. At least no visible aftermath was reported in some cases. Here is an occurrence related by CG: "When I was coming home from school, I saw an ʔɨnɨpi in the pine tree near my house. He seemed to be wearing clothes. It was getting dark. I was with two of my sisters. We saw a 'man' and thought it was Harry Williams. Then we realized it was a devil, and ran."

Again: "Three of the Williams brothers, Ed, Willie and Harry, saw an ʔɨnɨpi while they were driving a car up to the Piute Rancheria. 'He' came into the car and smiled at them. They kept talking to each other as if the devil were not there. When they approached the house, 'he' disappeared. They said, 'What was that? It was a devil!' They all had a very strange feeling."

"Another time a devil entered the car and sat down between them. The devil said, 'There goes Harry.' Later Harry was driving along this road and went off a steep embankment. The person riding with him was killed."

"The ʔɨnɨpi sometimes comes right in the house. Early one morning I heard one whistle in this house."

An old informant told of an incident that happened long ago: "People were hunting kangaroo rats at night. They set the brush on fire and then clubbed the rats as they ran out. Suddenly the people saw an ʔɨnɨpi sitting by the fire. They were afraid and ran home."

It is unlucky to dream of ʔɨnɨpi since it means that a *pohagadɨ* is trying to make you sick. Anyone who is so indiscreet as to keep talking and laughing in bed after the lights are out may expect to be frightened by ʔɨnɨpi. An elderly informant, however, insisted that it was the *pitadɨ*, the neighboring tribe to the south, that had the custom of remaining quiet in bed "until the ʔɨnɨpi passed." To invalidate the baneful effects of dreaming of ʔɨnɨpi, one should hurry to a mountain and there tell him to stay away. (The custom of "talking to the mountains" will be discussed elsewhere in this paper.) As one proceeds to the mountain, the ʔɨnɨpi might frighten one by whistling or becoming visible. One should not whistle at night or the ʔɨnɨpi will answer. Once when the informant's brother whistled at night, the ʔɨnɨpi whistled in response. One should not cut one's hair at night or the ʔɨnɨpi will call you (see under *Tuuwaruudidɨ* above).

When one's ears ring, ʔɨnɨpi is calling. Once the ears of Emma Williams' maternal great-grandmother were ringing. It was the ʔɨnɨpi summoning her. She heated her finger by the fire and put it in her ear (to avoid hearing the call). "She didn't want to go, but she had to go anyway."

The ʔɨnɨpi fears tobacco (*soʔodɨ*, *Nicotiana bigelovii*), the smoke of dried "wild celery" root (*kayeezi*, *Lomatium californicum*), and the smoke of burning blue sage (*tugubasidabɨ*, *Salvia dorrii*). To chase him away, one places a pinch of tobacco on the back of the hand between thumb and forefinger and blows it in several directions. The ʔɨnɨpi sleeping in the bunkhouse (cited above) was made to disappear when a man blew tobacco at him. Dried wild celery root is ignited and the smoke spread about the room. Emma kept some of the root wrapped in a cloth by her bed. Blue sage is either thrown into the fire at night or, according to one informant, put in a frying-pan over the fire.

In recent years several of the Kawaiisu women and their children have become members of a local Apostolic Faith Mission church. They now equate the ʔɨnɨpi with Satan who is rendered powerless by pronouncing the name of Jesus Christ. They tell of instances in which they protected themselves from the threat of ʔɨnɨpi in this way. One young man dreamed that he was chained by the "devil," but the word "Christ" broke the shackles.

In the house it was customary to hang charms which were believed to keep the ʔɨnɨpi away. One, the ʔanaguyuutɨ, was made of two bird wings stretched on a stick. The other, the cakoloʔwaazi[2], consisted of a long, thin strip of wood twisted into a spiral. Both were suspended and moved freely in the air currents. Some informants insisted that they were merely toys to amuse the children.

There are complicating and perplexing elements in the descriptions of ʔɨnɨpi as recorded over the years. It would appear that some individuals are "part ʔɨnɨpi" and some possess something "black and like a hair" which may be located internally, apparently about the heart, or externally about the neck. McCown gives the name of this item as 'uwa unup' though neither Cappannari nor I had encountered this term.[3] To quote in part John Nichols' statement to McCown:

> A man might dream of an uwa unup and he might come to possess it. He could wear it around his neck. This gave him the power to take it out of another person who had one inside of him. He could disappear and reappear at will. Also, it made him invulnerable.

But John thought it would not help a man against witches and witchcraft. McCown notes that "George Bowman has an uwa unup. His father had one, too, but he had to help George get his. Evidently it was not possible for George to inherit this thing." Bob Rabbit told McCown that the uwa unup will eventually kill its owner. "Bob thought they were very dangerous to play with. He knew about them [but] never wanted to have one."

Although Cappannari provides no name for it, the presence of hair is mentioned in his account of the exploits of the ʔɨnɨpi: "Twisted hair is a symbol of an ʔɨnɨpi. If someone dies because an ʔɨnɨpi has entered him, a twisted hair will be found by cutting his chest open." Such a hair was found around the heart of the killer 'bear' pogʷitɨ (see below).

---

[2]The presence of 'l' in this word seems to indicate that it is a borrowed term.

[3]'unup' is obviously ʔɨnɨpi (terminal vowels are frequently omitted in speech), but the force of 'uwa' remains unknown.

The feats of men who were "part ʔɨnɨpi" are described in an informant's recounting of an incident dating back to an early contact of the Kawaiisu with the "Mexicans." The Indians walked to Los Angeles where the Mexicans had locked their horses in a corral. At night one Indian "who was ʔɨnɨpi" unlocked the gate by spitting on his hands and opening the padlock. The horses ran out and were driven to a "rock corral" on the other side of the mountains. The ʔɨnɨpi "shot" the pursuing Mexicans through the ears (?). The informant explained that the ʔɨnɨpi wore twisted hair around his neck.

On another occasion two Kawaiisu men came into a camp of white men (apparently miners). One of the Indians saw a woman's clothes hanging on a line, and stole two silk handerchiefs. The woman's husband caught the thieves, stripped off their clothing, and found the handkerchiefs. One of the men was hanged from a tree, but he didn't die. The other was locked up in the house. When everyone was asleep, the latter spit on his hands, opened the lock, and walked out. He said "hello!" and jumped from the door to the top of a mountain. He walked a bit and then jumped to the next mountain. "He had dreamed of a little insect that jumps and that gave him the power to jump. He was ʔɨnɨpi. Anyone can dream and become ʔɨnɨpi." The man who had been hanged got back to the Indian camp the next morning. He was a rainmaker and made it rain on the white man's camp.

At the time of the Kernville massacre (more than a century ago), Indians of several tribes were rounded up and shot. When the Kawaiisu were led to the place of execution, one of the men suddenly sat down. The soldiers didn't see him and passed by him. "It was ʔɨnɨpi that made him invisible." He escaped.

That the characteristics of ʔɨnɨpi know no tribal boundaries is indicated by an incident that occurred in Yokuts territory when the Kawaiisu and the Tübatulabal were invited to a fiesta. For some reason fighting broke out and the Yokuts started shooting at their guests. A Tübatulabal woman fled and got as far as a hill near Bena (near the Kawaiisu-Yokuts "border"). "The Yokuts followed her; they wanted to kill her. She had on her basket-hat, and pushed it off the back of her head. Then they couldn't see her. They saw only the hat. It was ʔɨnɨpi. She got away."

## YAAH$^w$EʔERA

While the yaah$^w$eʔera has some of the characteristics of the ʔɨnɨpi, he is not associated with the spirits living or dead. Yet, like the ʔɨnɨpi he is indestructible, and his presence is an evil omen and ought to be avoided if possible.

One informant maintained that the yaah$^w$eʔera cannot be seen--only heard--but generally he is believed to have the form of a bird with a tail about a foot long. One of the difficulties about identifying him is that he has the ability of imitating the sounds made by men and animals. Emma related how one day she heard him "yelling" and thought it was a cow. A bit later he was farther away and sounded like a rabbit. Then he moved still farther and sounded like a grey squirrel. Once described as a "little hawk," he seems to have some relationship to the mountain quail. As to his indestructibility, one comment was, "It's a bird--how's it going to die?"

If *yaahʷeʔera* approaches closely, you become stiff and helpless. But if he is still some distance away, you can get rid of him by putting some tobacco on a rock and throwing it in the direction of the sound. He yells as he swallows it. You won't hear him again for several minutes. Then you hear him far away. "He won't come back." Setimo told how, when he and his family were camping out to gather pinyons, they were bothered by *yaahʷeʔera* every night. He would pick up a stone, spit on it, and rub some tobacco on the moistened area. Then, crying "hee!" he would fling the stone into the darkness. That would keep *yaahʷeʔera* away.

When he appears to you in your sleep, he takes the form of a female if you are a male, and a male if you are female. He will have intercourse with you all night, and the next day you will be weak and worn out. You won't be able to get up until the next evening. An informant recounted the experience of an old man who told him how *yaahʷeʔera* had slept with him on Piute Mountain. He heard *yaahʷeʔera* coming "like quail" but he couldn't move. He didn't remember anything after that, but *yaahʷeʔera* stayed until morning and the man slept the whole day.

It appears that *yaahʷeʔera* dwells in a "cave" deep in the earth. The entrance is difficult to find because it keeps changing and sometimes disappears altogether. Someone once tossed a rock down the "hole" and it took a long time before it reached the bottom.

There are two tales which, told with variations by several narrators, involve *yaahʷeʔera*. One of them is concerned with "*yaahʷeʔera*'s house" and will be told in the section on the Netherworld (q.v.). The other relates the story of a woman who, accompanied by her little daughter, was out pounding acorns. The girl misbehaved so her mother walked off and left her. When the mother returned to get her daughter, the latter had disappeared and could not be found. *Yaahʷeʔera* had taken her to his cave and made her his wife. A long time afterwards the girl's brother, out hunting, saw her in a field gathering tickseed leaves (*tɨhɨvidɨbɨ*, *Coreopsis bigelovii*, an edible plant). He did not speak to his sister but went home and told his mother who, thinking the girl dead, was about to prepare her clothes for the mourning ceremony. (According to one version, *yaahʷeʔera* fed the girl little fish, about six inches long. He had no fire but cooked the fish by placing one under each arm. When they dropped out, they were "done.") There are two versions of the end of the story: (1) Not long after the brother saw the girl, *yaahʷeʔera* brought her home after telling her not to reveal where she had been. He told her parents that she was pregnant and they were not to harm the babies that would be born. The girl gave birth to many babies who immediately ran off to the hills. The parents asked her where she had been and she told them. The babies threw rocks from the hills, destroyed the house, and killed everyone inside. (2) After a while, yaah^we?era told the girl to go home. She was pregnant, and he instructed her to keep the babies under a basket. There were many babies and they got out. She tried to catch them, but they ran away. They were mountain quail. Yaah^we?era picked up a rock, threw it at the house, and killed everyone.

THE ROCK BABY

There is a "baby" who dwells inside exposed rock areas. His name, ?uwan?azi, is explained as being derived from the sound of his cry: "?uwa ?uwa," though it is clearly related to ?uwa?iici, infant. Since he is linked to rocky regions, he is believed to be engaged in painting the pictographs found scattered throughout Kawaiisu territory. Though no reason was forthcoming from informants to account for this activity, the ?uwan?azi never stops working at it. Thus the patterns may change from day to day, and the Indians commonly react to a description of a certain group of pictographs by saying, "It wasn't like that when I last saw it." The suggestion that humans may have been the artists is invariably rejected as absurd. (It may be noted here that cave contours are also regarded as changeable, but these are not attributed to the Rock Baby. As for the numerous bedrock mortar holes, they are accepted as the "normal" shape of the rock formation.)

Both the Rock Baby and his pictographs are "out of bounds" for people. The paintings may be looked at without danger, but touching them will lead to quick disaster. One who puts his fingers on them and then rubs his eyes will not sleep again but will die in three days. Some informants said that this would be the consequence even if the eyes were not rubbed. Photographing the pictographs was thought in the 1930s to bring bad luck--the camera would break. By the 1970s, however, this unhappy outcome was forgotten.

But the real danger lurks in the ?uwan?azi himself. He is an omen of disaster. Though rarely seen, he is described as "just like a baby," but his sex is indeterminate. He has a little black hair. Usually he is heard rather than seen, and his cry is a tuuwaruugidi. A number of incidents are related in which the presence of the ?uwan?azi brings death. In the following two stories the people involved are said to be 'South Fork' (Tübatulabal) rather than Kawaiisu.

Some South Fork people went above Onyx (on the South Fork of the Kern River) to get chia. One of them heard a baby crying on a rock so he went up, got him, and brought him back in his arms. The man told the others to come and see him, but they put their hands over their eyes because they were afraid to look at him. Only two glanced at the baby. Then a girl told the man to take him back, and he did. But when the man put the baby down and stepped away, he could see that the baby had a cradle tied on him. The baby got up and walked right into the rock.

Sometimes that baby lives in the water near a spring. One day a Tübatulabal woman was going from South Fork to Tule River. She was

walking across the Greenhorn Mountains. She came to a spring and put
water in her water-bottle. Her baby, whom she carried in a cradle,
began to cry. He kept on crying so the mother nursed him as she
walked along. While he nursed, he kept looking at his mother's eye.
He started to swallow her breast. When she arrived home, her husband
tried to pull the baby away but could not do so. Finally the husband
cut off the breast. The baby swallowed it and ran off. The mother
died. The ʔuwanʔazi [at the spring] had turned the woman's baby into
an ʔuwanʔazi.

Sadie Williams heard the cry of the Rock Baby in the summer of
1947 and a few days later a neighbor died.

A couple were lying together on a cot out of doors. The woman
heard a baby crying under the cot. She told the man, but he said he
didn't hear anything. They looked under the cot but saw nothing. At
about this time the woman lost a grandchild. It was the cry of the
ʔuwanʔazi.

About a month before her baby died, GG heard the Rock Baby crying in the rocks. For several nights before the death, she heard a coyote
howling near the house. On successive nights, the howling sounded closer.
After the infant died, it ceased.

Henry Weldon had an experience at a pictograph site, but he did
not mention the Rock Baby or any other being as the cause. He was riding
his horse near a pictograph rock, but the horse stopped before the rock
was passed and refused to go farther. Dismounting, Henry attempted unsuccessfully to pull the animal. He mounted again, but the horse seemed
to be pulled down and fell over on its side. One of the horse's legs lay
on Henry's leg and neither could get up. When it looked as if they might
be held there all night, Henry pulled out his gun and shot toward the
pictograph rock. Then the horse got up and they went on their way.

## COYOTE'S SONS AND DAUGHTERS

The activities of Coyote's sons and daughters are limited to a
single pattern which would seem to stem directly from the proclivities of
their lecherous father. In the Kawaiisu version of the widespread tale
*Coyote Marries His Daughter*, Coyote's wife and children escape from him
by ascending to the sky where they become the stars in the Pleiades.[4]
Thereafter the "children"--apparently two sons and two daughters--return
to the earth to enjoy sexual intercourse with their sexual opposites. If
they come at night, they are seen in dreams and have their way with the
helpless victim. During daytime their chosen partner temporarily "dies,"

---

[4]There is a difference of opinion as to the identity of the constellation. One informant called it the "Little Dipper," another the
"Milky Way." Sapir (1930:533, ftn. 88) comments on a Paiute text: "A
constellation of seven stars is meant. Tony [his informant] thought it
was the Dipper (*Ursa Major*). . . but was not quite certain."

that is, either faints or goes into an epileptic fit. (The distinction, however, is not made by informants--they simply describe the human partner's condition as a "dying" for a period of a half-hour or more.) According to one informant, both daughters--and, by implication, both sons--appear to the partner who makes a choice, but in no case is the experience considered desirable, and ways are sought, not always successfully, to prevent it.

Two informants told of an "old man" who, tired of the repeated dream of being seduced by one of the daughters, hit upon a means of frustrating her. Before going to sleep he spread cholla cactus (*Opuntia echinocarpa*) all around him. Then he tied the sharp pointed leaves of yucca on his penis with the points projecting outward. That night the girls came down and found it impossible to get to him. They wept in their helplessness. He continued this practice every night until he was no longer disturbed by that dream. As one informant remarked, "They can't cross the cactus, and they are afraid of the yucca points. He didn't die anymore after that."

The daytime dying can occur in any situation and at any time. The attacks seem to begin at about the age of adolescence. A man of twenty-one may "die" as he sits in his saddle. Sometimes these sky beings draw you near water so that, when you "die," you will drown. An old Yokuts woman "died" at Tejon; she fell into a fire and then she really died.

John Marcus's daughter began her "dying" when she was thirteen. When I saw her, she was said to be twenty-four. According to one informant, she dreams of Coyote's two sons. Sometimes the attacks come frequently and then cease for several months. When John served as my informant, his daughter was kept in a shed surrounded by chicken wire. Neither John nor his wife ever referred to her, but it was clear that they treated her with kindness and kept her confined for her own safety.

LOCALIZED SUPERNATURAL BEINGS

In a number of places within the territory occupied by the Kawaiisu the sudden appearance and subsequent disappearance of "beings" has been indicated. Though usually taking the form of animals, there are instances in which the "beings" are "people." Their supermundane nature is evident from the fact that they come and go without leaving a trace, but the frequent tragic aftermath reveals them to be *tuuwaruugidɨ*. Although they are rarely seen, it is assumed that they are always there, and their unexpected visibility is taken to convey an ominous message. The disastrous consequences are not always specified, but this may be due to negligent reporting. In the words of one informant, "Anything might suddenly come out of the ground, but there wouldn't be anything there. It is a sign of death for some relative."

Several accounts were given of the unexplained appearance of "lots of dogs" in Kelso Valley. At least one such place is described as on a "little ridge" and is called *puguroʔoci*, 'dog-hole'. "Old timers saw lots of dogs there, but there were no tracks." Perhaps the same locality figures in this episode: "In Kelso Valley there are red rocks piled on one another. Under the rocks is a hole. A hunter passed on a trail which goes nearby. He saw white woolly dogs with beautiful hair and tails curved up like Eskimo dogs. He watched them on the rock and wondered where they came from. Then they vanished." There is another place above Walzer's Ranch. A couple of old women went down there to gather juniper berries. One of the women saw a big, black dog and thought it was a sheepherder's dog. "It went down the rock into the water below and wasn't seen again." The women picked the berries in a hurry and went home.

Hu?yupɨzi, transvestite,[5] was picking ku?u (seeds of blazing star, stickseed, *Mentzelia* sp.) and went to get water toward evening. At the spring he saw a dog which looked like a sheepherder's dog. Hu?yupɨzi ran and hid. He stood watching from his hiding place. The dog disappeared but Hu?yupɨzi didn't see where it went. When he returned to the spring, he could find no dog tracks. The informant's comment was "Hu?yupɨzi was afraid of a man [who might be with the dog]; that's why he hid."

Near Piute Ranch there is a spring where the water used to come out of the ground like a fountain. There were lots of reeds (*Phragmites australis*) growing there and so it was called *pagabo?ova?adɨ*, 'by the reed-water'. A white dog lived there. Old timers saw him lying off to one side. "Maybe he lived in the water."

When Emma Williams's brother was a little boy, he saw some animal in Lander's Meadow. "It was red and had no hair on it. Maybe it was a dog--maybe a bird." The boy went down to take a drink and then he saw many of these creatures. He ran away.

There are similar stories about the mysterious appearance of rattlesnakes. "Sometimes near a spring you see a bunch of rattlesnakes come right out of the water, but nothing's there. Near the hot springs in Thompson Canyon, Marie Girado saw lots of rattlesnakes in a hole. Maybe that's where Rattlesnake lives."

On one side of Bear Mountain there is a little lake on which a "basket" was floating.[6] By the side of the lake there is a pinyon tree whose pinyons are always green, and a Joshua Tree. Once a *kohozi* (Panamint) Indian, coming by with his little son, was told about the basket. He said, "It can't be there." He went to the lake and tried to pull the basket out with a long stick. It wouldn't budge. He pulled very hard. Two rattlesnakes "stood up." There was no basket there at all. The man

---

[5] The Kawaiisu word for transvestite is *hu?yupɨzi*, but, since all references in my fieldnotes seem to be to *one* transvestite, I treat the word here as though it is a personal name. No other name was ever used.

[6] A close parallel to this story is found in Voegelin's *Tübatulabal Ethnography*.

and his son were frightened away. When they got back to Caliente, blood
was flowing from their noses. Both of them died that night. That pinyon
tree and the Joshua Tree belong to the rattlesnakes. There are lots of
pinyons on the tree even in winter, but if you eat them, a rattlesnake
will bite you. The "basket" looked as if it had the rattlesnake-design
(*togowarkɨdɨ*) on it. The rootstock core of the Joshua Tree is used in
the making of this pattern. Later a Kawaiisu man looked for the place,
but he never found it.

In Walker's Basin there is a flat rock with many mortar holes
in it. The rock belongs to Rattlesnake and it is dangerous to count the
holes. Once two women, one a Kawaiisu and the other Panamint, came there
to pound their acorns. The Kawaiisu woman warned her companion about not
counting the holes, but the latter wouldn't believe her and proceeded to
count them. Just as she stepped off the rock, she was bitten by a rattlesnake and died right away. When the Kawaiisu woman got off the rock,
there was no rattlesnake around.

Many years ago Jim Manuel went deer-hunting near Big Bear Lake
where he had never been before. He found fresh deer tracks and followed
them to the lake. There he saw three holes in the ground and an enormous
rattlesnake several feet in diameter. The snake bit him, and Jim fell
down and crawled along until he reached a red-ant hill. Having eagledown with him (as hunters do), he put live ants in balls of eagledown
and swallowed them. Then he fell asleep and dreamed of the snake who
said to him, "I just bit you. You are not going to die, but will be well
when you get home. Why did you come here?" The next morning he woke up
and began to crawl home. Two men, who were looking for him, found him
and took him home on horseback. He recovered, but after that he never
went hunting and was afraid of snakes.

Near Monolith there is a little spring. Louisa Marcus's grandmother once saw a bunch of buzzards there. But actually there was nothing.

Two springs near the Piute Rancheria are said to be inhabited
by supernatural beings. One is occupied by a "seal" with "tusks." The
spring is called *cɨɨpɨɨpoʔoweena*, 'seal's water'. No one has seen the
"seal" for many years, but that is no indication that he is not still
there. The other is called *yaahʷeʔera kahniina*, '*yaahʷeʔera*'s house',
which is at or near the entrance to *yaahʷeʔera*'s cave.

Emma said that in "Tejon" (Kitanemuk?) territory there are more
springs inhabited by "animals" than in the Kawaiisu area.

In at least two instances the "localized beings" are "people."
A "little old woman" has been seen sitting at the mouth of a cave in Sand
Canyon. She is a *tuuwaruugidɨ*, and passers-by keep clear of the spot.
At a cave entrance in Kelso Canyon a young girl who had come to use a
mortar hole (probably to pound acorns) saw an "old man." When she told
her mother of her experience, the latter immediately had the girl undergo
the procedure of swallowing red ants in balls of eagledown. In her dream

the girl saw the old man who assured her that, since she had taken the ants, she would not die. Otherwise her use of his *pahazi* (mortar hole) would have meant death.

Two pictograph sites north of Monolith are apparently exceptions to the general rule that the rock paintings are made by the *ʔuwanʔazi*. The pictographs, too, differed from those of other sites in that, instead of the usual color, at least five colors were used: red (predominant), green, yellow, black, and white. One site is a small shallow cave and the other a large rock shelter perhaps forty feet in height and several hundred feet long. When seen in the 1930s, the paintings were in an excellent state of preservation. Subsequent vandalism, however, has almost completely erased them. In mythological times the animal-people held celebrations at both these locations. It may be that each of the participants painted his own picture. In any case, it was at the rock shelter that the world was created. A mortar hole marks the spot. It was Grizzly Bear who called the animals together although, according to one version, he was not the chief. He still lives in the rock and there is a fissure through which he can come and go. He is known to have growled at a non-Indian woman--and perhaps chased her--when she approached too near (see Offerings). Here the animals decided what they wanted to be. [A discussion of Kawaiisu mythology will be published elsewhere.]

## SKY CREATURES

Two ominous symbols are apt to appear in the sky, though there is some indication that at least one of them, in somewhat different form, has been seen on the ground.

White Coyote (*tugusɨnaʔavi*, 'sky-coyote') may be seen going across the sky. Many years ago two women were gathering chia (*Salvia columbariae*) when they happened to look up and saw White Coyote. The women were so upset they could eat no supper. A few mornings later one of the women was gathering willows for basket-making when she heard a baby crying in the rocks. Several days after three men were killed at Walker's Pass: her son, her sister-in-law's son and an old man. (This may have been the historic episode related by Powers in his *South Fork Country* [1971:30-1]. The Indian version of the tragedy, however, is quite different from that of Powers.)

One summer Benny Girado heard White Coyote howling. The next day he accidentally shot himself through the foot.

The Great Snake, *tugubaziitɨbɨ*, may be seen in the sky during the day or night. He is described as "reddish," about 200 feet long and three feet in diameter. When it rains heavily, you can see him hang down. He urinates out of his tail. He moves in "curves," and fades into clouds. If you see him, one of your relatives will die. Sam Willie's great grandmother saw him in the sky over Kelso Valley and at the same time he was seen in Cummings Valley (perhaps thirty miles away). Soon after the great grandmother saw the Snake, her brother died. One informant said it appears

"all lit up in the sky." The way its head points shows where people
(Indians?) are going to die. But the *tugubaziitɨbɨ* is also seen on the
ground "crawling just like a rattlesnake." According to AG, the home of
the *tugubaziitɨbɨ* is in the Tehachapi Mountains. The area is known to
be fraught with danger and the Kawaiisu seek to avoid it. Hunters have
died up there. One day AG and BF (a non-Indian) were riding through on
horseback with the cattle. They saw a lizard about 3½ feet long. It
swayed from side to side and moved its head as it went along. They
wanted to catch it, but they had no place to put it. AG thinks it was
a *tugubaziitɨbɨ*. After this experience, Sophie Williams, her son Joe,
and his wife Louise all died within a few weeks.

In Oak Creek Pass (near Tehachapi) there is a spring called
*tugubaziitɨbɨ poʔoweena*, '*tugubaziitɨbɨ*'s water', because someone saw the
Lizard there. The mud around it shakes--one can't pass through it--it
would bog you down. The water is no good for drinking.

The Great Snake which the sick man had to pass over in the
netherworld (q.v.) is a *tugubaziitɨbɨ*.

There are two giant beings that are involved in a number of myths
and, if seen, are *tuuwaruugidɨ*. One is the Man-carrying Bird (*nɨhnoovi*
or *nɨhnɨhnoovi*) who swoops down and seizes people. When a member of GLG's
family was in the hospital, another member caught sight of the wing of the
Bird and the hospitalized person died in a few days. The *haakapainizi* is
a large-sized grasshopper, but he is also a giant who can walk "from Inyokern to Onyx in one step." He relishes eating children though, in several
myths, they manage to escape. In one, a mother substitutes a redhot stone
(an arrow-straightener) which the giant swallows and dies. CP recalls that,
when she was a child, her grandmother (who had reared her) would frighten
her when she misbehaved by saying, "The *haakapainizi* is coming!"

## *MɨɨTIIPɨ*

With the data available, it is impossible to arrive at a clear
definition of the term *mɨɨtiipɨ*. Superficially it looks as if it combines
*mɨɨ*, 'only, just' and *tiipɨ*, 'dirt, earth', but no informant offered such
an analysis. In any case, it is used to designate an unfavorable and unlucky sight which, unless prompt counteraction is taken, may be the prelude to some dire consequence. But the relationship between *mɨɨtiipɨ* and
*tuuwaruudidɨ* was never indicated. Perhaps a *living creature* which is
*tuuwaruugidɨ* may be referred to as *mɨɨtiipɨ*. However, this is nothing more
than a guess. One informant described a *mɨɨtiipɨ* as follows: "When you
are out and see something you haven't seen before--a big rattlesnake or
other big animal--it is a bad sign. You will die in two or three days.
He will eat you. He is called *mɨɨtiipɨ*. But if you eat or drink nothing
after seeing him and you take red ants the next morning, you will live."
The formula was spelled out in Kawaiisu: *mɨɨtiipɨ meheciina taasuʔuvita
yɨʔɨgidɨnaamɨ hiʔɨkʷeevaaci*, 'When seeing *mɨɨtiipɨ*, they swallow red ants
in order to be well'. "After swallowing the ants, you fall into a deep
sleep at once like being drunk. The *mɨɨtiipɨ* comes to you in your dream

and says: *yuwaatɨ yuweʔikʷeevaanaami*, 'you will not die'. One can't tell where *mɨɨtiipɨ* comes from. He disappears and leaves no tracks."

A few sights considered *mɨɨtiipɨ* were mentioned, but it is unlikely that the list is exhaustive: rattlesnake, grizzly bear, the Rock Baby, a white man. (The inclusion of the last named must go back to the earliest period of contact.)

"When you go out hunting, you might step on a rattlesnake. Therefore they say to you: 'Be careful of *mɨɨtiipɨ*!'"

## "PRAYERS" AND OFFERINGS

As has already been indicated, the attempt to influence one's destiny is an important preoccupation among the Kawaiisu. Two techniques may be equated with procedures familiar to worshippers of the "western" religions. One, "talking to the mountains" or "to the darkness," roughly resembles a direct appeal to some invisible power. Its use as a preventative measure to ward off threatened disaster has been mentioned earlier, but there is a positive side to the practice. A man starting out on a hunting trip might first address "the mountains." Apparently his request would be stated aloud and, in any case, briefly. He would ask that he be permitted to see deer and no rattlesnakes (and perhaps no *mɨɨtiipɨ* of any kind).

Probably more common than "prayers" was the giving of offerings. A wide variety of situations might call for this type of action though, again, the basic purpose was to create favorable conditions and to avoid unfavorable ones. The verb stem *naahʷi-* seems to express the idea of scattering since the offerings were usually spread broadcast, though at times they may have been aimed in a specific direction. Such "scattering" accompanied festive occasions like "fiestas" when dancing was always a feature, the mourning ceremony, and toloache drinking. The offering might consist of one of several items: eagledown (probably the most highly regarded), beads, acorns, berries, or seeds. Pieces of meat are mentioned in one incident. Not limited to "formal" events, an offering might be prompted by unforeseen and spontaneous happenings. To insure success for his undertaking, a hunter might "talk to the mountains" and also scatter an offering. Though probably referring to eagledown rather than to "feathers," an informant told McCown: "Men sometimes put feathers on the brush, talked and danced. This helped in finding deer. Some men took tugub [beads] with them and scattered it about the ground and talked. This made the deer come quickly." Rafael Girado's statement to McCown is at variance with those of other informants: "Eagledown was put into little bags. The bags were tied to trees--would help the person who put them there in his hunting." (While eagledown was carried in little bags, the customary procedure was to cast it about loosely.) And there was still another technique to increase the effectiveness of deer hunting (see Magical Substances). A hunter might repeat the offering-ritual as he went along; when, for example, he was about to go through a mountain pass (and uncertain, presumably, as to what lay beyond). As Emma put it, "Whenever they came across something strange and unusual that didn't belong on that mountain, they would toss it a piece of meat" (or, doubtless, other things). A sight recognized to be *tuuwaruugidɨ* would warrant an immediate offering.

Here is an incident which was recounted, with variations, by several informants: Emma's father and Charlie Haslem's father had killed a deer and were skinning it when Charlie, who was with them, saw a little bird (a *puupizi*, species unknown). He shot at it with his bow and arrow but missed. The bird flew away, but soon two returned. Charlie was about to shoot again but didn't. Then birds came in great numbers. Charlie was frightened. Emma's father threw the internal organs of the deer-- heart, liver, lung (one version mentions only liver)--in the direction of the birds. One version says they ate what was thrown and another that they didn't. In any case, they flew away. Some time later a relative (apparently of the Haslems) died.

When Sam Willie and John Marcus took me to the rock-shelter site (mentioned above), they stopped a few hundred feet before we reached our destination and told me that, before we could proceed farther, it would be necessary for each of us to make an offering to an animal whose representation we chose to see. Otherwise we would see nothing. Unnoticed by me, Sam had picked some juniper berries along the way. He now divided them among us, and I was instructed to name the animal I wanted to see and then scatter my berries in the general direction of the site. Sam and John did the same. After having performed this ritual, I was assured that we should see pictographs--which we did. They told of a non-Indian woman who had come to see the pictographs but made no offering (possibly she was ignorant of the custom!). She heard the growl of a grizzly bear, fled, and never returned. According to one version of the story, she was actually chased by the bear.

## MAGICAL SUBSTANCES

To a number of substances supernatural potency is attributed, and it is quite likely that the magical properties of others have escaped notice. The efficacy of those recorded is diverse. Thus there is a rock standing about three feet high called *noʔozigadɨ*, 'one who is a little pregnant' because of its shape. Though no specific case was cited, it was said that a young woman who wanted to become pregnant would knock off bits of the rock and swallow them. (According to one informant, a sterile woman might become fertile by drinking a decoction prepared from the dried powdered paw of a mouse.)

Thirty-five years after squaw bush (*Rhus trilobata* var.) was described as having a limited use in basket-making (see *Kawaiisu Ethnobotany*), an informant recalled that her grandmother had told her that this material could be used only by women who have no relatives.

As previously noted, at least three plant substances are considered effective in keeping away the *ʔinɨpi*. Tobacco (*Nicotiana bigelovii* and probably *N. attenuata*) is potent against both the ʔɨnɨpi and the yaah^weʔera. The efficacy of the dried root of "wild celery" (*Lomatium californicum*) is indicated by the fact that Emma always kept some on hand. Perhaps the supernatural quality of blue sage (*Salvia dorrii*) is to be seen in its native name, *tugubasidabɨ*, 'sky/night *pasidabɨ* (chia)'. All of these plants also have medicinal usages.

A plant which figures prominently in Kawaiisu magical practices and yet, as far as is known, does not grow in the area normally inhabited by the tribe is *muguruuvɨ*, turpentine broom (*Thamnosma montana*). Men were willing to travel considerable distances to obtain it. Several functions are assigned to *muguruuvɨ*. Dried and crushed to powder, it is carried in small containers on hunting trips. When deer tracks are located, a small quantity of the powder is dropped into each deerfoot imprint. This procedure has the effect of slowing down the deer so that it can be overtaken and shot. The odor of the plant undoubtedly contributes to some of the beliefs about it. Thus it is said that the *kaap(ɨ)sɨkɨmɨ* (Yokuts) and the *pitadɨ* (a neighboring tribe to the south, possibly Kitanemuk) die from smelling it. While my Kawaiisu informants maintained that nothing except deer blood was ever put on arrows, Cappannari was told that, when fighting the Yokuts, the Kawaiisu treated "their arrows with a poison . . . made from a weed called muguruva . . . which caused [their enemies'] noses to bleed." Though he obtained no name for the substance, McCown recorded that "fighters used a medicine . . . to make the eyes of the enemy wink in order to facilitate killing them." This sounds like *muguruuvɨ*. The powder may be kept on one's person to keep rattlesnakes away, but, on the other hand, it attracts snakes and causes men and horses to sweat. If you keep *muguruuvɨ* with you, certain material benefits may accrue: you will win at gambling and, in recent years, the cashier at the supermarket will err in your favor as she totals your bill.

No substance is more puzzling or more mysterious both as to identity and to effect than *puyumaʔaku*. When, in 1975, at my request, a linguist asked his elderly Kawaiisu informant about the word, her response may have reflected the attitude of all previous informants. "She said it was 'poison' and a 'bad thing', and acted like she didn't really want to talk about it." While my informants referred to it as a powder, McCown was told by one man that it is "an ointment or salve" and by another that it might be "red, white or blue colored" and that "one type of puimak, a powerful charm, is a rock crystal." McCown notes: "I tried to get Bob [Rabbit] to describe what puimak looked like. From his statements it might be dirt, rocks, liquid." There are two possible causes of the confusion: it may be that no informant had ever seen the substance, or the term may have been used to apply to different materials. It might be appropriate here to point out that E. W. Voegelin, in her *Tübatulabal Ethnography*, refers to a substance as a "white powder (alum?) . . . white stuff that looks like flour . . . like baking powder." Although the name of the material, *ayi·p*, in no way relates it to *puyumaʔaku*, its usage in "bear shamanism" closely parallels one of the chief usages attributed to *puyumaʔaku* by the Kawaiisu.

McCown's informants made no mention of a bear-cult in any form, but both Cappannari and I were told of the role of *puyuma?aku* in what might be called "bear-impersonation." However, it was always maintained that the Kawaiisu never used it for this purpose, but knew of its use by neighboring peoples—the *kaap(ɨ)sɨkɨmɨ* and, especially, the *pitadɨ*. In some instances, as will be seen, the Kawaiisu are said to have obtained the substance from the *pitadɨ* at Tejon, but the avowed purpose had nothing to do with bear-impersonation. Indeed, the Kawaiisu picture themselves as the victims rather than the perpetrators of this sinister activity.

The actual situation is complicated by the failure of informants to make a clear distinction between a "real" grizzly bear, a bear-impersonator, and a human killer for whom the term $pog^witɨ$, 'grizzly bear' and *tuhugadɨ*, 'murderer' might be applied synonymously. The grizzly bear itself is invariably portrayed as "mean" and dangerous—a symbol of evil and malice. It will be recalled that the animal is a *mɨɨtiipɨ* and to dream of it is a "bad" omen (see under *Mɨɨtiipɨ* and Dreams). The bear is said to kill people in a special way—taking the scalp from the back of the neck upward and removing the limbs while leaving the upper part of the torso intact and usually sitting up. The bear-impersonator of the *pitadɨ* is, according to Kawaiisu informants, "able to behave like a bear by dressing in a bear skin. They used *puyuma?aku* to make him run and act like a bear." One informant said that "the *pitadɨ* made a 'bear' called *kaukau* [recording uncertain]. Maybe they put *puyuma?aku* on the man. He sits inside the bearskin. He has reins and carries lots of beads inside. That powder makes the hide alive—makes him run." Thirty-five years after these statements were recorded, the same beliefs persisted: "If a bear is killed and skinned, then someone with this substance can control or direct the bearskin from a distance by using some kind of rein or bridle-type mechanism, and it can be used to kill one's enemies. Perhaps the person doing the magic could hide a knife inside the bearskin to kill someone." Voegelin notes the use of a bear skin and a "white powder (alum?)" but states that the Tübatulabal (living adjacent to the Kawaiisu) "were aware of it but did not imitate [it]." She attributes the practice to the "Ventura Indians" and the Chumash, and says that the "bear machine" was "stored in a cave north of Tejon" (just south of the Kawaiisu) but the "white stuff" was obtained in Tübatulabal territory.

The operation of a bear-impersonator is described in an "actual" case:

> Someone in Tejon wants to kill someone over here. The "bear" waits for the man in the mountains. He hides in the willows near the trail. The man to be killed is a "South Fork" [Tübatulabal]. The "bear" cuts off his head and legs. They thought it was a "real" bear, but it wasn't. He stuck arrows with the points upward in a circle around the dead man. . . . The people, including the dead man's wife, went up there. The "bear" was watching from somewhere—they could hear him laughing. [This seems to be a habit of the bear-impersonator.] They thought it was a grizzly bear until they found the arrows. Then they knew it was a man.

Here is an enigmatic episode: Once some cowboys in Tehachapi saw a bear eating juniper berries. They threw a lasso and caught it by the hand. They pulled and the hand came off. Later, that "bear" was not in his "outfit" and he saw these cowboys. He said, "Look what you fellows did to me." His hand was missing.

Once two of the "bears" went through Kelso Valley on the way to the desert to get salt. "Real bears never go to get salt." On the way back they passed by Jim Haslem's place where there was a pine tree. One of the "bears" jumped up and swung on one of the limbs. Then they went through Tehachapi on the trail back to Tejon. Their tracks could be seen.

Emma told a grim and lengthy story about *pog<sup>w</sup>iti*, a "bad man" who lived in Old Town (usually regarded as in Kawaiisu territory but on the way to Tejon) and went about killing people for no apparent reason. Five men were murdered by him, but eventually a posse ambushed and killed him. The individual episodes were recounted by Emma to me in 1938 and to Cappannari in 1947. Our respective fieldnotes seem to indicate that no *puyuma?aku* was involved and that *pog<sup>w</sup>iti* was "just mean."

Apparently referring to the same individual, Marie said that after *pog<sup>w</sup>iti* was dead he was cut open. Around his heart was found a hair, and that hair was *?inipi*. (The assumption is that *pog<sup>w</sup>iti* was possessed by an *?inipi*.)

As already indicated, McCown obtained no affirmative data about the use of *puyuma?aku* (or, in McCown's transcription, puimak) in a bear-cult. McCown notes that Nichols "did not recognize my description of bear or rattlesnake shamanism." However, other unrelated usages of puimak were known to several of his informants. Both Emma (Williams) and John (Nichols) said that puimak was brought from Tule River. Only wealthy people could afford to have it as it was expensive. John said it was "strong" and could make people do whatever you wanted them to do. It

> might be used in business or in love to make the other party accede to your wishes. Also it was rubbed on the back during dances, for what purpose he did not explain. . . . A man might use puimak to make a girl come to him despite her parents' opposition. . . . It was often used by people who wanted to make money. If you had puimak people would come to your house to trade with you and you were always successful. It might be used by a man who wanted a certain girl, especially if she was reluctant.

Emma said that a rag "with some sort of medicine on it, possibly puimak, might be hung over the door of one's house and people would come to the house regardless of their wishes in the matter."

Bob (Rabbit) said that puimak

> was used by shamans and also other men. It would make them crazy. . . . Puimak might be used to make people go crazy or it might kill them. It works at any distance. One type . . . is a rock crystal. The possessor has to put the right kind of "dope" on it to insure its efficacy. It might disappear or kill the owner unless he knows how to keep and use it. . . . Once an Indian on a high mountain took out his eagle feather. He talked. . . . The puimak appeared. The Indian

knew how to make the puimak stay with him. [It has an] attraction for lightning. The lightning will come and take the puimak away. . . . This is why trees get hit with lightning. One Indian (Juan) was killed by lightning because he had puimak in his pocket.

Of three kinds of puimak--red, white and blue-green--according to Bob, the red "was for fighting. . . . The puimak that is best for [making] rain is blue-green like galena. . . . Puimak was no good against witches." Bob mentioned still another usage: To make pinyon trees bear, a cone on a large limb is painted with puimak. It brings good results for seven years. The same procedure is recommended for acorns and chia (!).

My informants, including John and Emma, and those of Cappannari, described *puyumaʔaku* as a "deadly poison" which, if placed anywhere on the skin, will sting like the bite of a red ant--and cause death. The *kaap(i)sikimi* are said to put it on their arrow points. It makes dead worms come to life and can grow flesh on bare bones. A *pohagadi* employs it against his victims. One *pohagadi* had grown flesh on [the bone of] a human finger. It was discovered in her nephew's trunk after she had died. Marie Girado told of an old man who had heard an owl hooting in a nearby tree. He shot it. The next morning he looked for the bird but found nothing but old bones. A witch had wanted to kill the man, and had brought the bones to life with *puyumaʔaku*. But the intended victim had not touched the owl and thus escaped harm.

As suggested by John Nichols, the "powder" is also an effective love potion. An informant knew of a Kawaiisu woman who had learned of its power from a *pitadi* Indian. If the substance is kept in the house, a couple cannot stay apart. They will spend their time making love. The woman used some on a man nicknamed *sinaʔavi*, 'coyote' (perhaps so called because of his sexual preoccupation, though in this instance it would seem more aptly applied to the woman!). It proved predictably potent. But the man's aunt disapproved of the match, and when, on one occasion, she found the couple out of the house, she looked under the pillow and saw some hair on which there was *puyumaʔaku*. She took the hair and threw it into the creek. The man had known nothing about the presence of the "powder," and soon left the woman.

An old *pohagadi* at Tejon lived across a creek from a couple. The young wife was alone while her husband was working in a nearby town. The *pohagadi* was about to put *puyumaʔaku* in the woman's chamberpot, but the latter saw her. When the husband returned, his wife told him of the witch's attempt to poison her. Pretending that he was going off to work, he walked a short way and hid. That night he knocked at the witch's door and, when she opened it, he killed her with an axe.

A Kawaiisu man called Pete wanted to marry a certain girl. He had some of that powder. He came up to her and sat back-to-back against her. There were people there and they all felt "pretty good." They started to sing and dance. An old woman who had been picking juniper berries came singing and dancing along the trail. "Maybe Pete rubbed against the girl. She jumped up and asked, 'What are you doing?' Then

everybody had to dance. He threw the powder away. He didn't get it here--
maybe at Tejon." The girl didn't marry him. "If we had the powder here
now, it would make us all dance."

Another story does not mention *puyumaʔaku* specifically, but it
may well be the substance involved. A *pohagadɨ* living in Kawaiisu territory "went to Tejon and came back with some kind of poison. All the
people got sick. Some children and old people died." Two men found the
witch taking a nap on a hill near where he lived. They hit him on the
head with a rock and killed him. They were his relatives. After that,
all the people got well.

Clearly my early informants regarded *puyumaʔaku* as having a
compulsive quality. "The *pitadɨ* have that *puyumaʔaku*," said an informant.
"If one of them calls you to come there [to Tejon], you have to go."

Although we have data on the substance covering a forty-five
year period, it remains, to the end, elusive and mysterious. It is
tempting to regard *puyumaʔaku* as a broad concept covering diverse materials and functions, and it is even possible to theorize that some of
the reputed usages may more properly belong to one or more neighboring
peoples. But it would appear unlikely that any meaningful reconciliation of the diverse testimony can be achieved at this late date.

## SHAMANISM

There is no Kawaiisu equivalent for the term "shaman," but the
idea of "specialist" or "expert" may be expressed through the use of the
suffix *-gadɨ*, 'possessor', 'one who has'. Thus *pugugadɨ* is 'dog-
possesor' or 'owner of a dog'. A *huviagadɨ* is a 'song-possessor' or curing shaman. An ordinary "secular" song is *kaapɨ*, but *huviavi* is a song
that has been received through a dream or vision and is therefore of
supernatural origin. While no authentic example was ever recorded--the
last alleged *huviagadɨ* died around 1930--a typical shaman's song is said
to have named the surrounding mountains and other phenomena of nature.
The important factor was that the song was received in a dream that might
be deliberately sought. There seems to have been no claim of ownership,
however. During a curing session a song introduced by the shaman could
be picked up by onlookers and repeated. The words *kaaciʔidɨmɨ* and
*kaaceʔeyawɨ* (no longer remembered in the 1970s), based on the root *kaa-*,
were said to refer to 'shaman's assistants', but it is not clear that
such roles were institutionalized.

Aside from singing, the *huviagadɨ* was apprised of his calling
through dream-images. The only one mentioned was deer, and especially
deer singing, but there were probably others. While Charlie Haslem's
competency as a *huviagadɨ* was questioned by some (see below), his account
to McCown is all that is available concerning the process through which
one became a curing shaman. Charlie said that as a young lad he thought
that he was "just dreaming" and for the first few years he did not realize that "his dreams were doctors' dreams." It might take four to six

years before one was "strong enough" to cure. Charlie's uncle (his mother's brother) Ramon, a well-established *huviagadɨ*, recognized Charlie to be a "dreaming man" destined to become a *huviagadɨ*. Ramon tried to cure Old George of a nosebleed or hemorrhage, but he was unsuccessful. Told by Ramon to try, Charlie stopped the bleeding. He

> had the power two years before he made his first cure. . . . He blew on George's head and the bleeding stopped. . . . Ramon did the singing the time that Charlie cured George. . . . The "man" in the dream gave Charlie the songs that he sings. He always saw the "man" before he made a cure. . . . He gets a new song for every cure. . . . Also this "man" gave him the crystal in the dream.

The techniques followed in a curing session were never clearly defined. Part of the confusion may stem from the fact that people were not reluctant to seek the services of shamans of any tribe if a reputation for effectiveness was widely known. This practice led to considerable differences of opinion as to what a Kawaiisu curing shaman usually did. Here are some of the features of the procedure as recorded: The singing continued throughout the night and was often--but not always--accompanied by dancing. The shaman was given a mixture of tobacco and water in a steatite bowl, and he chewed and swallowed as he worked. He laid his hands on his patient and, when he reached the affected place, his hands felt "as if they had been stung by nettles." The patient might also feel this sensation. Describing Charlie Haslem's movements, the informant said "he hopped on both feet like a bluejay. His arms were by his sides with palms facing forward and knees relaxed." Suddenly he produced his crystal and showed it to all present. He rotated his hand, but the crystal (or 'diamond') did not fall. He placed it on the sickness, sucked on it, and drew the sickness out. A little sore on the body marked the spot. Whatever was drawn out of the body (one informant insisted that nothing was removed), he took outside, put in a hole, covered up, and then stamped on. If the shaman was convinced that a witch (see below) was involved, he might go off to the mountains in the middle of the night to learn of the witch's identity. John Marcus said that the *huviagadɨ* might rub his hands together and produce a "snowball." He gave it to the sick man who swallowed it. On one occasion John (Marcus) was watching Charlie "doctoring," and relates the following conversation:

> I said to him, "How you going to make well? You got nothing with you." Charlie said, "You're right." After a few hours he said, "I think I fool you. I'm going to show you something." He put his open hand out the door and drew it back. In his hand was something very pretty--round like a sheep horn. "Who you think gave it to me?" asked Charlie. Night gave it to him. It speaks to him like us.

A *huviagadɨ* is paid for his services--usually in advance. He might receive $5 to $20 or be given a horse. If the patient dies, the payment is returned to the relatives. Charlie told McCown that "doctors" would refuse to take a case if they knew that the patient was going to die. The sudden death of a patient during a cure was due to the efforts of a witch. The *ʔɨnɨpi* will come back and haunt the one who killed him.

The bewitching shaman, *pohagadɨ* (possessor of *pohavi*, 'poison', but the word is a cognate of Southern Paiute *poa-*, 'supernatural power') also gains his power through dreams and visions (q.v.). The images are those identified as *tuuwaruugidɨ* and *mɨɨtiipɨ*. As noted elsewhere, stinging nettles may aid in preparing an aspiring *pohagadɨ* for his vocation. No mention is made of song either in connection with the preparation or the procedures of a witch. As to his techniques, there is the same kind of confused evidence that characterizes those of the *huviagadɨ*. Apparently the "poisoning" could be achieved both through direct contact and indirectly, at any distance. According to John Marcus, the *pohagadɨ* works at night. "You might be here and he is in Kelso Valley." When he wants to kill you, it appears in your dream.

> Maybe you see an animal, a rattlesnake or something else. He tells you you'd better go away or you'll be killed. He lies, because it won't do you any good to go away. You might feel all right the next day, but the next night you begin to feel sick and you go to bed. Sometimes the *pohagadɨ* has a small rattlesnake in his pocket. He makes it straight like an arrow, and shoots it at you with his bow. He may be far away. That rattlesnake might show like a spot on your leg. It gets bigger and bigger and then you die. You see him shoot at you in your dream.

The fear and hate that witches inspired are expressed in the statements of John Nichols to McCown:

> The sole function of witches was to kill people. They never used their power for spells in hunting. . . . If a witch was killed, that was all right because they were mean people and no one cared for them. They were better off dead. . . . Women are very bad witches; they are not "doctors" [i.e., *huviagadɨ*—this assertion is not supported by the testimony of others]. Devils [ʔɨnɨpi] help the witches and will carry poison for them. When a witch appears in a dream it means sickness. They have the power to change into wildcats and snakes.

Bob Rabbit told McCown that "[bewitching] shamans were often killed and when this happened, they were burned and not buried [in the usual way]. This was to prevent their coming back [apparently as ʔɨnɨpi]."

Though the goals of the *huviagadɨ* and the *pohagadɨ* were in sharp contrast, people were not always confident of the identity of each. The ultimate proof was in the result of their respective actions. If recovery followed upon the ministrations of a 'doctor', then his reputation as a *huviagadɨ* was advanced. But if, instead, death followed, he might well fall under suspicion. After several failures, conviction would grow that he was not a curer at all, but a witch. Under such circumstances his life might be in danger and, as already indicated, there were instances in which accusation led to murder. Depending upon experiences, one family might characterize an individual as a *huviagadɨ*, another as a *pohagadɨ*. Though reputedly a curing shaman, Charlie Haslem was accused by the head of one family of "never curing anybody." At least two attempts were made on his life, but he lived beyond the age of 90.

An important function of a *huviagadɨ* was to identify the

*pohagadɨ* whom he was convinced had caused an illness. This placed upon the *huviagadɨ* a grave responsibility, and it was generally believed that only a powerful one could risk making such an accusation. If bewitching was the cause, identification of the witch could lead to a cure.

It should be noted that, with the acceptance of non-Indian medical services, there has been a shift in the meaning of words. A modern physician is called a *pohagadɨ* (apparently with no pejorative connotation), and a *huviagadɨ* today is a musician.

In the area of healing, another specialist was also recognized—the *matasuk^wigadɨ*, 'possessor of medicine'. While John Nichols explained the term to McCown by saying that a *matasuk^wigadɨ* is "like an American doctor, a doctor with medicines," his assertion that "anybody could do this—all that was required was a knowledge of the weeds and how to fix them" would not be acceptable to others. Actually, with the many plant medicines known (my *Kawaiisu Ethnobotany* lists 107) and with the probability that other substances were believed to have curative powers, an expert in medicinal formulas should have been an important functionary. Speaking on the basis of personal experience with a *matasuk^wigadɨ* (who was, however, a Tübatulabal and not a Kawaiisu), John Marcus, whose evaluation of the profession differs from that of John Nichols, explained to me that the *matasuk^wigadɨ* was acquainted with all kinds of medicines, both beneficial and poisonous. This knowledge put power in the hands of the 'possessor of medicine' and John M. was convinced that the Tübatulabal expert was responsible for the deaths of his three sons who died in successive years. Nevertheless, "home remedies" were an integral part of traditional Kawaiisu lore and the people from whom I assembled my *materia medica* in the 1930s made no pretense to being "professionals."

When one suffers from an ailment, what determines the choice between seeking the services of a *huviagadɨ* and a *matasuk^wigadɨ*? "I failed to ascertain," writes McCown, "the distinction between sicknesses curable by herbs and those requiring a shaman. From talks with Santos [Phillips] who is always ailing and with John [Nichols], I rather think that the gravity and length of the sickness determines this. A bad cold is usually treated homeopathically at first but, if it gets worse or lingers and other pains or headaches develop, a doctor may be called in." It may be added that, if traditional medicines do not prove effective, it may be suspected that a *pohagadɨ* is involved. The next move, then, would be to consult a *huviagadɨ*.

More than a half century ago, the Kawaiisu had achieved preeminence as rain shamans. Kroeber refers to this talent in his *Handbook of California Indians* (1925). Voegelin, in her *Tübatulabal Ethnography*, mentions (1938:64) the "notable reputation" of "Bob Rabbit, Kawaiisu rain doctor"; and Steward, when doing fieldwork among the Owens Valley Paiute, heard of the "shaman in Kern County who predicted storms" (1933:311). The rainmaker, or more accurately, weather-manipulator, is called *ʔuupuhagadɨ*, a term whose derivation is not altogether clear. Rain is *ʔuwa-*, a stem sometimes shortened to *ʔuu-*. Thus *ʔuupuhagadɨ* may mean 'rain-witch' or 'rain-doctor', but there is an unidentified item in the rainmaker's kit called ʔuupuhɨvɨ, so that the definition may be 'possessor of ʔuupuhɨvɨ'.

In the land of the Kawaiisu, precipitation was of prime concern. The productivity of the wild plants is dependent upon rain in an area which often suffers from drought. On the other hand, water is capable of descending in overwhelming quantity. Flash floods were known and feared, and a dry creek bed could suddenly turn into a rampaging, destructive torrent. Therefore the services of a competent ʔuupuhagadɨ were in much demand.

Of a number of stories about rain-control, here are two recorded by Cappannari: There was a female rain shaman who lived near Caliente. She had not made rain for a long time and the people in Kelso Valley were hungry and worried about their wild plant crop. The drought was widespread. Three *kohozi* women walked over the mountains from Inyokern to Kelso Valley. They too sought rain and carried beads and baskets to give to the ʔuupuhagadɨ. They went on with the Kawaiisu women to Caliente and gave their gifts to the rain shaman, but "she just laughed." The women started back but, when they reached Sand Canyon, it started to rain. It was a moderate rain and soon the grass and edible seed plants came to life. The ʔuupuhagadɨ joined the women to gather seeds. It was raining in Inyokern also. "It rained all over."

There was a Kawaiisu rain shaman at Tejon who had not made it rain for a long time. The creeks were almost dry. Some Kawaiisu people and a non-Indian cattleman visited him and gave him money to make rain. He sang and danced all night. In the morning he told the people to look at the sky. They saw a huge black cloud. Soon it rained very hard.

Weather shamans were secretive about their procedures. According to one informant, "no one can watch them at work." The most detailed account of weather-control techniques was obtained by McCown from Bob Rabbit. Bob had been "around" a good deal and, as a result, seems to have brought together some eclectic ideas about rainmaking.[7] The emergent picture is not as clear or precise as one might wish. Thus Bob talked weirdly of a "rain-god" who comes from the "south" and speaks Serrano (?). Of the equipment which rain shamans used, McCown lists a steatite plate, chia, pinyon (seeds), acorns, a young fawn, eagle feathers, and special crystals or rocks. Songs were indispensable. Bob said he acquired his songs in dreams after he had eaten the tobacco-lime mixture as a young man. His songs would be effective even if someone else used them. Apparently into the steatite plate (which seems also to be designated a "bowl") mud, kept moist, is laid and seeds of all kinds are embedded. Over the whole the skin of a fawn is stretched. Bob smoked his pipe "three times" and blew through a bone tube "three-times--this is to make the wind." Then there

---

[7]Harold E. Driver, in *Culture Element Distributions VI*, evaluates Bob Rabbit as a "rather poor, erratic informant, but good on topics that interest him, such as deer hunting" (1936:89). I spent one day with Bob in 1936, and agree with Driver except that I do not recall any comments on deer hunting.

was something about tracing "a circle with cross lines pointing north and south." The important thing, according to Bob, was to be able to stop the rain after it had started. "Otherwise the whole world might be drowned." McCown records that "Bob chewed weeds (medicine) and water. He spat into his fire, steam rises and the rain stops in three days from that time." The use of blue-green 'puimak' (see under Magical Substances) was mentioned but no particulars of how and to what effect were volunteered. Bob emphasized that all those who benefitted from the rain were expected to pay for the services of the ʔuupuhagadɨ.

There is still another method of causing precipitation and, unlike those imperfectly described thus far, it is available to everyone. It is the use of the tree-lichen, paaziomoʔora (*Ramalina menziesii*). Bob had employed it himself and told how he went to Koso Hot Springs (to the north) and put paazimoʔora in the water there. He claimed that it brought rain with cool weather, "but it did not blow or freeze and there was a good stand of filaree" (probably *Erodium cicutarium*). But Bob was highly critical of the widespread use of paazimoʔora for two reasons. For one, its effects were unpredictable. When placed in water, it might produce rain; but, instead, it might bring cold, sleet, snow, and high winds. Secondly, "people all over the country would try to use it. It invariably made trouble and also kept the rain shamans out of work." Even as late as the 1970s, the older people testified to the effectiveness of paazimoʔora, and I was warned about its power when I took some away for taxonomic identification. LG explained that heavy winter rains were caused when some children sprinkled water on the lichen which she had hung on her kitchen wall. Thereafter she hid it in a can.

The possibility that some form of "bear shamanism" existed among the Kawaiisu is discussed above (under Magical Substances). No Kawaiisu word was ever suggested. The term kaukau is clearly alien, and informants insisted that bear-impersonators belonged to neighboring tribes. It is therefore doubtful that bear shamanism was a Kawaiisu institution.

## MISCELLANEOUS BELIEFS

When the sun goes into eclipse, it is sick. (When the moon is in eclipse, it is also sick.) People were frightened lest the darkness remain. They felt that they ought to stay at home so that they would not get lost in the blackness. During a solar eclipse, "pinyon birds" swarm over the earth. If it gets very dark, these birds will eat people alive. Once a couple were walking up a trail. Late in the afternoon there was a solar eclipse. They heard the pinyon birds coming. The woman ran away in the dark, but the man stayed and struck at the birds with a stick. The birds killed and ate him. When the woman returned, she found his bones picked clean. There were holes in all her baskets.

Sometimes the sun can be "cured" during an eclipse. Emma recalls an eclipse when she was a little girl. As it grew dark, an old man sang and danced. He had "dreamed" the song. The sun "got better."

Many years ago there was a great earthquake. Emma's mother and grandmother were crying. Marie's grandfather went outside and shouted three times. Then he lay flat on his stomach and struck the earth with a winnowing tray. He had dreamed what to do to stop the earthquake. The earthquake stopped.

When it thunders, one should remain quiet indoors. One should avoid loud talk, singing, or playing music because noise makes Thunder angry. You may talk to Thunder and tell it to go away, but if you yell or whistle or point a finger, it will get worse. But you may point with your thumb over a shoulder.

One may talk to the clouds--tell them to go that way and not come this way. They will obey.

Killing a trapdoor spider ("tarantula," *nɨwɨsooyagizi*) will cause the wind to blow.

Blowing on the "fluff" on rabbitskin will bring precipitation. CP remembers that, as a child, she and other children were blowing on a rabbitskin which they held between their hands. Her grandmother warned her that this would bring snow. The next morning there was snow on the ground.

Emma's great grandfather told her: "When you see a new moon in the winter, take a small stick and break it in the direction of the moon (?). This will shorten the long winter months." But only an older person can do this.

When clouds appear for three successive days, there will be rain for three days. A rainbow augurs an abundance of edible seeds. But one should point at the rainbow only with the thumb. Using a finger will cause it (the finger or the rainbow?) to break off.

If a pregnant woman looks at a waning moon, her child's face will be black on one side. She must keep away from foods and objects which symbolize closure or stoppage. She must refrain from eating the feet of animals lest her infant be born feet first, and from stepping over a mole tunnel lest he be born blind.

During pregnancy no one (in the family?) killed an animal that might harm the child--a rattlesnake, grizzly bear, mountain lion. Tule elk was not eaten because it is a big, slow animal, and the baby would be fat and slow. Deer is quick--it is good for the baby.

If the teeth of the pregnant woman remained white, the infant would be a girl. If the teeth turned black, it would be a boy.

Sewing with needles would hurt the baby's eyes. A head scratcher was used by menstruating and pregnant women. If they scratched with their fingers, their hair would fall out. Hot water was drunk by menstruating and pregnant women because cold water hurts the blood.

If deer meat were eaten before hunting, the hunter would have no luck because the deer would not show themselves.

If one steps on a rattlesnake's track, it makes one's legs ache. Instead, one steps across the track. If snakes' rattles were kept in the house, one would have a headache all the time. Also, snake rattles attract snakes and, if kept in the house, snakes would come in. If you wound a rattlesnake, it will wait for an opportunity to bite you. Sophie's brother injured a snake. The next year it was at the same place waiting, but he killed it this time. You never talk about a snake biting someone. "You don't even think about it."

If you tell myths in the summer, a rattlesnake will bite you. (This constitutes a problem for the ethnographer.) In the winter those who listened to myths the evening before must jump in the water no matter how cold. According to Emma, this was done because rattlesnakes are afraid of people who have just taken a bath. But her grandson, Harry, said it is because rattlesnakes drink water only in September.

For fear of grizzly bears, one would start on a hunt in the morning--never in the afternoon. When wounded by a bear, one is not likely to die right away, but might live a month and then die.

If a hibernating bear is located, one doesn't talk about it that night or the bear will move to another place (before he can be killed).

If you talk at night about birds' eggs which you have seen during the day, you won't find them the next morning. If you cast your shadow over a nest of eggs, they won't be there the next day. If you talk about birds before the eggs hatch, the eggs will be destroyed.

If you sneeze once, someone is saying (or thinking) something bad about you. If you sneeze twice or more, someone is saying (or thinking) something good about you. If your eye twitches, you will cry soon. If you nose twitches, you will fall on it.

One never touches human bones (they sometimes become exposed after burial). If one does so, the skin of one's hand will peel off. Once a woman stepped barefooted on bones in a graveyard. A few days later the foot became very sore and the skin peeled off. It stayed that way a long time.

One does not refer to the recently deceased by name. Instead, the word ʔɨʔɨnɨpi (cf. ʔɨnɨpi, 'spirit, ghost') is substituted. One does not give the name of the recently deceased to a newborn child, for to do so would be a sad reminder to the bereaved. However, after several years the name may be used again.

As you come to the end of life, your mind wanders to all the places where you've been (ʔɨnɨpi paginiidɨ, 'the spirit goes about'). Finally you come to the end of the trail and you die.

There is a spirit (or ghost) trail (ʔɨnɨpitoovɨ) where the spirits of the dead walk at night. It comes from the Piute Mountain area into Kelso Valley and then into the desert over Mustang Canyon. In the evening the ghosts come from the east to the west, and then, just before daybreak, they return eastward. You can feel the hot air as they pass.

The morning or evening stars may be seen bobbing up and down behind the mountains. Coyote threw these stars up there when he was playing ball, and they are still bouncing.

If pinyon cones or acorns are put in the pockets of a dead man, no pinyons or acorns will be produced for five years. Cones will grow, but there will be no seeds in them.

## THE AFTERWORLD

Informants claimed to have some familiarity with the abode of the ʔɨnɨpi after death since a few living individuals had visited the place and had returned to tell about it.

A long time ago a woman was bitten by a snake while she was gathering chia, and died when she reached home. She had three nephews who put beads around her neck (in preparation for burial) and cried all night. Her ʔɨnɨpi went along the trail eastward to the land of the ʔɨnɨpi. When she got there, she was told to go back where she came from. The ʔɨnɨpi of her deceased grandmother said to her, "You stink," and directed her to return home. Before she left, the woman saw many dances. The ʔɨnɨpi were dancing and singing just like human Kawaiisu and lived in the same kind of brush houses. As she ran home, she looked back at the hills where the ʔɨnɨpi were. She saw fires that looked like lights.

When she reached her home, she stood outside and heard her nephews crying. She was "bashful" (embarrassed?) and hesitated to go inside. Eventually she entered the house, and then she awakened. She asked for a drink of water. They took off her beads and gave her water. The next morning she was all right.

The account of Bob Rabbit's visit or visits to the afterworld may have suffered from the retelling. Perhaps all three versions available ought to be presented. The second and third versions were recorded by McCown.

(1) Bob was sick. He "died" and went to the ʔɨnɨpi's world. There he found his grandmother cooking acorn mush. His parents were also there, but they did not speak to him. The grandmother told him to go back. She said, "The ʔɨnɨpi here sometimes kill people. They might kill you." So he came back.

(2) Bob said he had visited the place of the dead. His relatives did not treat him well. They would not feed him although they had plenty of food. He saw his father, mother, sister, and grandmother.

(3) Bob made two trips to the soul land to see his sister but found the doors locked so he came back.

The inference seems inescapable: The world of the ʔɨnɨpi is not a hospitable place--at least for those who don't belong there!

## THE NETHERWORLD

As previously indicated under Yaahʷeʔera, this supernatural creature is apparently in charge of a netherworld where the spirits of animals are to be found. One informant called the place yaahʷeʔera kahniyeena, 'yaahʷeʔera's house'. While differing in some details--one version does not even mention yaahʷeʔera--the descriptions are alike in certain significant features. Perhaps two versions ought to be presented separately:

(1) A sick man who was seeking a cure came to the entrance-way which is in Back Canyon. Its opening assumes various forms and is sometimes shut altogether. This is the place where "all the deer you kill come." Someone once saw the tracks of three deer leading to it. To reach the bottom, the man had three nets tied together end-to-end, and one end was tied around his waist so that he could be let down the shaft. He said, "When I get to the bottom, I'll shake the rope." He did, and the people above pulled up the nets and went home. Down below, the man entered a tunnel of white rock. A large gopher snake (kogo) stretched across the tunnel and served as a "door" to yaahʷeʔera's house. The man climbed over it. A little farther on there was a larger snake, tugubaziitɨbɨ, and he climbed over it too. He passed the Brown Bear and the Grizzly Bear and walked on. Beyond it was sunny just like outdoors. Many deer were eating the leaves of sɨnaʔaruubɨ, mountain mahogany (Cercocarpus betuloides). Yaahʷeʔera told the man to sit down, and gave him acorn mush in an acorn cupule and dried deer meat to eat, but the food was never exhausted. Yaahʷeʔera asked what he wanted. The man said, "I'm sick and I want medicine." There were different medicines wrapped in deerskin. The man chose a song which was also wrapped in deerskin. Yaahʷeʔera told the man which way to leave, and said he would come to a spring. The man found himself outside again.

(2) A man was up at the cave above Indian Creek. He ate a large piece of tobacco because he wanted luck. After he ate the tobacco, the entrance to the cave closed. He began to walk through the tunnel and it had no end. He was very frightened. He saw many different animals-- deer, bear, and others. They spoke Kawaiisu just like people. Someone handed the man a basket with one pinyon in it. He ate it and there was still a pinyon in it. He was also given a never-emptying basket with one acorn in it. There were many different kinds of luck on the cave walls. He saw a bow and arrow of a good hunter in a prominent place. He took something for his luck. (The informant did not know what it was.) Finally he came to the end of the cave. He saw water that was transparent like a window. He came out through the water and found that he was way up in Back Canyon--a few miles from the cave entrance. That man had been gone a whole year. His relatives didn't know where he had been.

There is another ending which parallels that of a different yaah^we?era tale (see above): Yaah^we?era told the man that for five days he was not to tell anyone where he had been. The man resisted all questions for a time, but finally told his story before the end of the five-day period. He died.

## BOND OF FELLOWSHIP BETWEEN MAN AND ANIMAL[8]

"When Joe Williams [CP's brother-in-law] was a small boy, John Nichols took him under his wing to teach him to hunt, to track, and all the ways of the animals. One day John had tracked this mountain lion. It was a fresh track, and he took some of the sand from the track and mixed it in his [Joe's] food. He told him [Joe] now this would give him the ways of the lion, the ability to track, to scent, and to kill. Whatever he was stalking, he would manage somehow to kill it. As a rule they did this with the boys. His [John's?] comment was that they didn't usually tell the child when they were feeding it to him--usually afterwards. The name of the mountain lion is *tukuumɨci*. After that they felt a brotherhood between the mountain lion and the one who had eaten of his track. Joe Williams won't kill a mountain lion to this day.

"One time my father Andy Greene and Joe worked on a ranch. It was a cattle ranch and the boss told them, 'If you see any mountain lions, destroy them.' Of course, they were paid bounty on them, too. In the course of knowing that they should do this to keep the cattle from being destroyed, my father shot a mountain lion. He felt extreme remorse afterward because he had been fed the track of this mountain lion, and he felt the binding of this brotherhood. I don't believe he ever collected the bounty. If I remember right, he brought him home and buried him like you would a pet--something you felt a strong attachment to."

## IN CONCLUSION

Kawaiisu culture began to deteriorate at least 120 years ago as the presence of the non-Indian came to be an inescapable fact. One by one the traditional customs fell into disuse, although the order of their disappearance can no longer be traced. Groups of neighboring households, usually interrelated, continued some basic activities. Ritualized occasions like "fiestas" (often intertribal), the mourning ceremony, and toloache and red-ant swallowing, could not have survived far into the twentieth century. By the 1930s there were no curing shamans and but one rainmaker who was no longer interested in his vocation. There were those, however, who were suspected of being bewitching shamans in the 1940s and quite probably beyond. Pinyon gathering outlasted acorn gathering--it may be because the end-product was more popular. (I participated in a pinyon "expedition" in 1937, but was assured that "it was not like in the old days." In the 1970s one of the women promised to make me some acorn mush on her kitchen stove. Having gathered the acorns, she kept them for

---

[8]Transcript of a recording made by CP, 8/25/70.

more than a year and then died without completing the project.) A half-century ago modern cigarettes may have taken the place of the strong native tobacco for smoking by the men, but the women perpetuated the old tobacco complex at least into the 1940s because they enjoyed chewing the tobacco-lime mixture.

What has survived into the 1970s? Thirty-five people—none of them less than 35 years of age—can speak the native language, but they never do so except with close relatives. The common speech is English. No one attempts to teach Kawaiisu to the children since, as one mother commented, "Who are they going to speak to?" In only one family are both husband and wife Kawaiisu. Of the survivors, 26 live within an area of about 55 square miles, but they never meet together as a group.

As noted under Shamanism, 107 medicinal plants are listed in the forthcoming *Kawaiisu Ethnobotany*, but not more than a handful are still utilized. The people consult modern physicians and find no conflict in taking both modern medicines and those dictated by tradition. One elderly woman was given a prescription, but she didn't understand what she was supposed to do with it. She continued with her old-time remedy and, when she saw the physician again, he told her she was much improved. In the 1930s there was a sharp difference of opinion as to whether Mexican or Kawaiisu procedures should be followed to strengthen the crippled legs of the infant son of a Mexican father and a Kawaiisu mother. Possibly both were tried but, in any case, the physical condition was not improved though the son is now nearly forty.

Some of the ideas and beings of the supernatural world still live in the minds of a few people. To the women who have become faithful devotees of the local pentecostal church, the *ʔɨnɨpi* is very much alive, but he is now Satan and is kept under control by Christ. CW has told me that she is perplexed by the thought that the old-timers were somehow able to protect themselves from the evil machinations of the *ʔɨnɨpi* even though they knew nothing of Jesus Christ. She has tentatively decided that they must have had "very strong thoughts" through which they escaped disaster. A few of the women make the annual pilgrimage to the Church Assembly in Oregon. En route one year, one of them gathered some of what she believed to be the rainmaking lichen (*paazimoʔora*). She had no doubt as to its potency (see under Shamanism). There is no longer any *huviagadɨ*, *matasukʷigadɨ*, or *ʔuupuhagadɨ*. One must be somewhat less certain about witches (*pohagadɨ*) since suspicion about an individual, if held, would remain a dark secret to be shared only by members of one's immediate family. The sheer paucity of numbers, however, makes it quite unlikely that anyone now living can be considered qualified for that unfortunate calling. On the other hand, *tuuwaruugidɨ* may well lurk in the minds of the few who still have memories of the older beliefs. The occurrence of the "unusual" is an ever-present reality for all of us! AG's experience with the crawling *tugubaziitɨbɨ* falls within the present decade. And who can deny that some strange cloud-borne image might appear in the sky tomorrow?

No longer a viable way of life, Kawaiisu culture will have a fragmentary survival in the consciousness of a few people for another decade or two.

# Behavioral Patterns in Chemehuevi Myths
## by
## Carobeth Laird

The animals who were people, the forerunners of mankind as depicted in Chemehuevi mythology, hunt, gather, make artifacts, travel about, practice shamanism, make war, and conduct their sexual affairs very much like their aboriginal successors, but with vastly superior magic powers. Since Chemehuevi culture has been so rapidly swallowed up in the dominant white society, it would seem that the actions of the "people" of the myths might yield valuable clues to the day-by-day practices of the ancients, their actions and reactions, what they considered permissible and what not permissible. Naturally this comparison cannot be carried too far. To assume that one can deduce from myth a complete picture of aboriginal behavior would be like believing that the manners and mores of Victorian society might be reconstructed in their entirety from the novels published during that period.

The Chemehuevi did not regard their myths as fiction--or at least not altogether as fiction, although a clever story-teller had no qualms about embellishing the basic structure of a myth to suit his fancy or to accommodate it to changing times. The myths, let us remember, were both sacred narrative and superlative entertainment; and the People (that is, the Chemehuevi) had a notably light and ironical touch in regard to matters elsewhere treated with dreadful seriousness. There was probably no doubt in their minds of the truth of the creation stories; of the continuing existence of Ocean Woman, the creator; or of the former presence in semi-anthropomorphic manifestations of Wolf, Coyote, and their contemporaries. But always the exploits of these beings, with the exception of Ocean Woman, closely followed (the Chemehuevi would have said "set the pattern for") the conduct of everyday life, with the addition of those elements of exaggeration and shock which make fiction so entertaining.

When I began to record Chemehuevi myths, they impressed me as being very poorly structured. There is frequently a rather long opening episode, from which the myth may or may not take the name by which it is most often mentioned; then one or more of the characters sets off on a journey or quest, which becomes a thread upon which are strung four or more unrelated (or loosely related) adventures. Sometimes, as in the tale of the Yucca-date-Worm-Girls' search for a husband, the successive adventures form a prelude to the longer incident with which the myth ends. I frequently thought of these stories in a somewhat condescending manner as "rambling." They do indeed ramble; not because of any lack of ability on the part of the original narrators, but because they reflect the experiences and interests of a roving people. To a Chemehuevi, "traveling about" was what made life worthwhile.

The doings of Mythic Coyote, as the exemplar (the People say, "We followed Coyote"), must have been the very mirror of everyday behavior, although with emphasis on its least approved elements. The more admirable Wolf spends his time hunting big game. Coyote also hunts, and frequently leads hunting parties; however he also roams aimlessly, wondering (that is, querying his penis or tail) what he should do next, always receptive to adventure, preferably sexual or warlike. Coyote and all the other heroes of that era have a passion for paying visits to relatives, friends, strangers, gambling opponents, or known enemies.

Southern Fox, almost as typical a Chemehuevi as Coyote, on his long treks to visit relatives in the north, amuses himself by shooting arrows, outrunning them, and dodging them where they come to earth. (Swiftness and agility were much prized in the days of the hunters.) Southern Fox also enlivens his journeys by duels with his Enemy, unprovoked attacks, and ambushes. He shoots at a woman rocking her babe at the entrance of a cave; but she is a bird (Flycatcher) and rises from earth more swiftly than the arrow flies toward her. Southern Fox treacherously kills a Goose Girl who has ferried him across a stream, turns her carcass into the carcass of a buffalo, and magicks a huge pine tree into growing in the desert, all as part of an elaborate scheme to entice Coyote and his family to their deaths.

Death, when it happens to Coyote, is never final. If he dies with his companions or warriors, in battle or of thirst, he is revived last of all by Shamans who carry the *poro*, the crooked stick or rod of power. If he dies on a lone adventure or with his family, sometimes he is willed back to life by his destroyer, sometimes nothing is said of his being revived; but the listener can always look forward to his reappearance in another story. The majority of tales include the death of Coyote, perhaps in unconscious acknowledgment of the mortality of mankind.

However, for certain mythic characters death has finality--which is not to say that they will not reappear in this present time as spirit helpers to shamans or as the animals of today. There occurs in many myths a certain grim, unaltering sequence. "He got mad" is always followed by "he killed" the object of his wrath. Great Horned Owl is a good provider for his wife and son. Every evening he brings home jackrabbits. However, he always eats with his back turned and this arouses suspicion. Spying upon him, his wife discovers that he is keeping the fattest ones for himself. Immediately she "gets mad." Now there is outside their house an area of hard-packed snow where the returning hunter habitually stamps to shake the loose snow from his garments. Here Owl's wife buries sharp slivers of jackrabbit bones. When Owl stamps his feet as usual, the bones penetrate his flesh. Feeling the pain, he thinks he has been frostbitten. At night, as his condition worsens, his wife, pretending to help him, drives the pieces of bone further in. Towards morning Owl knows he is about to die. He tells the woman and her son to travel to his cousin, Hawk, who will be a good provider for them. After several narrow escapes, all brought about by her disobedience and curiosity, the widow reaches the end of her journey, marries Hawk, and presumably lives happily ever after.

To the white man's way of thinking, this would be the logical end of the tale; but to the Chemehuevi sense, Coyote, appearing towards the end of the story, has not been dealt with adequately. Another grimly humorous episode is added. Hawk becomes angry with Coyote and flings his bow. Coyote, fawning, avers that he was "just saying" (loosely translated, "only fooling") and implores Hawk to recall his anger. Hawk says, "Then dig yourself a place where you may stay alive." Coyote hastily digs himself a pit, but is so fascinated by the progress of the returning bow, devastating the whole mountainside as it flies along, that he keeps sticking his head out. The bow, whizzing along at an immense speed, severs Coyote's neck, then falls at the feet of Hawk. This incident seems to indicate that anger, once loosed, is an implacable lethal force with a life of its own.

In the story called "Struggle for the Handstone," two brothers who have been fighting for possession of the *mano de metate* "get mad" because their mother has gone away and allowed the seed she was toasting to burn. They follow her, find her cohabiting with an old man called Rattlesnake, and kill them both. Then they press their mother's belly with their feet and various reptiles come out, also a mouse. These they kill. Last of all, Packrat emerges, and they decide to cherish her as their little sister. They set out on a long journey with an apparently fully anthropomorphic female child. As they travel, they make packbaskets for the little girl out of the ribcages of various animals, beginning with very small ones and progressing to larger game as the child grows. Later it appears that one of the brothers is *Kɨ'atsi*, a species of insect; the other remains nameless.

In these tales murderous rage and its consequence is seldom followed by grief or remorse. Sometimes the offense which precipitates murder seems trivial; while conduct which in a "civilized" society might lead to killing, provokes no such reaction.

One myth gives an instance of prostitution. Coyote and his followers, being without women, see Hawk's wife sitting in a provocative attitude. They determine to hire her services. She refuses several offers, but ultimately one is made which she finds attractive. The men of Coyote's band approach one by one, but because she is sitting with her legs spread apart and they stare at her as they draw near, all but a few reach climax without touching her. (Those who stared at the woman's genitals have yellow eyes in their present animal manifestations; therefore it is said that if a youth wishes to grow up with eyes of the proper dark brown color, he must avoid looking at a woman's private parts.)

Hawk watches the whole transaction from his aerie, then flies off to gamble with his opponent, Blue Beetle. The wife, also a Bird, casts a hypnotic spell to make him too weak to fly till she can overtake him. She follows swiftly, high against the vault of the sky, singing as her hair waves in the wind. Then she gives Hawk two of her eggs to substitute for balls in the game they are about to play. Husband and wife fly on together. The substitution safely made, Hawk and his companions triumph over their opponents and rescue the wife, who has been left as a pledge. But now she is baked brown--formerly she was cream-colored--because Blue Beetle has left her warming by the fire preparatory to cooking her when he should have won the game. Instead it is Blue Beetle who is boiled and eaten.

These hints of cannibalistic practices occur throughout the myths. A race of giants, believed to have been ancestors of the Mohave, were reputed to be cannibals, ready to gobble up anyone who laughed at them. (And George Laird, who furnished virtually all the information I have on the Chemehuevi, stated--as fact, not myth--that there was a Shoshonean speaking tribe "who hunted people as we hunted the deer and the mountain sheep.")

Mythic characters gamble incessantly. Hunters on the way to the localities where they intend to lie in ambush or to make their drives, engage in wrestling, footraces, and archery contests as they go and bet on the results. Bat's grandsons, Sky Brothers, are pictured as leaning disconsolately on their bows after they have wagered and lost all their arrows in such contests. Serious gambling is carried on night after night or day after day. The loser first bets his property, then his wife and children, last of all his own life. But frequently, at the very end, an element of magic enters in to change his luck.

One story tells of a particularly gruesome game between Chipmunk and a Giant. It is called "Cutting off the Testicles" and consists of an attempt to castrate the adversary by a single knife stroke. . . . Did such savage contests take place in reality? And what sort of knife was pictured in the minds of those who listened to the tale? Southern Fox sings of a stone knife, and the boy who was divided into Dove Boys fashioned a knife out of hardwood.

In discussing Chemehuevi marriage customs, George Laird insisted that marriage between siblings or cousins was absolutely forbidden. Mythic Coyote had no sister, so we have no way of knowing whether he would have violated this particular taboo. But in the above cited "Struggle for the Handstone," he puts a hypnotic spell upon Kɨ'atsi to cause him to lie with his own sister, now become a woman. Coyote himself will go to any length to commit incest with his mother-in-law or daughters.

Widows are shown as availing themselves of the protection of a deceased husband's brother or cousin. But also in myth (as in fact) women exhibit considerable independence in the matter of choosing marriage partners. In the myth variously known as "Yucca-date-Worm-Girls Went to Look for a Husband" and "Yucca-date-Worm Girls Got their Eyes Punched Out," two young girls wander, naked and nubile, over the trackless desert. In the first four episodes they are deceived (or rather, the younger is deceived and the elder allows her to have her way) by the magic of various worthless fellows into believing that they have found a good hunter. As soon as the deception is uncovered, they walk away and resume their quest. The fifth husband is Redtailed Hawk, a mighty hunter and a powerful shaman. He at once sets about making buckskin clothing for his new wives. Later, by sleeping in a cave they have been forbidden to enter (a typical act of disobedience), the wives become the victims of an old man called Grasshopper, who gouges out their eyes with a single kick and robs them of their belongings. When their eyes have been replaced by the eyes of female mountain sheep, property restored, and the crime avenged, the properly chastened young women live happily with the husband of their choice.

In a tale called "The Bluebirds Went to War with Wolf," the menfolk of a band of Bluebirds are out hunting small game. Left behind, the women see distant smoke. They find it comes from the womanless camp of big game hunters led by Wolf, Mountain Lion, and Coyote. Ever ready for change, the Bluebird Women join themselves to these hunters, thus initiating a war in which all their former marital partners are killed.

Perhaps more realistically, another myth tells of a woman taken captive and forced to leave her living infant among the corpses of her relatives.

The duties of women are clearly defined: to gather and to grind seeds, and to cook the products of these labors; to weave baskets and other items made out of plant fiber; and to bear burdens. (The rationale for this latter requirement is that men must have their hands free to handle weapons.) Young women are frequently represented as headstrong and disobedient; but youths and young men display the same traits.

The articles of women's apparel most frequently mentioned are aprons and rabbitskin capes (blankets of woven strips of rabbit skin worn as capes). In a typical instance of Coyote-ish behavior, Coyote, walking behind his mother-in-law, suggests with lecherous intent that she throw her skirt over her head to protect herself from thorny shrubs, as she goes along stooped over looking for jackrabbits he has shot.

Women are associated with the killing and preparation of all animals smaller than a jackrabbit. A magical boy (whose name, that of a bird species, is revealed only after he has performed certain exploits) grows up in the charge of his grandmother and Coyote. As he grows, he traps progressively larger animals in progressively larger and stronger snares. All those from a head louse up to and including a woodrat he brings to his grandmother, who gives them names and illustrates the manner in which they shall be killed. All larger animals (with the exception of the mythical Person Carrier, who carries off the boy!) he drags in for Coyote to name and kill. Coyote ties up the jackrabbit, the deer, and the mountain sheep, and pretends to ambush them before he shoots them.

Men use the products of trees and shrubs to make weapons and to build houses thatched with brush. Coyote has a stone with a groove in it. He heats it in the fire and employs it to straighten reeds for making the shafts of arrows. He also illustrates the proper method of affixing flints and feathers. (Wolf would have done all these things "the easy way," by magic; but "we followed Coyote.")

Everything pertaining to the hunt belongs in the masculine realm. Jackrabbits and cotton-tails are "small game"; deer and mountain sheep (and presumably antelope) are "big game." Hunters unaccompanied by women bring in small game themselves, fastening the carcasses to their belts. The hunter of big game kills his animal, returns and tells a woman of the household its location, and she backpacks it home. Then the man takes over, butchering his kill, tanning the hide, and using his awl to sew clothing for himself and his family. Hunters operating from a womanless camp of necessity pack in their own game. In the myths there are instances of both men and women cooking meat. (But according to George Laird, it was the duty of the hunter to cook the animal he had killed.)

Mention is made of armor, perhaps reflecting the prevalent belief that certain articles of clothing had magical protective power. Wolf and Coyote fight their last great battle in rainbow-hued warclothes (Coyote wears one at a time the pale shades of the secondary rainbow; Wolf is resplendent in the dazzling colors of the primary rainbow, worn all at once). Gila Monster and Turtle have "stone shirts"--Gila Monster's is hidden by his wife ("the captive woman," in league with his enemies) and he has to fight unprotected. It is to be noted that the wildest fantasy is rooted in keen and accurate observation of the natural world.

Mention is also made of a charm which had power to warn the possessor of approaching danger.

In this collection of myths I have not found an account of any rite of passage from youth to manhood. But in the story called "Coyote Went to Gather Basket-Making Material," which illustrated Coyote's androgynous nature, he ritually roasts himself for four nights after moulding breasts out of mud. Coyote also commands his "daughter" (the child whom he has delivered of a dead mother and nursed through infancy with his artificial breasts) to gather wood and roast herself at the time of her first menstruation. This latter custom was observed within living memory.

It has been positively stated that the Chemehuevi always buried their dead and burned the possessions of the deceased. But in the myths there are at least two references to cremation. The body of Great Horned Owl is burned inside his house, after his wife and son have removed their personal belongings; and Coyote, feigning approaching death, tells his wife and children to place his body on a funeral pyre, ignite it, and leave "without looking back"--it being his intention to roll away from the flames unobserved, make off, and return with a new identity.

At some distant time magic apparently attached to the bones of a slain adversary. Wildcat changes the luck of his maternal grandfather, Sun Spider, who has lost everything but "his life and a little charcoal" while gambling nightly with the Sky Jackrabbits, by making peon sticks out of the leg bones of a jackrabbit he has killed and substituting them for sticks regularly used. And Bat makes himself wrist protectors out of the bones of the maniacally vicious Yucca-date-Worm Girls, when he is planning to kill their husband, the ancient Rattlesnake.

Here we note that these dreadful sisters are in every way the reverse of the naive pair who wandered in search of a husband, being either a later development, or as George Laird once suggested, "a different race." In either case we have in the Yucca-date-Worm Girl stories one more instance of the dualism which pervades Chemehuevi metaphysical thought; only here we have two opposing pairs instead of two opposing individuals. One pair is innocent, gullible, and harmless, the elder sister being more intuitive and prudent; the other sisters of the same name are motivated solely by the desire to kill, and the younger is dominant. The only other mythological dyad in which the younger (the last created) is promoted to a position of dominance (and actually called the elder) is that of Wolf and Coyote. Wolf dominates because he is wise and good, the younger Yucca-date-Worm Girl because she is wise and superlatively evil.

Myth, like fiction, gives at best a distorted picture of a culture. To take one example only, it must not be assumed because of the frequency with which rage equals murder in the myths that the Chemehuevi were unreasonably belligerent. The reverse is probably true. A decent restraint in speech constituted (and still constitutes) good manners--perhaps for the very reason that an intemperate expression of wrath might be equivalent to the launching of a curse that could not be called back. The Chemehuevi were brave and well equipped for war but not prone to provoke combat, preferring rather to maintain an alert but not necessarily provocative demeanor while visiting strangers or potential enemies. Neither does the delight experienced while listening to Coyote's sexual exploits imply that incest and rape were rife among the People; in fact, we might be justified in the inference that these pleasurable thrills were due to a customary decent restraint in such matters.

Nonetheless, the customs, manners, and material achievements of everyday life must be the background against which the narrator paints his vivid verbal pictures. Fantasy gathers its basic material from reality. Therefore a judicious examination of the lifestyles portrayed in myth provides a more comprehensive view of the aboriginal way of life of this people than would otherwise be obtainable.

# Native California Concepts of the Afterlife
# by
# Richard Applegate

INTRODUCTION

    This paper is an overview of California Indian concepts of the afterlife, stressing correlations with other aspects of culture such as mythology, religion, and world-view. These concepts of the afterlife were not merely mythological or cosmological speculations for the native Californians--at least for certain members of a community--these were matters of experiential knowledge. People dreamed of visits to the land of the dead, their souls might go part way there during a coma or a serious illness (e.g., Steward 1934:427), and shamans often visited the land of the dead in spirit journeys. In addition, the Orpheus myth found in much of California (cf. Gayton 1935) seems to have been regarded not as a myth but as a factual account of events in the not-too-distant past.

    It deserves mention at the outset that the soul was of interest to the native Californian not just as a postmortem phenomenon; soul concepts impinged on daily life in a number of contexts, such as disease, curing, witchcraft, the vision quest, and power in general. Hultkranz' encyclopaedic work (1953) on North American Indian concepts of the soul devotes considerable space to Californian soul concepts and these related beliefs. My purpose here is to supplement Hultkranz; I discuss variations in major themes of what befalls the soul after death, as well as the more striking beliefs unique to particular California tribes.

    As with many other aspects of aboriginal Californian culture, the lack of a standardized or orthodox version of beliefs concerning the soul and afterlife is evident everywhere. This reflects the lack of centralized political and religious power, as well as a rather experimental and individualistic approach to the supernatural. Indeed, alternative versions and disagreements or even outright contradictions are most frequent precisely in those tribes which encourage each individual to approach the supernatural on his own (e.g., Atsugewi, Wintu, Mohave). One ethnographic example of this lack of orthodoxy will suffice, from the Yuki:

> Tillotson believed that all souls, regardless of merit, went to heaven, after first crossing water. . . . The idea of punishment was not considered by him (Tillotson). Ralph Moore denied that the soul

crossed water, and was joined by George Moore in insisting that the
souls of bad people remained on and under the earth . . . (Foster
1944:206).

An important variable is how interested people themselves were in questions of the soul and what befalls it after death. The Mohave, for example (Devereaux 1937), were obviously quite concerned with these matters, as might be expected from the inturning dream orientation of the culture. Other tribes, often culturally marginal groups such as the Wappo (Driver 1936:217) and Washo (Lowie 1939:322) seem to have had much vaguer notions.

Sources are extremely uneven. There is an excellent monograph on Mohave soul concepts (Devereaux 1937), and many full-scale ethnographies which devote space to discussions of the soul and afterlife, such as Dixon (1905:259-262) on the Maidu and Hooper (1920:342-343) on the Cahuilla. Cultural Element Distribution lists are sketchy and often contradictory, although they sometimes contain valuable data, particularly on more obscure groups. Narrative texts may contain much valuable information on the afterlife, such as Blackburn's collection of Chumash texts (1975:texts 10-12, 25, 59). Mythical references to the afterlife are nearly always in the form of the Orpheus myth (cf. Gayton 1935), which provides much useful data, but the text of the myth itself often presents many details which are either lacking in other accounts of the afterlife in the same tribe, or are in outright contradiction to it. Thus, the reference in the Maidu Orpheus myth to crossing over a torrent on a rope to reach the land of the dead (Powers 1877:339-340) is utterly unlike the Maidu beliefs which Dixon discusses. Another serious problem with relying on the Orpheus myth for data is that it is missing from most of north-central and southern California, as well as the Colorado River area.

Some Concepts

An overview of soul concepts is a necessary background for any discussion of the afterlife. Hultkranz' premise is that concepts of dual or multiple souls tend to evolve toward the concept of a unitary soul. A typical dualistic concept of the soul appears among the Tübatulabal (Voegelin 1938:62). Here life is embodied in one soul--the life-soul--symbolized by the breath, which stays in the body as long as life remains. Another soul--the free-soul or dream-soul--leaves the body during dreams, faints, and other unusual psychic states; it resides in the head, although its name is synonymous with 'heart'.

According to the evidence presented by Hultkranz (1953:95-101, 136-139), California is divided on this point roughly along the lines of the major culture areas. The concept of multiple souls appears in the Colorado River area (Mohave, Yuma, Kamia). Soul dualism characterizes much of northeastern California (Modoc, Shasta?, Achomawi, Atsugewi, Wintu, Northwestern Maidu) and the adjacent Karok in the northwest, as well as the Eastern Pomo; it is typical of most Shoshonean peoples in southern California (Juaneño, Luiseño, Tübatulabal, Owens Valley Paiute). The concept of a unitary soul characterizes the south-central area (Yokuts, Western Mono, Chumash), a western bloc of the north-central area

(Coast Central Pomo, Yuki, Nomlaki, Bear River, Sinkyone, Kato) and some southern tribes (Cahuilla, Chemehuevi).

## CONCEPTS OF THE AFTERLIFE

Here is a bare outline incorporating key themes of the afterlife and land of the dead. These themes are not necessarily present in all tribes; certain themes are usually accentuated at the expense of others.

(1) The soul leaves the body a set number of days after death, though sometimes before death.

(2) The soul lingers for a while around its familiar haunts, or revisits all the places it had been in this life.

(3) How this life was lived affects the afterlife, either in terms of who goes to the land of the dead, what occurs along the way there, or the ultimate destination.

(4) The soul sets out for the land of the dead after the funeral.

(5) On the way to the afterworld, the soul encounters water in some form: it crosses a body of water or bathes.

(6) The path to the land of the dead may fork; the left branch is the more auspicious.

(7) There is a gatekeeper or guardian of the afterworld, often stationed at the fork in the trail.

(8) There is a point of no return, beyond which living souls in fits of unconsciousness or visions cannot go; it is often the guardian who bars their way.

(9) The soul faces trials or tests along the way, often administered by the guardian of the afterworld.

(10) The soul undergoes a rite of passage symbolizing its new status as an inhabitant of the land of the dead.

(11) The soul can return to the land of the living, to appear to the living in dreams; the ghosts seen in this world are often the souls of those who never left for the land of the dead.

(12) Conditions in the land of the dead show symbolic reversal of conditions in this world; the land of the dead is more pleasant than this world.

(13) Beliefs in the ultimate fate of the soul are not uniform, but the soul may undergo transformation into animal or plant form; a belief in reincarnation is rare.

### How This Life Affects the Afterlife

All over California one finds beliefs that how this life was lived--and how it ends--affects the afterlife. Not every soul goes to the land of the dead, and of those which do, not all go to the same place there. But concern with one's fate after death does not seem to have been as pressing a motivation for ethical behavior as it is in the world's major religions; for the California Indians, ethical behavior was reinforced more in this life by social and supernatural sanctions. There is, however, one clear example of a desirable afterlife being mentioned as among the benefits of ethical living: the Luiseño told boys and girls being initiated into adulthood that if they heeded the wise counsel of the initiation homily, they would rise to the stars after death (Sparkman 1908).

There is much variation in beliefs of how this life affects the afterlife, revolving around notions of soul dualism, ethical conduct, social status, manner of death, and still other points. Among some tribes which believe in dual souls, one of the souls regularly remains in this world as a ghost, while the other--the soul which is the vehicle of individual consciousness--goes on to become an inhabitant of the land of the dead (Eastern Pomo, Wintu, Tübatulabal, Owens Valley Paiute, perhaps Juaneño and Luiseño).

By far the most common belief is that the souls of bad people remain on earth as ghosts or fail to reach the afterworld, or--less often--have a harder time getting there and find it less pleasant. This belies a notion sometimes expressed that California soul beliefs have little reference to ethics or morality. Bad people, among the Pomo, are "those who lied, stole, and killed" (Loeb 1926:296); among the Cahuilla, the good people who entered the afterworld are those who "have lived good lives, been generous at all times, thoughtful and respectful to the old people, and have obeyed all of Mukat's [the culture hero] orders" (Hooper 1920:342).

The belief that the souls of the bad or wicked may remain on earth as ghosts is particularly common in the northwest (Yurok, Wiyot, Hupa, Tolowa) and north-central California (Yuki, Pomo, Achomawi, Atsugewi, Wintu). This explains partly why ghosts were so feared, since generally only the souls of evil people remained around the living. The souls of evil people may be transformed into animals (often insects and reptiles), plants, or even rocks (Bear River, Atsugewi, Foothill Maidu, Cahuilla). Among the Chumash, the souls of murderers, poisoners, and other evil doers turn to stone from the neck down outside the entrance to the land of the dead (Blackburn 1975:text 12). In a few cases, even if the souls of evil doers enter the afterworld, they have a more difficult time getting there (Nomlaki, Foothill Maidu). So, moral judgement is a near universal criterion of post-mortem existence in California; it is simply not as obvious as Western notions of heaven and hell.

The fate of the soul may depend on its social status in this life, where the status marked for special treatment might be either socio-political--the chief or rich man, or religious--the shaman. This notion is best developed in the northwest, where social distinctions are most finely drawn. The Hupa emphasize religious status: the souls of shamans go to the sky and live forever, and participants in the great dances go to a place of perpetual dancing, but the souls of commoners go to a dismal underworld, where they are not immortal (Goddard 1903:74). The Yurok emphasize social status: the souls of the rich go to the sky (Kroeber 1925:47). Shamans occasionally have a special destination in the north central area (Bear River, Foothill Nisenan).

Social differentiation also appears in southern California. The souls of Gabrielino chiefs become stars, while others go to a western island (Harrington 1942:41, 46). Social differentiation is clearest and most dramatic among the Juaneño (Kroeber 1925:642): the soul of an initiate, a bite of whose flesh is ritually eaten at his cremation (reflecting the southern California dying god motif), goes to the sky and becomes a star, while the souls of all others go to an underground region of feasting and dancing. The Luiseño version of this Juaneño dual destination reflects a belief in a dual soul: the soul goes north to the Milky Way, the ghost goes underground.

When the Soul Leaves the Body

The soul might leave the body before the death of the body actually takes place, according to some tribes in southern California and along the Colorado River (Cahuilla, Luiseño, Diegueño, Yuma, Chemehuevi). This belief also occurs in the northeastern area (e.g., Shasta, Achomawi, Atsugewi). In the case of the Cahuilla, Achomawi, and Atsugewi the soul might leave the body months before death, seemingly in conjunction with a belief in soul loss as a common cause of illness and death.

Elsewhere, the soul often leaves the body some set number of days after death. This period usually corresponds to the ritual number which recurs in myths, formulas, and public and private rituals. It is three in the south-central area (Salinan, Chumash, Yokuts, Western Mono), four in much of the north-central area (Kato, Sinkyone, Pomo, Wappo, Nisenan, Northern Sierra Miwok), and five in the northwest (Karok, Yurok, Hupa, Tolowa, Mattole).

Occasionally there is a special place in the afterworld, or a special way to get there, for those who die unusual deaths, particularly those who are slain or drowned. A Yuki girl dying during her first menstruation follows the rainbow to the land of the dead in the sky (Foster 1944:207). Those slain in battle may go to a special place in the afterworld (Yurok, Bear River, Yuma), but the relative weakness of this concept may reflect the relatively minor importance of warfare in California. The souls of improperly buried persons may remain on earth (Karok, Achomawi, Wintu, Yuki--if blood is spilled on the ground). A unique Mohave notion is that the souls of those killed by witchcraft do not go directly to the land of the dead, but are hidden away by the shaman until his own death, when all proceed together to the afterworld (Devereaux 1937:419).

Various other factors may determine the soul's fate. In the south-central area, the souls of those lacking supernatural guardians may fail to enter the afterworld (Chumash, Yokuts, Western Mono): any soul that falls from the treacherous bridge to the land of the dead becomes some sort of water creature (e.g., fish, snake, turtle). Among the Yuma and Mohave, the souls of twins go to a special afterworld in the sky, where they are immortal (Drucker 1937:48; Devereaux 1937:417). Physical characteristics may be important: among Yuman peoples (Mohave, Diegueño) the soul of a person who was not tattooed does not reach the land of the dead, and among the Yana (Spier and Sapir 1943:284) the fate of the soul is determined by whether its nasal septum was pierced or not.

Before Setting Out for the Afterworld
-------------------------------------

The soul may have the option of setting off at once for the land of the dead (Wappo, Northeastern Maidu), but much more often it lingers for a while in this world. The soul often spends this time revisiting all of the places it had ever been during life. In particular, among the Valley Maidu and the Yana (Dixon 1905:260; Sapir and Spier 1943:284) the soul must revisit every spot where it had spat while alive, and the Valley Maidu show the soul re-enacting every deed it had ever performed in the flesh. The period thus spent is often specified. It may be immediately after burial or cremation (Chumash, Desert Diegueño Yuma, Chemehuevi), or after some set number of days, again the ritual number (e.g., four in the case of the Huchnom, Eastern Pomo, Coast Central Pomo). The Yuki allow the soul up to a month for its wanderings, but only around a week for the souls of children, since their lives have been shorter (Foster 1944:206). Where the time allowed the soul to wander is either indefinite or does not correspond to the ritual number, it is almost always between three and five days.

This common Californian belief in reviewing the scenes of the past life finds a parallel in the Western folk belief that just before death or at a time of great danger, one's life passes in review before one's eyes. With greater cosmological sweep, the Tibetan Book of the Dead says that after each incarnation, the soul reviews its past life in order to work on its shortcomings and bolster its strengths in the next life. So widespread a belief undoubtedly reflects an actual psychic experience of the dying person.

The Location of the Land of the Dead
------------------------------------

A survey of native California cosmologies sets the stage for discussing the location of the land of the dead. A tripartite division of the universe into upper, middle, and lower worlds is a basic cosmological assumption throughout California, as summarized by Bean (1975: 25-26). The middle world is the world of men, usually circular and surrounded by sea or void; each tribe considers its own homeland to lie at the geographical center of this middle world. The upper world is the world of powerful supernatural beings--including creator figures, culture heroes, the first people of mythic times, and other largely anthropomorphic beings--who are often benevolent toward man. The inhabitants of the lower world are more often malevolent; in form they are frequently water creatures or distorted humanoids.

The land of the dead might be located in the upper world; in the lower world; or, often, at the uttermost end of this middle world. It might lie in any direction, but west is the commonest orientation. In the case of a land of the dead located in the upper or lower worlds, the cardinal direction specified seems to refer to the direction taken by the departing soul to reach it.

Customs among the living often refer to the direction of the afterworld. The dead were almost always buried or cremated with their heads in the direction of the land of the dead, to facilitate the soul's journey. Among the Modoc and Cahuilla (and doubtless many other tribes between these geographical extremes), it is considered bad luck to lie sleeping with one's head in the direction of the land of the dead, although the Modoc did lie thus when seeking a vision (Ray 1963:80). The Yana count it a bad omen to dream of travelling that direction. Among the Chumash, 'to go west' is a euphemism for death.

For a large block of south-central tribes (Chumash, Salinan, Costanoan, Yokuts, Western Mono), the land of the dead is on an island or at least across an expanse of water at some distant point on this middle world. For the coastal peoples this meant across the sea to the west, but further inland it might be located to the north or northwest (still further inland, the Lone Pine Shoshone, neighbors of the Owens Valley Paiute, say that the dead go *east* to the ocean [Steward 1933: 307]). This south-central concept of an afterworld across water extends into adjacent tribes in the north-central area (most Pomo groups, Wappo, Patwin, Nisenan), as well as some adjacent southern California groups (Fernandeño, Kitanemuk).

Elsewhere in southern California, the afterworld is to the south or east, apparently usually in this middle world, although the Juaneño and Luiseño and perhaps Gabrielino seem to place the land of the dead both in the upper world among the stars and underground in the lower world. The Yuman peoples generally place the afterworld to the south on this plane (Mohave, Kamia), although it is east for the Diegueño, and the Yuma have a unique concept. The soul traverses four planes successively higher and further south; prematurely dead persons spend more time on each plane, so that their loved ones can overtake them, and those who lived together on earth join one another in the afterworld (Forde 1931: 179-180).

In the northwest, the land of the dead is generally in the lower world across a river (Yurok, Hupa, Tolowa), although some souls go to the upper world; among the Bear River Athabaskans, all souls go toward the rising sun to the upper world (Nomland 1938:93). In much of north-central California, the land of the dead is in the upper world. This location of the afterworld correlates roughly with a belief in a high creator god, usually anthropomorphic, as among the Yuki (cf. Loeb 1926). The route to the upper world is indirect among some of the tribes further east. Among the Wintu, the soul first goes north on this plane, then ascends and travels south along the Milky Way, but more often the route is west and then back east along the Milky Way (Shasta, Atsugewi, Valley Maidu).

The land of the dead may not be differentiated from that of the living spatially (Kato, some Pomo groups, one Washo version). Among the Kato, the soul goes to live with the creator Nagaicho in the mountains in Kato territory (Loeb 1932:14).

How the Soul Travels to the Afterworld

The soul seldom simply 'goes' to the land of the dead; various aspects of its progress are highlighted. Occasionally the soul is escourted to the afterworld by the souls of those who have died before (Bear River, Northwestern Maidu, Kamia) or by spirits (Sinkyone). In the northwest, a ferryman takes souls across an underground river--a Californian Charon (Yurok, Hupa, Tolowa). In the south-central area, the soul crosses water over a bridge (Chumash, Yokuts, Western Mono). A localized north-central concept of the soul's crossing water among the Eastern Pomo is that it rises above the water (Loeb 1926:290), while among the Wappo it wades or else the water dries up as it crosses (Driver 1936:217). Among the Luiseño, the soul was evidently assisted in rising to the sky by participants blowing ritually three times at the funeral (Sparkman 1908).

The soul may have a specialized vehicle. It is a common idea all over California that ghosts travel about this world during the day in whirlwinds; sporadically, the whirlwind is also the vehicle of the soul to the afterworld (Mohave, Wintu). The Huchnom mention the whirlwind, the smoke of the cremation fire, and the rainbow as alternate means to reach the afterworld (Foster 1944:232).

The Foothill Maidu speak of a trail to the afterworld; according to another account the soul rises and follows the sun to the zenith, and from there ascends straight up into the sky. A person dying in the afternoon follows the sun to the west and then through the underworld and on the following day at noon ascends into the sky world (Dixon 1905:261).

The Guardian of the Afterworld

A guardian figure very often stands at the entrance to the land of the dead, or else along the path to it, often at the point where the path forks. This guardian has several overlapping functions. In the northwest, the guardian ferries the souls of the dead across an underground river to the afterworld. In the Yurok version of the Orpheus myth (Kroeber 1925:47), a man overtook the soul of his beloved at the bank of the river and smashed the ferryman's canoe; for ten years no one died on earth while the canoe was being rebuilt.

The guardian often sends back the souls of the living--people who have only fainted or who are journeying in a dream. This is a particularly common northwest and north-central concept (Yurok, Hupa, Tolowa, Pomo, Atsugewi, Maidu, Nisenan). A Yurok flourish is that the ferryman has a dog which sometimes bites his paddle and breaks it; he cannot ferry the soul across and the person revives in this world (Driver 1939:413). The guardian may also discriminate between the souls of the good and the bad (Tolowa, Atsugewi, Yana) or test the souls: the Cahuilla guardian Montakwet challenges souls to make various cat's cradle figures, among other tests (Hooper 1920:342).

In south-central California, the guardian is elevated to the status of chief of the land of the dead, presiding over the games and activities of the inhabitants (Chumash, Yokuts); among the Western Mono, the chief directs the soul to the place in the afterworld where it will find the souls of its own tribe and family (Gayton 1948:237). This figure may be connected with supernatural power (particularly among the Yokuts, where there is a suggestive similarity in the word for supernatural power, *tipni*, and the chief's name, *tipiknits*), and it might function as a possible guardian spirit (Yokuts, Wintu).

## Trials along the Way

The concept of the soul undergoing trials on its way to the afterworld is restricted to south-central and southern California, but it is often quite elaborate. Commonest, of course, is the theme of crossing over a bridge that is very narrow, or slippery or rickety, or which rises and falls (Chumash, Yokuts, Southern Sierra Miwok, Nisenan). Not only is the bridge itself a problem to cross, but usually some bird or monster also rises up to startle or frighten the soul. Weak souls, meaning those without supernatural power derived from a guardian spirit, fall into the water and become snakes, turtles, or fish. Among the Nisenan, a soul may be afraid to attempt the crossing, and so it turns into a coyote, as it also dies if it falls off the bridge while crossing (Beals 1933:380).

Among some Yokuts groups, the soul must also brave falling or precipitous rocks (Gayton and Newman 1940:102), and the Chumash and Cahuilla elaborate the theme of the soul's passing between two clashing rocks or hills. Among the Cahuilla, the souls of the wicked are caught between these hills and become bats, butterflies, rocks, or trees. A person may visit the afterworld while unconscious and then revive, but if he reveals what he saw before three years, he dies and his soul is caught between the clashing hills. The Cahuilla also elaborate the theme of tests administered by the guardian of the afterworld (Hooper 1920:342).

## The Rite of Passage

Often the souls of the dead undergo a rite of passage on their way to the afterworld. The guardian figure may administer this rite, which formalizes the soul's new status. Either the rite of passage is denied to the souls of the living who are passing by in a faint, or after the rite the soul is a ghost forever or else cannot return to the world of the living. The concept of the rite of passage partially overlaps with the notion of the point of no return.

The rite of passage most often involves water; it is interwoven with the motif of crossing water on the way to the afterworld. The simple fact of crossing the bridge over water is a rite of passage in south-central California, as is being ferried across the underground river in the northwest. In the northeast, the soul bathes (Atsugewi, Nisenan), or the guardian of the afterworld bathes the soul or washes its face (Valley Maidu, Northeastern Maidu), or the soul drinks from a special spring along the path to the land of the dead (Wintu, Atsugewi). Bathing for power and ritual face washing appear elsewhere in central California religious and ritual practice; water itself is a supernaturally charged medium. The parallel to baptism in Christianity is obvious; in all of these cases, water symbolizes the transition from one state of being to another.

A more unusual south-central motif is that the eyes of the soul are replaced. This is found in its most elaborate form among the Chumash (Blackburn 1976:text 12). Partway along the path to the afterworld, two ravens peck out the soul's eyes, which it replaces with poppies; when the soul reaches its final destination, it gets permanent new eyes of blue abalone. A simpler version of this theme appears further east among the transitional Yokuts-Western Mono and the Tübatulabal.

The Point of No Return

The souls of the living could go to the land of the dead in dreams, faints, and trances; but there is usually some point at which a living soul is turned back or committed to remaining in the afterworld and dying in this world. In the northwest and north-central areas, the guardian of the afterworld often turns back living souls (Yurok, Tolowa, Pomo, Atsugewi, Maidu, Nisenan). Among the Yurok, a soul must stay in the land of the dead once it crosses the underground river, while among the Hupa a living soul goes only as far as the fork in the path on the way to the river (Driver 1939:413; Goddard 1903:74).

The Atsugewi elaborate details of the point of no return. A soul seldom returns if it gets as far as the Sacramento River, from an island in which it rises to the Milky Way, but definitely if it goes past the fork in the trail along the Milky Way and drinks from a spring on the left branch of the trail, it will never return alive to this world (Garth 1953:193). A more unusual concept appears among the Owens Valley Paiute. On its flight south to the land of the dead, if the soul sees and takes hold of the "soul stick"--a slippery pole about five feet high--and looks back toward the land of the living, it will return (Steward 1933:307). This detail appears in an autobiography: after a long illness a man dreamed that he was dying, but he grasped the "soul stick" in his dream and awoke to recover (Steward 1934:427).

A living soul may actually enter the land of the dead, according to some tribes, but it must observe certain precautions there. Among the Wailaki, the souls of the living can visit the afterworld, but if they eat anything there, they must remain, very much like Persephone in Hades (Loeb 1932:95). Among the Mohave, a person could visit the afterworld under the guidance of a shaman specializing in the cure of witchcraft, but he must not let go of the shaman's hand or the dead will keep him with them (Devereaux 1937:420).

Conditions in the Land of the Dead

Conditions in the land of the dead are nearly always better than in the land of the living. One remarkable exception is the Hupa afterworld: the souls of common people descend to a cold, dark, foggy place;

they eat dead salmon and other unpleasant things, and they are given to brawling and fighting (Goddard 1903:74).

Where details of the land of the dead are given, a number of common themes emerge, showing a symbolic reversal of conditions in this world. This life is fraught with work, hardship, hunger, disease, and death; so the afterlife is nearly always specified as free from death and disease, with an abundance of food which is easy to obtain, and with much more time given over to feasting, gaming, singing, and dancing. Some desert-dwelling groups also specify that the afterworld is a green place (Yuma, Lone Pine Shoshone). The dead opt for ritual housing and activities: instead of following the humdrum daily round, they feast, dance, and play at games; and in north-central California they live in sweat houses and underground dance houses rather than in ordinary dwellings.

In more specific instances of symbolic reversal, the dead are active only at night; during the day they sleep, become skeletons or piles of ashes, or disappear. A south-central motif is that the smell of the living is offensive to the dead (Chumash, Yokuts, Western Mono, Southern Sierra Miwok), coinciding with the area of California where the Orpheus myth appears in its fullest form. The chief of the land of the dead sometimes has an inexhaustible basket of food (some Yokuts groups, Western Mono, Foothill Maidu).

The land of the dead may be crowded with the dead of all tribes; among the Tachi Yokuts it is overpopulated so rapidly that every two days it must be cleared out. The chief orders the people to swim: most become water creatures, while a few emerge from the water still in human form (Kroeber 1907:218).

## The Soul in the Land of the Dead

The soul in the land of the dead often retains the identity it had in this life. The most important aspect of identity in the afterlife is family ties. This theme is underlined by the belief that the spirits of dead relatives guide the soul to the afterworld (Northeastern Maidu, Kamia) or that the chief of the afterworld tells a newly arrived soul where to find its family and friends (Western Mono). When a Mohave shaman visits the land of the dead, he must not tarry lest his dead relatives induce him to stay (Devereaux 1937:418). Social identity is not so often preserved, except among tribes like the Mohave, who specify that "one remains in the other world what one has been in this world" (Devereaux 1937:418), and among tribes where there are distinct destinations for chiefs, shamans, and other notables (Yurok, Hupa, Bear River, Nisenan, Gabrielino, Juaneño). The material trappings of this life seldom contribute to the soul's identity. Although disposal of the personal belongings of the dead is a nearly universal custom, the notion crops up only rarely that the dead take these things with them--in essence or spirit form, of course (Valley Maidu, Sierra Miwok, Yuma, Kamia).

Almost always, the soul is free to visit the land of the living at times, even after it has reached its final destination. There are sometimes restrictions: among the Bear River Athabaskans, only the spirits of shamans and malevolent common people return, but not well-intentioned common people (Nomland 1938:93). Occasionally the soul must remain in the land of the dead once it has arrived there (Yurok, Tolowa, Valley Maidu, Cahuilla implicitly). There are sometimes explicit statements that the dead may return to this world to lure the living back with them, particularly among the Yuman peoples (Mohave, Yuma, Kamia). This notion is also implicit in the wide-spread belief that dreams of the dead are a bad omen, meaning a visit from a ghost. Dreams of the dead often cause illness and even death; sometimes shamans specialize in curing dreams of the dead. The dead might also return if some of their personal possessions had not been properly disposed of (Pomo, Wappo). There is no intimation that mentioning the name of a dead person evokes the ghost; mentioning the dead by name is anathema all over California, but Kroeber (1925:360) believed this to be a social rather than magical tabu.

In the land of the dead, the soul is generally in more direct contact with supernatural power than in this life (cf. Bean 1975). This is obviously the case where the dead go to dwell with the creator or culture hero (Yuki, Kato, some Pomo groups, Foothill and Northeastern Maidu, Serrano) or the mythical first people (as Hupa shamans do). Even where the dead are not in direct contact with these powerful figures, they are close to the source of power if they leave this middle world and go to dwell in the upper world of the three superimposed worlds so common to native California cosmologies. If the dead go to the underworld or to the distant edge of this world, this still means access to greater power, since as Bean (1975:27) points out, potential danger and power increase as one moves further from the known and safe homeland. Whatever the final destination of the dead, they merge into the general category of spirits: powerful and potentially dangerous supernatural entities.

The power of the dead is implicit in the often disastrous consequences of their contact with the living: this is unfocused power which is dangerous to those who come in contact with it. Misfortune, illness, and even death may follow dreams of the dead or waking visions of them; to be touched or even looked at directly by the dead is sometimes considered particularly harmful. Power can be beneficial as well as harmful, however, and the dead may confer some of their power on the living, or at least act as a channel of power from the supernatural world to the living. Thus, in the northwest and in the eastern part of the north-central area, the ghost of a dead relative may act as a guardian spirit, often conferring shamanistic power. This largely coincides with the area in which the dead (or at least dead shamans) dwell in the upper world. The notion of the dead as guardian spirits occurs sporadically down into south-central California (Yokuts, Tübatulabal).

The Ultimate Fate of the Soul

Speculation on the ultimate fate of the soul is sporadic. Belief in reincarnation in a human body is rare; in the northwest (Hupa, Kato), the only mention of reincarnation is that after a miscarriage or stillbirth, the spirit of that fetus is born in the next baby the woman bears (Driver 1939:413). There is evidence of a belief in reincarnation in the south-central area; it is clearest among the Ventureño Chumash, who believed in reincarnation after twelve years and who regarded their children as reincarnated ancestors (Blackburn 1975:texts 10 and 11). A Yokuts and Southern Sierra Miwok belief that the souls of the newborn come from the land of the dead may imply reincarnation; a Yokuts myth (Hudson 1902:105) portrays the souls of babies about to be born wandering in silence in a long column along the road from the land of the dead to that of the living.

Belief in the transformation of the soul into animal, plant, or even rock form is quite common. The animals mentioned are usually insects, serpents, and water creatures like fish, turtles, and ducks. Such a transformation is often the fate of the souls of evil persons and of those who fail to enter the land of the dead. Among the Tachi Yokuts, even a soul which has arrived safely in the land of the dead may be transformed into a water creature when the afterworld becomes too crowded. Sometimes shamans by choice turn into animals after their death, particularly bear shamans. With the obvious exception of the cunning and dangerous bear, there is apparently nothing special about the individual animal or plant into which a soul has turned.

The immortality of the soul is denied, at least in part, by some groups. When a soul has been transformed into an animal or plant, for whatever reason, its immortality is in serious question. Immortality may be selective. Among the Hupa, the souls of shamans and ceremonialists are immortal, but not the souls of common people in their dismal underworld. The Yuman peoples (Mohave, Yuma, Kamia) believe in a multiplicity of souls, but all but one of these perishes or vanishes with the death of the body. Even that one soul which survives may undergo a series of transformations. One Yuma account has it that ultimately the soul ends up as a bit of cinder, although the more general belief is that the soul lives indefinitely (Forde 1931:180). Among the Kamia and Mohave, the soul in the land of the dead lives, dies, and is cremated by its fellow ghosts through four successive cycles. It metamorphizes with each cycle, going through a series of owl or insect forms and ending up as a black beetle (Kamia) or as nothing (Mohave). The exception among the Mohave is the souls of twins, which are not only immortal, but are also exempt from this series of transformations. Considering how prominent the theme of the dying and resurrected god is in southern California, one might expect a corresponding emphasis on reincarnation or immortality of the individual soul, but this certainly does not seem to be the case.

Mythic Themes and the Afterlife

Concepts of the afterlife are tied in with other mythic themes, but these ties are often rather loose. The land of the dead may be mentioned in connection with the creator or creation. The soul may go to dwell with the creator, culture hero, or mythic first people (Hupa, Yuki, Kato, Pomo, Foothill and Northeastern Maidu, Serrano). In southern California, since Chingichnich came from the stars and returned to them, it is possible that souls which rise to the stars join Chingichnich. The Orpheus myth among the Modoc (Ray 1963:26-27) and one Chumash version (Blackburn 1975:text 25) show the culture hero himself visiting the land of the dead. The Cahuilla specifically mention how the creator Mukat made the land of the dead, and among the Diegueño the dead go east to a place in the desert where mankind was first created (Waterman 1910:278). In an interesting shift, while the Tübatulabal, Chemehuevi and Owens Valley Paiute name Wolf as culture hero, the Western Mono under clear Yokuts influence have remodeled Wolf as chief of the land of the dead (Gayton 1948:237).

Some of the motifs connected with the afterlife in particular tribes have a broader distribution in California, among tribes where these motifs make no reference specifically to the afterlife. One is the theme of the inexhaustible basket of food, possessed by the chief of the land of the dead (some Yokuts groups, Western Mono, Foothill Maidu); without reference to the afterlife, this theme also appears among the Chumash, Washo, Tübatulabal, Kawaiisu, and Luiseño. The theme of a living soul not being permitted to disclose what it saw in the land of the dead (Cahuilla), usually in the context of the Orpheus myth (Yokuts, Western Mono), may extend to not disclosing supernatural adventures in general (Kawaiisu, Luiseño).

The theme of bathing or crossing water as a rite of passage to the land of the dead also has a much broader distribution: water is a powerful supernatural medium which can transform persons and objects from one ritual status to another (Blackburn 1975). Thus, participants in rituals often bathe before or after the ritual, such as purification after contact with a corpse, or ending mourning restrictions. Bathing is part of the vision quest, preparing one for contact with the supernatural. Water can effect actual transformations: a bear shaman may bathe upon turning into a werebeast and upon resuming his human form, and in myth the dead may be revived by immersion. Ritual paraphernalia may be imbued with power or divested of it by contact with water.

SUMMARY

Summarizing eighteen versions of the Orpheus myth from the San Joaquin Valley, Gayton (1935:269) concludes that the local distribution of motifs is apparently random and has no geographical or linguistic significance; it is rather their overall uniformity which counts. Much the same is true of California in general: the local distribution of many motifs of the afterlife is apparently random. But some do show significant correlations; these have been noted already, but they deserve summary here.

The concept of the land of the dead in the upper world is largely centered in the north-central area in conjunction with a belief in a high god or anthropomorphic creator. The north-central area is often uniform in ritual (e.g., the Kuksu complex), but in concepts of the afterlife, the more southerly tribes (all Pomo but Northern and Northeastern, Wappo,

Hill Patwin, Nisenan) align with the south-central area.

The concept of moral distinctions in the afterlife is widespread; in the northwest and north-central areas the souls of the wicked are likely to remain on earth as ghosts; the south-central and southern areas achieve the same effect by imposing tests and trials on the soul seeking to enter the land of the dead.

Social distinctions affect the destination of the soul most often in the northwest, a highly status-conscious region.

Speculation on the ultimate fate of the soul is concentrated in south-central and southern California, where mourning ceremonialism looms larger than elsewhere in the state.

# Wealth, Work and World View in Native Northwest California: Sacred Significance and Psychoanalytic Symbolism
## by
## John and Donna Bushnell

INTRODUCTION

In the ethnographic panorama of aborginal North America, the Indian tribes of northwestern California--the Hupa, Yurok, and Karok, along with a number of lesser-known peoples such as the Tolowa, Whilkut, Chilula, and Wiyot--are usually seen as standing out in somewhat sharp relief when compared with California tribes in general. This relatively high visibility is, in part, a function of frequency of appearance in the anthropological literature, growing out of the studies of a series of scholars such as Goddard, Kroeber, Wallace, Erikson, Goldschmidt, Bushnell, and Gould (among others).

A constellation of cultural features apparently unique to this area prompted Goldschmidt (1951) to formulate an essay that has received considerable attention since its appearance 25 years ago. In this paper he suggested that both the structure of Northwest California society and the ethical precepts that furnished the rationale and motivation undergirding the system bore a remarkable resemblance to the structure and Protestant ethic of early European capitalism. The parallels were limited, of course. Industrial production, exploitation of labor, and the profit motive were integral features of the Western world but totally foreign to the native peoples of North America. Nevertheless, the elements that appeared to him to be isomorphic constituted a compelling roster. A listing of the key items would include, on the socioeconomic side, the private ownership of resources, wealth as an indicator of status and a determinant of power, an open class system (at least in theory), and money as a medium of exchange; on the ethico-religious side it would include work as a moral act, individualized responsibility,

---

[1] Field research on the Hoopa Reservation has been supported by grants from the Department of Anthropology, University of California at Berkeley (1948), the National Academy of Sciences-National Research Council (1956), and the Wenner-Gren Foundation for Anthropological Research (1965). The authors acknowledge with gratitude the assistance that has made these studies possible.

asceticism with respect to food and sex, and the concepts of guilt and sin.[2]

Goldschmidt believed that his analysis served two purposes: first, it provided a better understanding of Hupa-Yurok culture which, although it has surfaced frequently in theoretical contexts, has also in the author's words "remained enigmatic and inadequately comprehended"; and second, it offered a refinement of the concept of functionalism insofar as the cases being compared demonstrated the interrelatedness of cultural forms: i.e., "a specific interdependence of a particular ethic to a particular social structure which is societal and hence transcends the individual culture" (1951:523).

With respect to these two goals, it will be the former—a deeper insight into the core aspects of Northwest California culture— that will be the subject of this paper, while the latter will be viewed as lying beyond the scope of our present endeavor. However, needless to say, the validity or relevancy of the analogy developed by Goldschmidt will be strengthened or weakened by the extent to which the Hupa-Yurok-Karok data fit his model.

At the outset we would like to express our concurrence with Drucker's (1965:50) admonition that "intercultural comparisons are useful for purposes of explanation, but they must be interpreted with care. Close examination of two cultures may reveal similarities, but if the similarities are superficial, masking different basic concepts and functions, the comparison may be misleading. The wealth complex in North Pacific Coast culture [defined by Drucker to include the Northwest Coast proper and Northwest California] and that of modern Western society appear broadly similar. In both cases wealth and prestige are closely correlated; in both cases wealth and its acquisition occupy a large share of men's thoughts. There, however, the similarities end." While Goldschmidt was comparing the Hupa and Yurok not with contemporary European capitalist society but with sixteenth century Protestantism/capitalism,[3] we nonetheless are wary of inferring analogous functions and

---

[2]Posinsky (1957:4, 19), writing from a psychoanalytic frame of reference, cites Goldschmidt but pushes the comparison to an extreme: ". . . the exaggerated and basically unreal emphasis on wealth and property colors Yurok culture with a crassness which is difficult to match except among certain segments of a modern commercial society." And ". . . the Yurok are a primitive caricature of full-blown Western capitalism and puritanism."

[3]At the presentation of this paper Walter Goldschmidt was kind enough to call to our attention essential differences between earlier and later aspects of the Protestant ethic which has become increasingly secularized with the passage of time. While this is certainly the case, we still feel that the distinctions between European institutions of whatever era with their associated ethical systems and those of native Northwest California are intrinsic and fundamental.

structures from what seem to us to be phenotypic resemblances rather than genotypic commonalities.

WEALTH

The traditional ethnological treatment of the wealth complex among the Hupa, Yurok, Karok, and other culturally-related Northwest California tribes lays stress on the pecuniary value and use of 'money', that is, dentalia, and of other articles of worth, those items which Kroeber has designated as "treasure"--the white deerskins, redheaded woodpecker scalps, large blades of obsidian or flint, mink, otter and fisher fur quivers, and the like. While some writers have noted the aesthetic quality of dentalia (which were frequently skillfully and beautifully incised, decorated with red feathers, fishskins or snakeskins, and occasionally colored with dyes from wild plants or even human blood), and while Kroeber especially has commented on the personal meaning and sentiment that strings of dentalia could acquire within the traditions of a family line,[4] they nonetheless have nearly always been considered primarily a medium of exchange, with a fixed value set for shells of designated lengths and qualities, and only secondarily (in the case of smaller sized shells) as decorative items such as necklaces, trim for clothing, and other ornamentation (Kroeber 1925:23-24; Goddard 1903:19-20,48).

While it is clear that the dentalium shell was, indeed, somewhat akin to currency, we are inclined to the view that there apparently was no true money in the Americas; Driver (1969:221), for example, classifies dentalia along with clam shell discs, wampum, cocoa beans, etc., as a medium of exchange only approximating money.[5] It is also clear that

---

[4]This point is illustrated by the selective manner in which a Yurok man from a good family accepted or rejected offers of dentalia strings and other wealth from various relatives while accumulating a brideprice. His criteria included the affection or esteem which he felt for a particular individual, the fear of incurring obligations or other unpleasant entanglements, and the purity of the property under consideration: i.e., whether it was deemed 'clean' or 'unclean' as, for example, with the proceeds of gambling (Spott and Kroeber 1942:144-147). Wealth looted in a raid represented property "not obtained 'in the right way' and would do its possessor no good" (Wallace 1949:8).
"Wholly typical [in a narrative under discussion] is the way particular objects of wealth, and to whom each belonged, and how it had been acquired, are remembered seventy-five years later. Each string of shell money, woodpecker band, or obsidian has its own history which makes it more or less desirable, apart from its intrinsic or market value" (Spott and Kroeber 1942:147). Contrast the negative attitude or note of opprobrium regarding "too new Indian money" [dentalia newly-arrived from Vancouver Island in the 1920s] (Pilling and Pilling 1970:101-102).

[5]Earlier thinking on this point is reflected in Kroeber's

such other items as woodpecker crests, which have also been likened to money since, as with dentalia, they were translatable into US currency values (Goddard 1903:50; Kroeber 1925:26), and flaked obsidians, or deerskins, etc., were, in fact, greatly treasured both for their intrinsic beauty and for their purchasing power vis-à-vis brides, land, services of shamans, or the payment of indemnities. Nevertheless, we feel that the view, quoted and requoted, which holds that wealth among Northwest California Indians was accumulated, hoarded, and displayed, even flaunted, primarily or exclusively in order to attain, validate, or exalt one's personal standing within a status-oriented, hierarchical social structure fails to take into account the all-important symbolic significance of wealth for these peoples. That which has been interpreted as the quest for riches, social position, and power is seen by us as but one part of a more basic and deeply meaningful search for the sacred, the sanctified, and the spiritual aspects of life.

Although men yearned and strove for dentalia, sometimes with greater and sometimes with lesser success, it is clear that this most prized of wealth objects ultimately belonged to the gods and partook of their magical, godlike qualities. For the Yurok Kroeber (1925:74) refers to Dentalium Land (also translated Dentalium Home [Kroeber 1976: 323,400] and Money's Home [Waterman 1920:Fig. 1]) across the ocean at the north end of the world where the ceremonial dances never cease. Great Dentalium (also Large Dentalium or Great Money) is a supernatural figure often endowed with human characteristics and sometimes portrayed as a creator or institutor (Kroeber 1976:95,200-204). His wife is Great Abalone (Ibid.:209) and he is one of three (sometimes five) Money Brothers who represent gradations of dentalium shells according to size, provenience, and status (Ibid.:117,251). Depending on whether they entered or passed by a given village or house, that place was rich or poor (Ibid.:200-204). Great Dentalium appears in myths not only as a sacred personage or as a generic personification of 'money' but also as "a magnified, free-swimming, fishlike dentalium" resembling a salmon or sturgeon (Ibid.:261,388).[6]

The beach at Dentalium Land, though usually described as barren and sandy, in one account at least is depicted as totally covered with dentalia. The hero in this tale, at the direction of his supernatural mentor, a giant condor, picks up what appear to be two dentalia

---

(1925:26) opinion that "dentalium currency is wholly and purely money," and in Goldschmidt and Driver's (1940:117) paper in which they reported "a true money" for the Hupa. For another discussion of indigenous wealth items as either a specialized form of currency (Du Bois) or all-purpose money (Drucker, Gould), see Gould's (1966:67-68) summary for the neighboring Tolowa.

[6]Nearly identical imagery is found in an origin tale in which Red Obsidian "running in the water like a salmon" permits himself to be caught so that a few villages might possess him and therefore be rich (Kroeber 1976:46-47).

joined together[7] and places them in a storage basket, whereupon they multiply to fill the container every five days (Ibid.:174). In a variant of this theme, the youth is given one small dentalium and one woodpecker scalp, each of which magically fills a basket at five-day intervals until he is incalculably wealthy (Ibid.:348).[8] Another, who has gone to Dentalium Land to gamble, although ultimately triumphing with the aid of extraordinary supernatural power, is up against great odds when the god who is his opponent places as a stake the contents of his carrying case which prove to be living dentalia that move about--and presumably constitute a potent and limitless supply (Ibid.:403). A Karok maiden who disappears from her home for two years returns, married to a giant and bringing, in addition to her baby, five baskets made of dentalia and filled with native treasure[9] (Ibid.:63-64).

Just as the Indians of Northwest California had fish weirs, so too the immortals had dentalium weirs. A young man, so fleet of foot that he could shoot an arrow and beat it to its mark, was accustomed to pilfering one shell from each basket in the dam and escaping from the pursuing dentalium owners across ten ridges, while Coyote, also a swift runner, attempted the same maneuver but could not resist overloading himself with dentalia and thereby jeopardized his escape (the outcome varies according to the version cited; Kroeber 1976:74-76,322-323).

In a Karok narrative in which Coyote is portrayed variously as a creator, a liar, a glutton, and a lecher, he schemes to arrive first at the Klamath Lakes (Upriver Ocean) to suck out dentalia[10] and to return home with bunches of the longest and most prized shells on his moccasins. However, his behavior leads to a state of extreme thirst and he ignominiously defeats himself by violating the sacred stricture against drinking water when engaged in such a quest (Harrington 1930:141; for a Yurok counterpart, see Kroeber 1976:267-268). In other stories, however, Coyote is depicted as wealthy and successful. "They thought he was a rich man from some place. He was nothing but money (there was money all over him). Even on his shoes money (i.e., large dentalia) . . ." (Harrington 1930: 156).

---

[7]This imagery suggests sexual union. Cf. an unelaborated reference to man-dentalium and woman-dentalium by one of Kroeber's informants (1976:385).

[8]The replenishing basket motif also occurs in connection with that item most valued and desired in the spirit world, tobacco. "Your people there [humans beings] think your tobacco does not reach us [the spirits], but we receive it all [offerings of tobacco 'blown out' from the hand]. We put one grain from you in our basket and in the morning it is filled. That is why we are always thankful" (Spott and Kroeber 1942:230).

[9]A belated brideprice?

[10]Probably both to eat the flesh of the univalves and to obtain the valuable shells.

When in a mythic Yurok tale an amorous divinity, Widower-across-the-Ocean, magically traps his son in a treetop for ten days with the intent of killing him, and blinds his grandson in order to seduce his daughter-in-law,[11] the son ingeniously escapes downstream and in retaliation takes with him all the dentalia in the world. He is intercepted, however, by his father, who recovers a sufficient number of the precious shells to replenish the supply for Indians (Kroeber 1925:73).

The gods worked out among themselves a rationale for the creation and accumulation of wealth. Great Dentalium said to the others, "Let it be that a man will buy a woman. He will pay much for a rich woman. A poor woman will be low priced; and it will be well" (Kroeber 1976:423). In explaining why one must pay before he can call a woman his wife, the gods said, "If he has children without buying her, they will be just like dogs; it will be like a bitch breeding pups"[12] (Ibid.: 444). Great Dentalium also decreed that settlements be paid for slayings. "When they kill a man, let them pay. Then they can be friends again and it will be well . . . [otherwise] there will be fighting all the time" (Ibid.:423). Again the gods reasoned: "For if they do not pay, many would think, 'I will commit murder again,' or 'I too will kill.' But since they have to pay, they are afraid. Therefore few kill" (Ibid.:444). "They will not want to be quarrelsome, for they have property. They will behave well . . . for they will think so much of what they have, of their dentalia and other things, that they will not want to pay them out in settlement" (Ibid.:364).[13] One who received wergild should "hide the money somewhere. Sometimes, when you want to see your dentalia, and go to look at them, you will feel sorry, because you will remember your poor kinsman who was killed" (Ibid.). When the pre-humans were preparing to leave, some to the mountains and some to the sky, only Dentalium chose to be left behind: ". . . 'it would be a

---

[11] In the version reported by Erikson (1943:272; see also Roheim 1950:278) the child, about to witness the quasi-incestuous primal scene between his mother and grandfather, is blinded by the old man's semen. Later the boy, though blind, is depicted as shooting birds which fall into his hands so that he does not have to search for them while, in like manner, dentalia money flies into his hands. In many versions the child's vision is restored by application of water from a pool or spring created by his father's tears (Kroeber 1976:287,318,355-356).

[12] The native rationale for the institution of marriage seems to have been misinterpreted by Posinsky (1956:607), who states that the Yurok rationalize "that women are little better than animals. (Was not the human race sired on a bitch? What can we expect from our women—are they not bought?)" The social significance of the brideprice, i.e., formation of kinship ties, elevation of status, "becomes overlaid with hostile sexual attitudes. Thus, women are inferior (damaged, castrated), yet sexually seductive and promiscuous, like bitches."

[13] In the event that blood money was not paid within ten days, it was believed that the vindictive grief and rage of the mourners would have a cumulative and overwhelming lethal power that would destroy the slayer (Kroeber 1976:140).

bad thing if I went off. People would not live well.' So Dentalium remained to be kept in the [elkhorn] purses of human beings" (Ibid.:438; for the Karok, see Kroeber 1925:28).

From Hupa texts collected by Goddard it can be seen that the realm of the immortals abounds with dentalia. A culture hero, Dug-from-the-Ground, goes to the abode of the gods at the edge of the world and demonstrates his supernatural prowess as he successfully shoots an arrow at a white bird which Indians can never hit, causing a shower of dentalia to fall about him. He is served a basket of "money's meat," that is, dentalium soup which only the divinities can eat, and later magically defeats his rivals at shinny, winning ten strings of dentalia and other great treasures (Goddard 1904:148-149). Another hero, the Scabby Young Man, who transcends his ignominious beginnings by gaining the power to fling himself great distances by arrow, is also able to eat soup made of dentalia meat prepared by two maidens who have come from the shore of the eastern world to be his wives (Ibid.:212). In a nearly identical Chilula text, Scabby Boy twists ten strands of twine, instantly converting them into strings of dentalia which he presents to his ten brothers (Goddard 1914:359).

In another story a Hupa woman who habitually wove baskets while sitting by the river gives birth first to a girl and then a boy who, unbeknownst to her, were fathered by a water sprite. The children, abandoned by their mother, survive by wishing each night for food which miraculously appears by their heads as they sleep. As the boy grows, his sister wishes for bows and arrows for him and for strings of dentalia. Their desires are always granted and thus they live until at a time of famine they are able to share their abundance with their mother, her husband, and ten half-siblings, after which, with their father's supernatural intervention, the girl and her brother go to live under the water (Goddard 1904:193).

By recounting the formula of medicine for making baskets, Hupa women can attain success and a long life. At dawn the story will come to them of the woman who wove by the shore each morning until one day her half-finished basket was blown from her hands out onto the water. It traveled around the world and returned next morning with its hazel ribs covered with sucking dentalia. She stored the dentalia shells in a tiny canoe which had come into existence at the same time she had, and each day her basket floated around the world to all the places where Dentalia Maker caused the dentalia to grow. It returned to her each dawn in the same manner and so she left her formula for Hupa women (Ibid.:326).

In one ritual for the purification of those who have handled the dead, a culture hero with wood basket and digging stick searches for medicine in a sacred location, the ridge where one finds Dentalium Maker and the fishers with dentalia clinging to their armpits. His formula calls for a sweathouse fire made from buck brush (*Ceanothus*), a plant upon which it is said that dentalia feed. The brush is made dry during the night by the sucking of the dentalia but it blooms anew in the morning and the dentalia return to feed each evening after the sun has gone down. When the wood has burned, the sucking of the dentalia can be heard in the sweepings of the ashes (Ibid.:367-368). In a second purification formula that reiterates the symbolism of renewal, sacred plants that daily are eaten down, one by deer and one by dentalia, regenerate each night. The god that loans this medicine says, "You will travel again in the Indian world. Your body will be renewed [cleansed of its contamination]. . . . You shall hunt and the deer will lie still for you. It shall be the same in regard to dentalia" (Ibid.:358).

Medicine for a "spoiled stomach" is made from the inner bark of the yellow pine that stands in the middle of the dentalia pond. Nightly, dentalia and abalones strip the branches so that by morning it stands bare, growing again each evening when the wind blows through it. Across the ocean to the south dentalia also feed upon the vine maple for which Dentalia Maker is always searching (Ibid.:349,368).

Hupa women may shorten the period of confinement following menstruation if they observe the ritual that prescribes bathing in dentalia's saliva. The traditional formula relates how a body of water came into existence to which bands of deer of different colors come from specified directions. The does stand in the water up to their ankles and by the next day the pond is deep with their drool. "Dentalia crawl in their armpits. The pond is filled with their spit. As far as the water reaches, the dentalia crawl." The woman always thinks to herself, "It is dentalia's spit I have bathed in" (Ibid.:312). Parenthetically, a Chilula formula for the purification of men who have buried the dead contains a similar theme involving variously colored deer swimming in the water of dentalia, while for bereaved women it is the water of abalone that is efficacious (Goddard 1914:376).

The supernatural attributes and spiritual power associated with dentalia are also evident from informants' accounts regarding vision quests as reported by Kroeber (1925:41; 1976:25,381) for the Yurok but applicable to the Hupa, Karok, and, no doubt, other adjoining tribes. A young man searching for sacred sweathouse wood abstains from water and from sexual contact, fasts, prays, sings, weeps, may lacerate and scarify himself, and thinks continuously about dentalia until such time as he might see them along the trail or hanging and feeding in the upper branches of the fir trees, or even feel them wiggling in his hands. Once in the sweathouse, he would concentrate on 'money', willing it to appear until, at last, it did--for example, with the shells looking in through the door at him. Or he might perceive in the river a dentalium as large as a salmon with gills like those of a fish.

A formula for ritual sweating further delineates this quest. A youth lay in the sweathouse thinking of going for firewood. And thus he would sleep. Every morning for ten days he went to the mountain thinking, "They [the fir needles] will stick on me, on my body; because I break [the branches] off, they will fall on me, all kinds of dentalia." Coming down the mountain he would cry and talk of the dentalia that he had gathered. Later in the sweathouse he thinks, "These [branches] are the ones I am putting into the fire, every kind of dentalia, and they will fasten to me. . . . This that is burning is dentalia. And it is smoking, and all the smoke is fastening on my body." The Douglas fir[14] itself would speak to him: "Whoever seeks me will have good luck. He will do well by thinking of me. That is how I leave it to be in the world" (Kroeber 1976:403-404).

In a similar sacred experience a Yurok woman in the course of her tortuous novitiate as a shaman thought and spoke constantly of dentalia as she remained alone in the sweathouse with angelica root (a sacramental plant considered highly potent among Northwest California tribes) placed in and around the fire. Kroeber (1925:65-66) has recorded one such example in which the neophyte would arise at daybreak and face the door saying, "A long dentalium is looking in at me." On her way to the mountain to gather sweathouse wood she would repeat to herself, "The dentalium has gone before me. I see its tracks." Of her loaded wood basket she said, "That large dentalium, the one I am carrying, is very heavy." As she swept clean the stone platform in front of the sweathouse she would tell herself, "I see dentalia. I see dentalia. I am sweeping them to both sides of me." Having repeatedly undergone such rituals as well as prolonged fasting, sweating, abstention from water, and suffering the pain of self-inflicted gashes, she did induce with the aid of prayers and piteous supplication the spirits to send dentalia to her. They came to her, she believed, just as in the middle of the sky they had come, together with redheaded woodpecker scalps, to feed on the leaves of the angelica plant (which is why its root is always withered).

In addition to dentalia, most if not all of the other greatly prized and highly valued objects (especially white deerskins, redheaded woodpecker crests, and obsidians) are intimately linked to the world of the immortals and characteristically emit supernatural power that redounds to the good fortune and health of those who possess them. In myth after myth and legend after legend, gods, heroes, and a panoply of other sacred or magical personages, creatures, and spirits are associated with native treasure which is always symbolic, usually endowed with beauty or splendor, and frequently super-abundant or larger than life.

Thus, while a Hupa, Yurok, or Karok house was traditionally made of cedar planks with a terrace of river cobbles in front, the dwelling of the gods in a Hupa tale was constructed of bluestone with a terrace of pure black obsidian (Goddard 1904:148). Again, the houses in the legendary village to which Rattlesnake Wife took her young husband were completely lined with obsidian and the platforms outside were of greasy-stone [bluestone] (Kroeber 1976:409). A Hupa culture hero traveled not in the indigenous redwood dugout but in a canoe of red obsidian, while a second mythological figure used a boat of black obsidian (Goddard 1904:

---

[14]Branches of the black or tanbark oak or of buck brush (*Ceanothus*), all considered to have highly efficacious properties, are mentioned in the Hupa texts as being utilized for sweathouse wood (Goddard 1904:213,367,368).

147,213). In those days when the pre-mortals inhabited the valley of the Trinity, the gods slept in a sweathouse with a door constructed of rare red obsidian rather than a slab of wood (Ibid.:205), and south of the river guarded by ten men hung a blanket made entirely of scalps of the pileated woodpecker (Ibid.:205,212). In a Karok tale a beautiful young medicine girl traveled nightly to the outer world where the ocean and sky meet. There she donned a scarlet cloak fashioned of hundreds of closely-sewn woodpecker crests for her role in the Life Renewal ceremony (T. Kroeber 1959:108). A scabby young man, the Yurok equivalent of the previously cited Hupa and Chilula culture heroes, outdoes his brothers and countless other youths by winning two sky-maidens and by escaping with two precious sky-blankets of pure red woodpecker feathers (Kroeber 1976:449-450).

Vast numbers of large redheaded woodpeckers lived across the sea in the Land-Beyond-the-World where Upriver-Ocean-Girl, a Yurok, went magically by canoe to meet Across-the-Ocean-Girl, the Shining One who makes the horizon glimmer at sundown. In that barren, treeless, sacred land the girls covered the boat with rush mats to prevent its being eaten by the voracious woodpeckers (Spott and Kroeber 1942:250-251). The spirit power and magical efficacy of a Yurok hero are symbolized by the flocks of large and small redheaded woodpeckers that perched continuously on the crossbars of two poles standing at the front corners of his house (Kroeber 1976:70). Similarly, an especially beautiful sacred sweathouse came into being framed with woodpecker scalps around the doorway and fronted by a dead tree that 'grew up' there covered over with brilliant red crests or, in Kroeber's opinion, more probably with living pileated woodpeckers (Ibid.:181).

At the upstream end of the world a lecherous deity desirous of a young woman brings sweathouse wood for ten days, each time with a large woodpecker magically appearing on top of the load as it is passed into the sweathouse, thereby providing a scalp for each of her ten brothers who marvel at what manner of man he might be (Ibid.:281-282). In a variation of the same theme, this Yurok god travels far into upper Karok or Shasta territory where his amatory exploits are unknown, and daily brings a load of sweathouse wood from which each time fall two scarlet scalps for the two brothers of the maiden whom he is intending to seduce (Ibid.: 336-337). Among his own people who were generally on to his tricks, he sometimes transformed himself, for example, into a baby or a small boy but, even so, he might be identified by the tufts of woodpecker pileum (or sometimes dentalia shells) that covered or adorned his hair. His son could be recognized in like manner and, additionally, each wore a woven rabbitskin blanket lavishly ornamented with woodpecker scalps (Ibid.:284,335,339).

Again and again the resplendence of the scarlet plumage is associated with supernatural persons, places, or phenomena as the following imagery reiterates: red-crested woodpeckers swarm over a boat that is beached beyond the end of the sky and the hero decapitates them, returning home with a full cargo of scalps, far more than the number needed to create enough headbands to initiate the Jumping Dance (Ibid.:164); the giant Sky Condor was woodpecker scarlet all over until his feathers blackened in the sweathouse as he tried for ten days to outwait the brave young man who had finally wrested away from him and hidden the largest and finest of his ten crest-covered sticks (eye gougers, like those used for salmon--Ibid.:230) that would bring great wealth to its possessor (Ibid.:170,347); from the sky came an enormous albino deer with skin like snow and antlers of red pileate plumage so large that they obscured the river (Ibid.:310); the killing of woodpecker-crest-covered Deer-in-the-Sky is the requisite deed set for young men who, variously, seek reunion with an estranged mother or marriage with two highly prized (and higher priced!) young sisters (Ibid.:294,324,325); a magical guardian deer, captured as a fawn and raised as a pet, is overlaid from the neck up with woodpecker scalp feathers (Ibid.:183); a dog that can make itself invisible and helps its master to defeat Earthquake at shinny was covered with sores until cured by an infusion of angelica root after which his back was coated with red crests (Ibid.:216); after a ten day ordeal on a distant off-shore rock during which the hero barely escapes being turned to stone and manages to fight off a water monster, the magical aspect of his adventure and ultimate rescue are highlighted by the woodpecker crests that cover the crossbar (the 'necklace') at the front of the canoe (Ibid.:184-185).

Origin tales for the woodpecker account not only for its creation but also for its beauty and value, and reinforce the rationale for the acquisition of wealth. When the Hupa creator-god first made all the birds, one of these, a very large woodpecker, requested that he be made red all over so that an Indian who killed him would become rich at once. But when he flew down from his tree, the creator sprinkled ground charcoal over him and he became Crow (Goddard 1904:131). In Yurok versions the creator, in gratitude for having been freed by pecking birds from imprisonment in a tree trunk, rewards them with touches of red plumage. Crow, however, demands so insistently that he be made entirely red, even rejecting an offer of woodpecker pileum color on the upper half (or, in a variant, that he can be red all over on condition that he always remain hidden in the depths of the forest), that the irritated god tricks and punishes him by telling him to close his eyes and then blackening him with coals (Kroeber 1976:112,114,266,317). In a Karok tale Coyote creates boys out of his urine and turns them into birds which he paints by squeezing semen of different colors from his penis. He makes Crow black, promising falsely that he will turn scarlet at a later time. He then colors Older Brother (Western pileated woodpecker), Younger Brother (California woodpecker), and Youngest Brother (Western gnatcatcher) but decides not to make them red all over.[15] "Only on the head I am going to make it. . . . [A man] will have to work hard . . . to kill lots before he can buy a woman with them. . . ." In a variant of this theme, Coyote cuts himself and paints the feathers scarlet with his blood

---

[15]In contrast to the Karok conception of woodpeckers as brothers, in at least one Yurok myth the large and small red-headed woodpeckers are depicted as two young women from the same house, presumably sisters (Kroeber 1976:245,246).

(Harrington 1930:156-158).

Although salmon clearly are not to be classified as wealth, they nonetheless are associated with many of the same attributes. They are valued, revered, viewed with respect and sentiment, endowed with power for good, and surrounded by taboos. In addition to being closely identified with Great Dentalium and Great Obsidian as previously noted, they are personified in Yurok myth and ritual by the figure of Great Salmon who comes from Salmon Home to the west across the ocean and is never killed (Kroeber 1976:207,218-221). In the Hupa land of the immortals, the "salmon are woodpecker color all over, and their scales are as broad as a winnowing basket. Tkey are knee-deep along the shore where the wind blows them out from the water" (Goddard 1904:368).

Originally, according to Hupa lore (and in like manner in Yurok legend), all the salmon were kept dammed up by a pre-mortal woman until a culture hero cleverly discovered their whereabouts and devised a strategy for releasing them into the rivers and streams for the people who were shortly to come into existence (Goddard 1904:124-125; Kroeber 1925: 73). It was much the same for the sacred deer that were kept inside a mountain and guarded by another of the immortals. These, too, were freed by the creator for the benefit of all the Hupa people (Goddard 1904:123-124). Of all the deer, the rare albino was, and still is, the most highly prized and revered by Northwest California tribes. In the White Deerskin Dance the stuffed heads of these and other beautifully or oddly colored deer are adorned with redheaded woodpecker scalps on the eyes, ears, throat, and dangling buckskin tongue. According to Hupa legend, if a sacred white deer is encountered in the forest, it can be seen to have eyebrows the color of woodpecker crests as do the gods themselves (Ibid.: 368). An individual who in all other respects appears to be an ordinary mortal will be recognized as one of the immortals when it is perceived that he has woodpecker-colored brows (Ibid.:188,367).

Thus, to recapitulate, it seems abundantly clear to us that any view of Hupa, Yurok, or Karok wealth which fails to take into account the extraordinarily sacred symbolism and magico-religious power of these desiderata misses the essence of their meaning and significance. Of course these people did concentrate upon 'money' but not simply money qua money. While they endeavored to obtain and to retain as much wealth as possible, its possession attested not simply to their social rank and influence but, more importantly, to their spiritual power and supernaturally-ordained 'luck' in hunting, fishing, gambling, games, and, indeed, in the acquisition of even greater sacred treasure. Furthermore, the wealth associated with a given individual reflected not only to his own credit but also to that of his family and, through ceremonial display, to the pride and affluence of the whole village or tribe. Snyder (1975:160) in her perceptive paper on the sacred component of the potlatch, commenting on similarities between certain cultural features of the Skagit and the Yurok, makes much the same point: "The Yurok tendency was to accumulate wealth creatively. But rather than give away property in potlatch, they converted it to beautiful treasures of ornamentation, the display of which enhanced the prestige of the whole tribe. There is not a great difference, then, between the motive of the potlatch where it occurred on the North Pacific Coast and the Yurok handling of wealth. Both were for display purposes and both elevated the standing of many more persons than the one principal who displayed it" (Cf. Erikson 1943: 297).

A position seemingly quite different from our own regarding the quest for wealth in Northwest California has been developed by Gould (1966) for the Tolowa. Like most students of the subject, he links the acquisition of items of high value with the striving for prestige. However, his special focus is upon the rational, conscious, manipulative means by which wealth is accumulated by Tolowa men. He dismisses Drucker's assertion that inheritance is the only realistic road to riches and proceeds to delineate other options available to a clever, shrewd, or enterprising individual.[16] He argues that, in addition to the possibilities afforded by litigation, gambling, and trading, a major resource for the acquisition of material gain is women. The brideprice brings significant increments of treasure to the father of daughters, and for the man who can purchase more wives there is always the possibility of yet more daughters who in time will bring a substantial price. Under certain conditions unmarried sisters may be swapped for brides. The role of women as food processors and preparers is described by Gould as a means of converting surplus foodstuffs into currency by selling in times of shortage or even in times of abundance to the chronically improvident.

While we do not question Gould's basic data, we are not fully convinced that these means for accumulating wealth would be applicable in a sufficient number of cases to warrant his conclusions. Polygyny, while permitted and perhaps even preferred[17] by the Tolowa, Hupa, Yurok, Karok, et al., seems to have been practiced only by a very few rich and powerful men (Kroeber 1976:400n). Occasions for selling food in any quantity must have been extremely limited, not only because of the typically bountiful nature of the region,[18] but also because of the

---

[16]The more traditional view regarding the relative fixity of social and economic status in Northwest California is typified by Kroeber's (1925:40) statement that "life was evidently so regulated that there was little opportunity for anyone to improve his wealth and station in society materially." And "the poor man was inherently inferior. . . . It was impossible that he should ever kill a white deer or have any other great piece of fortune" (Ibid.:118). Wallace (1965:237) concurs: "Though it was theoretically possible for an individual to better his station in life or that of his children, upward mobility was only rarely achieved." He adds that ". . . [shamans] were the only persons who could hope to accumulate a quantity of wealth by means other than inheritance" (Ibid.:242).

[17]Hupa and Yurok legends are replete with instances of polygyny among the gods and culture heroes.

[18]For discussion of such factors as food shortages and famines, geographic variation, and seasonal fluctuation in natural resources as

expectation and, from our observation, the practice of the more affluent headmen looking after poor relations and being generous with food, even to strangers.[19]

We also find a considerable discrepancy between Gould's (1966: 74) description of a dowry: "This return gift included a dowry of dance dresses. . . . Such dresses were valuable but were not composed of 'treasure' items and in no way approached the value of the brideprice" and Kroeber's (1925:29): "When the bride arrived . . . a considerable amount of property accompanied her. Ten baskets of dentalia, otter skins, and other compact valuables, a canoe or two, and several deerskin blankets seem to have passed in this way among the wealthy without any previous bargaining or specification [in contrast to the brideprice which was carefully negotiated]." The Yurok pattern lends support to Du Bois' contention for the Tolowa that "in reality there was at marriage an exchange between families which was only slightly in favor of the woman's family when the dowry and the bride price are translated into dollars and equated. Nevertheless the fiction existed that a man was enriched by marrying off his daughter" (Du Bois 1936:56 as cited in Gould 1966). Goddard (1903:55) reports for the Hupa that an approximately equal exchange of gifts took place between the families of bride and groom but that this was a matter distinct and separate from the brideprice. In any case the issue of whether or to what extent the dowry gift offset or largely cancelled out the brideprice will probably remain an open question.

For present purposes, however, our major concern lies with Gould's scant attention to those nonrational, supernatural, or sacred components of the wealth quest which are conspicuous by their virtual absence. Beyond an acknowledgement of an emphasis upon 'luck' in Tolowa folktales and narratives, his only other reference to 'luck' is made with respect to gambling: "They would 'train' in advance with fasting, cold night swims, and long treks through the forest, hoping to enhance their luck" (Gould 1966:85). We suggest that this fleeting glimpse of the quest for spirit power is only the tip of the iceberg so to speak, and

---

economic determinants with respect to the origin and function of the potlatch, see Suttles (1960) and Piddocke (1965); for an extensive critique of these positions, refer to Drucker and Heizer (1967:137-154) in which they confirm "the classical anthropological picture of the Northwest Coast as a region prodigal in foodstuffs for its primitive inhabitants" (p. 149).

[19]Spott and Kroeber (1942:167) graphically describe one such man: "He was also generous with food. His second wife . . . would set out extra baskets of acorn soup for whoever [sic] might come by, each basket with dried fish or meat in the cover basket. Then when Sra'mau would come from the sweathouse to the living house for breakfast, he would glance over at them, and if he saw none of them empty, he would say, 'I don't feel well.' When they asked him what was wrong, he would say, 'No one has yet stopped in to be given breakfast.'"

that whatever good fortune a Tolowa gained by his wits, ingenuity, and acumen (traits which also characterize many of the Hupa, Yurok, and Karok, we might add) was made possible only by virtue of a lifetime of devoted, probably obsessional, dedication to winning favor with the supernatural powers. The question in our mind in not one of either/or but one of emphasis.

OWNERSHIP

There is a considerable divergence of viewpoints regarding the ownership of property in Northwest California. Goldschmidt, Kroeber, and Wallace lay stress on individual ownership, while Driver, Drucker, Du Bois, Gould, and the present authors tend to see property as pertaining to the family group even though title was nominally held by the head of family. Goldschmidt (1951:507) in discussing resource property (i.e., hunting, fishing, and gathering sites) states: "Like no other hunting-gathering people of which I have knowledge (and very few primitive peoples generally), these resources are held as private property by individuals for their own use and control, and not in trust or as titular head for some larger group. The ownership was individual . . . complete, with free right of alienation."[20]

In contrast, Driver (1969:276), speaking of the Northwest Coast in general, reports that the most favored sites "were nominally owned by rich men, each of whom granted permission to his house or village mates, most of whom were his relatives, to exploit the land. That such permission was never refused proves that the use of the land belonged to the entire group of kindred rather than to a single individual. What at first appears to be individual ownership turns out to be a sort of stewardship. . . ." Similarly, Drucker (1965:50) in referring to the greater North Pacific Coast area (that is, Northwest Coast and Northwest California) asserts that "the social units--localized kin groups--were the owners of wealth, not individuals. An individual could regard himself as the owner of personal valuables such as robes and canoes, but major riches such as lands, houses, and important wealth tokens were group property. Even the objects possessed by the individual were made available to the group in case of necessity. Though the highest-ranking member of each group spoke of himself, or was spoken of by the others, as the 'owner' of his group's house or houses, its real estate and most of its treasures, he was the administrator of his group's possessions, not an individual owner." With specific reference to the Yurok, Driver (1969:294) states, "All property, both real estate and chattels, belonged to the extended families, nominally to the single headman of the family."

---

[20]In his discussion of this paper during the symposium, Dr. Goldschmidt indicated that since the writing of his 1951 paper he has modified his position considerably on individual ownership of property although he feels that he was essentially correct with respect to the individuation of moral responsibility and personal liability.

In the *Yurok Narratives* one can find indications of this concept; for example, "Her house owned an acorn-gathering place" (Spott and Kroeber 1942:220). Or, "If a whale came ashore between [specified] points, it belonged to the house *layekw* at Rekwoi. . . . The same house also had rights to the flippers of all sea lions that were brought ashore between two points on the coast" (Ibid.:182).

To the north the Tolowa provide additional confirmation of this point. Du Bois (1936:50) speaks of Tolowa fishing sites that were privately owned, but "ordinarily these were used freely by any person within the village group." Gould (1975:152,156) reports that the exploitation of acorn groves was always a family matter and that ownership of these trees was usually by families. Similarly, fishing gear, traps, and weirs were "built and used by small groups of closely related individuals, mainly individual families."

This concensus corresponds closely to our own view that among the Hupa land tenure and use as well as ownership and disposition of many other forms of property are usually a family affair. Thus two brothers living in separate homes with their families freely shared the ancestral dugout canoe for setting the nets which they took turns using, drying, and repairing, sometimes with the aid of an elderly uncle or one or another of their young sons. Their preferred fishing spot had been acquired by one of the brothers as part of a dowry gift received from his father-in-law at the time of the reported payment of the outlawed brideprice. Or again, a cluster of relatives comprising at least two extended families was living temporarily in donated mobile homes following a severe flood. The women had gathered abundant quantities of acorns from family sites and had stored them jointly in the dry attic of one of their water-damaged homes. The men fished cooperatively and had prepared substantial catches of salmon and eels by drying and by freezing. In a somewhat different vein involving an incorporeal family heritage, a man who had few living relatives and little in the way of tangible property took pride in possessing the power to cure--which ability, he believed, he had inherited directly from his grandmother and great-grandmother. Although he had successfully treated several cases, for the most part he had resisted the 'call' to become a shaman,[21] considering himself to be primarily the guardian and transmitter of this power. It was with the hope that his young daughter would also prove to have shamanistic capabilities that he and his mother were inculcating the child with Hupa language, legend, and lore (Bushnell 1970:798).

The centrality of the family is especially important in the matter of ownership of aboriginal artifacts and sacred dance paraphernalia.

---

[21]Among Northwest California Indians it is atypical for a man to become a shaman. It is interesting to note in this connection that this individual received extreme scores on an abstract figure preference test, being far below the other Hupa male subjects on a masculine dimension and far above his peers in his preference for complex, as opposed to simple, figures (Bushnell 1970:799).

A noted Yurok singer and formulist "owned the property of the house *tsekwel*. . . . On his deathbed there was a squabble about them [the ceremonial regalia] between his wife and his niece. . . . He raised himself on his pillows, pointed to the trunk which contained the property, and said that the things were not his, but belonged to the house *tsekwel*. Thereupon [the niece] took the trunk away" (Kroeber 1976:308). In another case a Yurok family that had paid a handsome brideprice for a Wiyot girl received in return a generous dowry that included among other treasures a great black obsidian presented with the stipulation that it never be paid again for marriage or settlement. Even though the direct line of descent can no longer be recalled and although the obsidian had been entrusted to the safekeeping of a non-relative whose children and grandchildren have continued to keep it in their possession, it nonetheless belongs to the house *sohtsu* to which it was originally given (Spott and Kroeber 1942:210).

The sense that Indian possessions are part of a family heritage rather than a matter of strict individual ownership is underscored by the very terms that are employed to describe the occasional disposition of such articles. Several examples have come to our attention in which a relative outside the direct line of descent has managed to acquire all or a large portion of the family's heirlooms. In such instances, even those in which a cash payment was involved, the items are often considered to have been lost through connivance, deception, or cheating.

When, a number of years ago, a Hupa ceremonial leader turned over his family's aboriginal collection to a man of another kin group in exchange for sorely-needed money, the transaction was, and still is, conceptualized as an instance of pawning rather than of selling. On the occasion of the ceremonials, this regalia is returned temporarily to the original owners (that is, the leader and his family) who in turn distribute it to the dancers under their sponsorship. The other man has attempted to assign himself leadership of this sector of the tribe on the basis of the indigenous treasure that he has come to possess but has consistently been rejected in this role. As one woman put it, "The inheritance and respect are what count. We still recognize [the leader] even though he lacks the wealth, and drinks." Driver (1969:292) has noted this phenomenon for the entire North Pacific coast, emphasizing that "social and religious statuses [are] more highly valued than material goods."

Over and above the actual or ascribed value of aboriginal items of wealth or the interrelationship of ownership and status is the intangible supernatural factor that takes precedence over individual and even family proprietorship. Goddard (1903:84) states categorically that the sacred white or other uniquely colored deerskins displayed in the White Deerskin Dance are the property of the Hupa people and are only held in trust, as it were, for the tribe by various individuals.[22] This

---

[22]In commenting on Goddard's view that these deer hides were, in a sense, a part of the public domain, Goldschmidt and Driver (1940:

conceptualization is carried a step further when, in Hupa mythology, a major deity who gives ten dances each night "comes through the valley every evening and collects the dance regalia from the Indians' houses and takes them in his boat to his home. In the morning the things return of their own accord" (Ibid.:76-77). The Yurok immortals also dance nightly in their Land-beyond-the-World. Each night a god and his son gather up all the dentalia and ceremonial finery, one from the upstream people, the other from the downstream villages, and they meet across the ocean for the Deerskin Dance (Kroeber 1976:287-288). In other versions boatloads of dancers shrouded in fog nightly travel down the Trinity and Klamath rivers, across the sea to the west, and return each morning at dawn (Ibid.:34; for the Karok, see Kroeber 1976:159; T. Kroeber 1959: 104-108).

Goddard's view of the tribal trusteeship of ceremonial regalia corresponds more or less closely to our own observation that such sacred items must be retained and used by the group to which they have always belonged and only in the traditionally ordained manner. Thus a Hupa family had obtained a ceremonial dress from an in-law, only to learn that 'medicine' had been made upon it for Down-river (i.e., Yurok) use. The anger of the parents and their concern over what ill might have befallen their daughter in the role of medicine girl had she worn this Yurok dress in a Hupa dance has been reported in a different context (Bushnell 1969:322). In another case that came to our attention, one with tragic sequelae, a young boy danced in an Indian show outside the reservation carrying a long flint intended for use in the White Deerskin ceremony, which must be performed only at the sacred dance sites along the Trinity River and on Bald Hill. As relatives had forewarned, the breaking of the injunction resulted in misfortune, the boy dying of leukemia within a year (Ibid.). Goldschmidt and Driver (1940:121) cite an instance in which staging of the White Deerskin Dance at a commemorative General Grant celebration in a town near Eureka contrary to tribal interdiction constituted a breach that was considered to have "spoiled the world."

Even when the proper use or misuse of sacred paraphernalia is not an issue, there is a potent spirit power for either good or evil with which this class of property is believed to be imbued. In a previous paper the case was presented of an informant who as a boy was terrified of approaching the trunkful of Indian relics in his grandmother's house unless he was carrying a piece of burning angelica root (Bushnell 1970:

---

118) report they were bought and sold among tribal members and considered to be private property. However, in our opinion a change in ownership does not invalidate the concept of holding sacred paraphernalia in trust for the benefit of the tribe. Also note the virtual absence of buying or selling white deerskins. "The Yurok state that fine white skins did not change ownership. Their possession was known far and wide and to part with one on any consideration would have been equivalent to a king selling his crown" (Kroeber 1925:26; see also Kroeber 1976:21n,37n).

791).[23] Another man lost the entire contents of his home during one of the Trinity-Klamath river floods with the sole exception of his case of valuable artifacts and dance regalia which, atop a floating mattress, was, he believed, saved from destruction by the sacrosanct nature inherent in these items (Bushnell 1969:323). This sacred quality pertains not only to the property of individuals, families, and family lines but also to the communal or tribal properties such as the river, ceremonial dance grounds, old village sites, Indian graves, restored semi-subterranean houses, and sacred pools, summits, and stones.

## WORK

We turn next to a consideration of work in Northwest California cultures. Goldschmidt (1951:513) speaks of an ethical pattern that consists of a "demand to work and by extension to the pursuit of gain." Citing Wallace, he describes these California tribes as "a busy and creative people" and notes "a strong compulsion to work heavily emphasized in childrearing supported by religious beliefs and demands, and expressed as a basic element in behavior." Wallace is further quoted by Goldschmidt: "Both a man and his wife are constantly busy. . . . Some seasons of the year are marked by more activity than others, but during none of them is anyone idle for long. The life is one of continuous routine work, although not necessarily of drudgery" (Ibid.:513n). Since, with rare exceptions, food resources were plentiful and relatively easy to come by, Goldschmidt concludes that work among Northwest Californians had become a moral value.

Although Goddard's (1903) monograph presents a rather detailed account of the Hupa hunting-gathering-fishing economy and related subsistence technology, he was apparently not sufficiently impressed with the degree of industriousness or the intensity of production activity to make a point of it in his published work. The major economic pursuits of men centering on deer and smaller game; salmon; steelhead; eels; and, for the coastal towns, surf fish and sea lions were intermittent or seasonal in nature although, needless to say, there were always potential tasks at hand--crafting wood, horn, or bone; tanning hides; weaving nets; making arrow and spear-points; or occasionally splitting and adzing house planks. Nevertheless, as Goddard (1903:38) points out, "The man's only routine work was the bringing of wood for the sweathouse. This was usually done in the early morning." Apparently the schedule of activities for the balance of the day was largely optional and contingent upon the exigencies or whim of the moment.

In the traditional Hupa pattern the day's work was completed prior to taking a light breakfast. "In the afternoon, the old men, and

---

[23] Goldschmidt and Driver (1940:120) seem to have missed the magico-sacramental nature and protective function of 'Indian root' when they note that "Angelica and a native weed were used for moth-proofing the trunks in which [dance] articles were stored."

the religiously inclined young men, took a sweat in the *taikyuw* [sweathouse], followed by a plunge in the river. After the bath they sat in the shelter of the *taikyuw* and sunned themselves. As they sat there, they engaged in meditation and prayer." After the evening meal the men "retired to the *taikyuw*, where they spent several hours in converse" (Ibid.:57).

Similarly, for the Yurok Kroeber (1925:84) states that "most men at least attempted to do a day's labor or much of it, before breakfast, which came late." (The epitome of this pattern, indeed almost a caricature, is expressed in the legend in which the inhabitants of Weitspus [Weitchpec], described as a chronically quarrelsome people, considered their most important pursuit to be fighting, a task that ideally was always undertaken and completed before breakfast!--Kroeber 1976:88). In detailing the daily round of the Yurok, Kroeber (1925:96) notes that "the flute . . . was played by . . . elders as they sat on sunny afternoons before the sweathouse in idle meditation" (cf. Kroeber 1976:312,347n). This recalls to us Theodora Kroeber's (1959:99-117) recounting of the Karok tale of the flute player who, though he worked to accumulate the treasure with which he would finally purchase his bride, also spent hours sitting by the river, dreaming and playing his flute.

Wallace (1965:239), discussing the leisurely aspect of native life, reports: "But industrious as they were, the Hupa found ample time for visiting, games, story-telling and other diversions." Our first impression of the Hupa a quarter of a century ago was, for the most part, of an informal, easy-going, non-competitive, non-compulsive, rather passive people, a scene which has changed but little in the interim despite modernization, improved educational facilities and job opportunities, and a shifting Indian-white demographic balance (Bushnell 1968). Visiting--talking, gossiping, joking--with friends and family, then as now, is still a high-priority activity; and trips up and down river or to the coast, for example, reflect many elements of an aboriginal tradition (cf. Wallace 1965:239). Indian games and gambling, once an accompaniment to virtually any gathering, are largely gone now except for the occasion of a major ceremonial or intertribal tournament. In an earlier paper (Bushnell 1970) a detailed examination of the lives of individual Hupa men studied longitudinally over a 20-year period suggests that the flexibility and freedom to attend social or ritual events; to take off for hunting, salmon or surf fishing; to travel with a delegation; or to participate in tribal council activities may have played at least some role in the tendency of many Hupa men to work at part-time, seasonal, or loosely-scheduled jobs although, needless to say, other determinants of an intrapsychic, interpersonal, or socio-economic nature were also operative here.

It may well have been the women of Northwest California rather than the men who more closely approximated the ethnographic description quoted earlier: i.e., "a life of continuous routine work," since meal preparation; child care; and, to a lesser extent, basket making were more or less year-round constants. They were expected to arise, pray, bathe in the river, and bring in wood for the fire before the men were astir in the sweathouse. The daytime hours customarily included the laborious grinding, leaching, and cooking needed to prepare the acorn soup that was a major feature of the diet as well as the gathering and processing of such supplementary foodstuffs as seeds, nuts, bulbs, and berries and, in accordance with the supply as provided by the men, the preparation of fresh or dried fish and game. In the evening it was the women's role to serve the principal meal of the day and to sit respectfully in silence in the presence of the men with feet hidden and basket hat removed (Goddard 1903:57).

However, the perennial performance of essential domestic tasks is hardly to be equated with a "compulsion to work." In discussing the White Deerskin Dance at Hupa, Goldschmidt and Driver (1940:125-126) note that "for the old women who were in charge of the cooking it was a period of work. . . . But even for them the dance was not entirely drudgery; long hours were spent leaching acorns or preparing food together in a leisurely way, talking or playing dice or guessing games. . . . The capacity of the women for sitting silently doing nothing, not even talking, was notable and rather astonishing to the whites, unused to such complete inactivity and repose."

We have also observed this phenomenon but have found it to apply to men as well as to women. Kroeber, too, was struck by the facility with which Yurok men could assume a passive posture. Thus in describing the Yurok household of one informant he refers to "an aged kinsman who appeared hopelessly bedridden but was only spending his days in the recumbent stupor into which aged Indians often seem to let themselves fall until some necessity rouses their waning faculties. . . . Once or twice [she] appealed to the old man, who answered, and then lapsed into his yogi-like unconcern . . ." (Kroeber 1976:315). Or again, "The northwestern [California] Indians, especially the older men, have a faculty of spending indefinite periods lying in a somnolent condition, although this does not seem to prevent them from rousing their full faculties on occasion. Nothing much would have been thought [by the villagers in the legend] of the young man's appearing to sleep day after day and night after night" (Ibid.:220n). This note makes it clear that retreat into passivity is not solely the prerogative of older men. Witness another Yurok tale in which the hero "brought in sweathouse wood and slept during the day," to which Kroeber (Ibid.:408) adds the comment, "This practice is called *atskei*."

Significantly, Kroeber in his insightful paper on Yurok national character does not emphasize either busyness or a compulsion to work. In the final sentence of his treatise, Kroeber (1971b:390) types the Yurok personality as compulsive but is nonspecific as to which areas of activity the designation applies. The distinct impression conveyed by this and his other writings on Northwest California is that this compulsivity finds its main expression in the myriad supernaturally prescribed and proscribed ritualistic behaviors with which these people were so frequently preoccupied. In this context the hours, even days, devoted to penance and prayer, the self-imposition of ordeals via fasting, sweating, vomiting, laceration, prolonged exposure to icy waters and winds, or the confrontation of monsters in river, ocean, mountain pool or forest, while clearly entailing endurance and arduous effort must, at the same time, from the standpoint of work be viewed as essentially nonproductive activities of a magico-religious character.

If work as a moral end in itself were truly central in the aboriginal setting of this region, we would anticipate that many of the paramount influences brought to bear on the growing child would reflect such a cultural focus. Therefore it is remarkable that, insofar as we can ascertain, at no point in the earlier stages of the life cycle was work deliberately and directly instilled as a central value, either in terms of being productive or as a virtuous activity in its own right. The approach to childrearing is noteworthy for the 'hands-off' attitude which prevailed. Wallace (1947:23) has detailed this laissez-faire approach with its "paucity of conscious instruction" which constituted an enculturative process whereby "children gradually and, for the most part, unconsciously, take over the culture. . . ." Deliberate instruction was largely limited to training in the rules of etiquette with the stress on proper eating habits and the inculcation of standards of deportment, including exhortations to show restraint, behave in the 'right way' (e.g., avoid precipitating a lawsuit), exhibit good manners, and adhere to the values of respect for elders, honesty, orderliness, and industry (Ibid.:18). The medium through which industry was to be manifested is not further explicated. Erikson (1943:289) in his observations on Yurok childhood does speak of teaching older children in "schools," that is, groups of five to seven (apparently boys) assembled under the aegis of an older man especially skilled in hunting, fishing, boating, etc. This 'teacher' would also impart the relevant stories and show them "how to live right."

Such instruction corresponds, at least in a general way, with our data for the Hupa except that learning was most likely to take place informally and usually within the context of a kin group. For example, a young boy or perhaps two or three brothers or cousins would accompany a father, uncle, or grandfather deer hunting--learning the trails, the art of tracking, the habits of the quarry, and possibly a medicine song or formula to enhance their luck, as well as the strict taboos that surround the entire undertaking from the preliminary preparations to the cooking and eating of the venison. To cite another instance, the medicine woman for a Brush Dance taught her young adolescent granddaughter the traditional formula in which the elusive magical basket cup is finally filled from the sky with the bark of the yellow pine (cf. Goddard 1904: 248-251). She trained her in the details of the ceremony, its meaning and purpose, the varieties and locations of the requisite herbs, the precautions to be observed, and instilled in her the frame of mind and spirit essential to the proper performance of her role as medicine girl.

We should like to point out, however, that for the child lacking sufficient aptitude or interest, no pressure or exhortation would be brought to bear. Also the learning would take place in the normal course of on-going, culturally apposite activities, not within a structured situation specifically designed for instructional purposes (cf. Wallace

1947:19-20). In any case, it was never a matter of work for work's sake.

Morality tales and myths were told which underscored the parental admonitions to practice restraint, moderation, and self-discipline. Erikson (1943:287-288) lists ten "teaching fables" for the Yurok, and Wallace (1947:18n) reports identical stories for the Hupa. These animal fables often constituted "Thou shalt not's" communicated by reciting the dire consequences of excess; lack of control; or rash, heedless behavior. We will have occasion later to discuss a number of myths and legends in which, in contrast to the so-called teaching fables, flagrant, blatant, or rampant misconduct or opprobrious behavior go entirely unpunished. At this point, however, the relevant observation centers on the fact that none of the aforementioned instructional tales carries a message that could be construed as portraying work per se either as a value or a virtue. In Erikson's (1943:287) words, ". . . the keynote of these fables is the ugliness of lack in restraint and conformity."

## THE SACRED QUEST

The one case in which youths were specifically instructed in what might be characterized as diligence and industry, and apparently the only instance cited in the literature in support of the viewpoint that the Hupa-Yurok-Karok esteemed work as a moral end in itself, was the obligation to gather the sacred sweathouse wood. The significance of this ritualistic endeavor, in our view, lies primarily in the unique combination of intense religiosity and purposive striving which it represents rather than a commitment to productive labor or a putative Northwest California "compulsion to work."

In commenting on the dedicated effort that was channeled into the religious side of the quest for wealth, Kroeber (1971b:386-387) says, "The greatest reliance for acquisition is on the supernatural and one's own will--a willing through abstinence and deprivation, and by sheer pertinacious wishing, weeping, insistence, and proclaiming--devices psychologically effective because they direct and focus volition. In short, the Yurok depend more on concentration of mind to acquire wealth than on extraverted activity. . . . It is through [self-] punishment, through self-deprivation and self-pity, that fulfillment of such wishing is heightened."

It is highly diagnostic, we think, that even in the story of the Inland Whale, the myth that perhaps comes closer to reflecting a work ethic than any other for the Northwest California area, the ultimate success of the hero would have been impossible, notwithstanding his assiduous efforts, had it not been for the factor of supernatural intervention in his behalf as the following synopsis indicates.

In Theodora Kroeber's (1959:17-38) beautifully written version, the young boy whose mother was of an aristocratic family but who was fathered by a young man of humble origin and who therefore could not pay the prideprice, was a bastard in accordance with Northwest California law and custom. He and his outcast mother lived with the lover's mother in poverty and ignominy. As the child grew, his maternal great-grandfather taught him to gather feathers which he kept, then to shoot birds and later small fur-bearing animals. With great-grandfather's guidance, he learned to carve small chests and then larger ones to hold his ever-increasing store of treasure. It came to pass that after attending an up-river dance he and his mother arrived weary at a mountain lake where the Inland Whale, herself a bastard, had been cast from the ocean by a tilting of the earth. The whale took pity on the boy, instructing him in dreams to pray to the bastard winter moons. As he grew he learned to fast, to purify himself, and to practice self-control. "He went far off to gather [sweathouse] wood . . . ; he prayed long and exhausting hours at the shrines in the hills. . . . When he fasted and prayed, he cried out to his great-grandfather and to the bastard winter moons as [the whale] had said to do. . ." During his youth and then as a man, he became ever more wealthy and respected until at last he returned to his ancestral home and brought his mother there for a time before she died.

While the magical intervention of the guardian helper is poignantly woven into the story, it is not conspicuous, with the young man's rise to riches and high rank seeming to be attributable in large part to his own persistent efforts, his dedication, industry, religiosity, and single-mindedness of purpose. However, in a shorter, less elaborated version published earlier by Spott and Kroeber (1942:224-226), the essential role of the supernatural helper is more explicit. Here the Inland Whale says to the young man in a dream, "It is I that have given you this wealth. Keep on doing as you are."

In a different narrative tale (Ibid.:219-222) the Inland Whale proved to be a guardian spirit to another Yurok, a woman desirous of becoming a shaman and who, through vision quests entailing travail, discipline, self-denial, and a consuming passion for her calling, at last came to be an outstanding and exceedingly wealthy doctor, an effort that would not have succeeded, however, had it not been for the spiritual power loaned to her by the Inland Whale. In one trance she received her Doctor Dance song and heard the flapping of the whale's tail. Later in a vision she saw the lake and the whale who said to her, "It is I who helped you. You will be a great doctor. . . ."

Exceptional good fortune and supernatural favor sometimes seemingly come to one as if by chance, though undoubtedly not without merit, and probably often in the context of an unexpressed need, wish, or longing. A Hupa man who loved to gamble but consistently lost, having arisen early to gather sweathouse wood, saw a strange, slimy, fish-like creature crawling along. He wiped off some of the slime which he wrapped in grass and took with him. This brought him great luck at gambling and he won everything his opponent had (Wallace 1948:354). Mythology and legends of the region contain a number of themes in which a supernatural pet, usually found when small, is raised and sometimes kept for a period of years bringing, at least for a time, luck in hunting, success in the acquisition of wealth, aid in overcoming obstacles or defeating enemies, and the like. Some of these pets serve as, or at least approximate, guardian helpers in that they have magical powers, come to occupy an important place in the lives of the persons to whom they are attached, and contribute to their welfare as in the case of a pet deer that provided abundant game not only for its owner but also his family while he was away and for whomsoever would live there in the future (Kroeber 1976:181-183). In another tale an old dog who had left his master was seen by him in the forest transformed into a white-rumped deer. Later his dog talked to him in a dream: "Sing this song, which I will teach you, and your luck will return. I know you feel badly about my going, but I left you on account of your son. If I had stayed I should have taken your son [in death] and you would have lost him. Now sing with me" (Spott and Kroeber 1942:235-237; see also Kroeber 1976:216,234,447-451). Perhaps the most frequently kept pets were water monsters, but their benefits were more often than not offset by the problems or misfortunes they generated, a subject to which we shall return later.

One water monster, although it was not a pet, became a guardian spirit for a man who in his youth had sought power and had become uncommonly brave with the aid of a dangerous woodland supernatural. The monster, like the man, frequented hazardous places and had been waiting for him in its underwater nest when he arrived.[24] The man's child had been abducted by other water monsters of the same kind as his spirit helper who consequently was knowledgeable regarding the motives, intentions, habits, and whereabouts of the culprits, information which it carefully imparted to its ward. Not only did the monster offer advice and counsel but provided direct assistance in the form of transport up and down river and to the monster village at the offshore seastack where the child was hidden. At a propitious moment under the monster's direction, the rescue was effected, the man thereby proving his unquestionable bravery to himself and to the monsters who had been testing him. Five days later the guardian spirit came upstream and crawled up the bank to receive a prearranged offering of ten baskets of sacred tobacco[25] (Kroeber 1976:397-398; see also pp. 36-37).

While inanimate objects sometimes serve in the role of an important but passive helper to men or gods as, for example, when a deity's

---

[24] This theme commonly appears in tales where the hero seeks supernatural assistance in his pursuit of strength and bravery. A youth whose first spirit helper was a rattlesnake felt dissatisfied with the feats he could perform. On a quest for the acquisition of even greater power, he found himself in the undersea house of the Thunders, one of whom said to him, "It was we who made your grandfather take you out to the [seastack]. It was we who told you to come here, though you did not know it." Later he was told, "Now you see that you are strong and brave. When you have returned, anything you wish for when you go in your boat will come true because we shall be with you" (Spott and Kroeber 1942: 288,230).

[25] An enormous quantity considering that the customary offering consists of but a few grains or crumbs of tobacco.

pipe aids in the weaving of the sky and the creation of the clouds and stars (Ibid.:127-128), or when a flute of another god at his command continues playing when he leaves so that it will be thought that he is still in the sweathouse (Goddard 1904:124), objects of this sort, when animate, have a more active nature and may be endowed with intentionality, especially of a beneficent or helping kind. Thus the pipe of a pre-human immortal of its own volition would roll about and point the direction--north, south, up in the air, etc.--from which another divinity for whom he was waiting would arrive (Kroeber 1976:95-96). Similarly, the mink hair tie of a young woman pointed the direction her brother had taken, lengthening itself and forming a walkway across the ocean (Ibid.:191). The sacred pipe kept in a village at the mouth of the Klamath and greatly dreaded by the Yurok for its power was responsible for the return of the salmon each season. A young man of the town who nightly traveled across the ocean to the home of the salmon was told by the headman (Great Salmon) always to feed angelica to the pipe for it is alive. It will then bring salmon in abundance; otherwise it will refuse (Ibid.:220-222).[26]

In two tales seemingly ordinary articles are actually devoted and concerned supernatural helpers, playing critical roles in the lives of their owners. An aging god who lay near death as a consequence of having been given poisoned food makes medicine, cures himself, and with the aid of his guardian quiver saves himself from further attempts at poisoning. When he is again served the same noxious fare, he says to the quiver, "Eat it," whereupon the quiver swallows the basketfuls of food while the god substitutes his own meal previously hidden in the quiver (Ibid.:158). A wealthy young man, a sponsor of the Deerskin Dance and devoted to the ritual of gathering sweathouse wood, finds himself drawn to Dentalium Land where he has been brought ostensibly to be the husband of a young woman but, in fact, to be tricked and killed. However, time after time his anthropomorphized weasel-skin pipe case warns him of the strategy his captors are about to employ. "And now his pipe case began to speak. It said, 'Keep yourself in control! Do not eat when they offer you food.' . . . Then it ran ahead to the sweathouse saying to him, 'I will go in and see how it is in there.'" It returned and warned him of a treacherously slippery spot to be avoided lest he slide into the fire and burn, cautioned him against smoking their deadly tobacco, and told him of the danger of hot coals being blown into his eyes if he should fall asleep. Whenever he felt sleepy, the pipe case would scratch him. In such a manner his guardian spirit continued to save him from ever greater hazards and impending death at the hands of the evil ones at Dentalium Home. When at last he returned to his own land, he gathered sweathouse wood ten times in one day, built his sweathouse fire, and prepared to move the sweathouse ten times, each stop marking a ceremonial site for the route of the Jumping Dance (Ibid.:255-260).

---

[26]In fact there were not one but two such sacred pipes, conceived of as being male and female, and married. When the house in which they were kept was destroyed by whites and one of the pipes broken, a new pipe was made so that the unbroken one would not depart in disappointment over the loss of its mate (Spott and Kroeber 1942:171-172).

On a ridge near the junction of the Trinity and Klamath rivers is a place where five white stones stand in a row across the trail. Legend has it that these are the ritual quartz cutting stones (*peihpegos* or *peihpergers*) used for slashing the flesh while gathering sweathouse wood, a practice called *ki-pehpego*. These were left behind by five brothers, the variously-sized dentalia, as they were separating in order to disperse themselves throughout the world before the arrival of human beings (Ibid.:251-252). Indians who sought sweathouse wood, especially those doing penance as part of a search for extraordinary power, supernatural favor, spirit helpers, or visionary experiences, would gash themselves with such jagged pieces of quartz[27] in order to enhance their piteousness, and hence their worthiness, and so invite special attention on their behalf (Ibid.:252n,254n,381; see also Kroeber 1925:66; Wallace 1949:3).

From all that can be adduced regarding the sacred quest in its various manifestations, it seems evident to us that its role in Northwest California is of greater import than has heretofore been acknowledged. The traditional view is echoed by Garbarino (1976:177), for instance, when she states in her recent textbook on North American Indians that "guardian spirit quests were not very important among the Yurok." It is significant that Kreober himself in the years intervening between the writing of the *Handbook of California Indians* in 1917-19 and the publication of the *Yurok Narratives* in 1942 shifted his own position considerably regarding the importance of the vision quest. In this latter work he concluded that the ordeal of the female shaman in Northwest California, after all, partakes of the guardian spirit quest "in the customary American Indian sense" with the spirit appearing in a dream or trance state (Spott and Kroeber 1942:155).

While Kroeber here was addressing himself to the quest as it pertains to the shamanistic experience, it is by no means limited to shamanism as we have seen, being evidenced in a number of other circumstances; for example, in the descriptions of the ritual gathering of sweathouse wood delineated earlier with their quintessential intensity, emotionality, and hallucinatory phenomena. Another instance of questing for a vision as recorded by Kroeber (1976:349-351) for the Yurok involved a search for the home of the Thunders who might serve as guardian spirits for youths seeking supernormal strength and valor. "The lake is still there, but invisible. A man who has been gathering sweathouse wood

---

[27]White quartz was probably employed for this purpose not only for its sharpness but also because it seems to have been endowed with potent magical properties. Wallace (1948:354n) cites evidence from Sapir (n.d.) that white quartz was believed to strike terror into a grizzly bear and that the Hupa would carry a fragment of it for protection. In a Yurok narrative a young man whose adoptive grandfather had instructed him to carry a piece of *peihpegos* while hunting for an albino deer, succeeds in his quest and drops the stone on the fallen animal, saying, "Your hair will always remain as white as this rock" (Spott and Kroeber 1942:245).

(ceremonially) for ten days might see [hallucinate] it, but he must think of the lake daily as he climbs the hill. If anyone tries to injure a person who has been in that lake, Thunder is heard running (rolling) [to his assistance]." In a detailed account of Hupa warfare, Wallace (1949: 3) reports: "The procedure for achieving military power was the same as that followed by a man seeking wealth or any other form of good fortune. Eating alone and sexual continence preceded the journey to the selected spot. The young man kept a lonely vigil during which he smoked himself over a fire of green pineboughs and gulped quantities of smoke until he vomited; he cut himself with a sharp stone on the arms, chest, and thighs,[28] wept, sang special songs, and recited innumerable prayers and formulas. Following this he bathed in the icy waters of a stream, river, or lake, and fell asleep. A dream or vision during the night gave promise of future braveness and invulnerability. If a youth dreamed [of success in battle], 'it would be that way all his life.' A dream involving the chicken hawk was also favorable."[29]

Goldschmidt (1951:514n) acknowledged certain parallels between the Hupa-Yurok sweathouse wood-gathering ritual and the Plains vision quest--"a lone act, performed in the wilderness by youths, [with] a deep religious and ritualistic involvement." He felt, however, that there the similarities ended. In Northwest California the "act was productive.

---

[28]This example of self-laceration by men, together with others cited previously, argues for a broader application of this practice in Northwest California than has generally been recognized. Erikson, for example, in discussing self-inflicted gashing by female shamans as symbolic menstruation, states that to his knowledge the only occasion for a Yurok man to cut himself would be in the event of 'contamination' by intercourse with a menstruating woman. Posinsky (1956:629-630), in reiterating Erikson's interpretation, carries it a step further: ". . . the Yurok have a general abhorrence of mutilation. It is absent from the wealth magic of the men, and is paralleled only in one type of masculine behavior [gashing for menstrual contamination] . . . a symbolic or displaced castration (Fn.). He, too, 'menstruates'."
Goddard (1914:360) has recorded a Chilula formula in which an immortal who has sexual relations with two perpetually menstruating women, signifying the ultimate in contamination, purifies himself with an unidentified herb, thereby restoring his luck with regard to deer and dentalia. Recitation of the formula and cleansing with the medicine presumably would have sufficed in lieu of drawing blood.

[29]Compare a shaman's acquisition of her second 'pain': ". . . She was at the same place on the hill, again dancing for more power. . . . She saw a chicken hawk soaring overhead. She became drowsy, lay down, and dreamed. She saw the chicken hawk alight and turn into a person. . . .'I saw you and came to help you. Take this.' And he . . . gave her something [for the pain, a dentalium]. . . . She swallowed it. At once she became unconscious." In her practice "if she sees a chicken hawk overhead . . . she knows she will be able to cure . . . the patient." If not, the prognosis is poor (Spott and Kroeber 1942:160).

". . . The hardship might be viewed as a concomitant to work rather than as a masochistic rite. . . . The visions were specifically directed to the ends of wealth-getting rather than the attainment of vague supernatural power. . . . The 'visions' of finding wealth were dreams of a more-or-less conscious, controlled sort rather than those received passively while in a comatose state." By now it should be apparent that in many important respects Goldschmidt's viewpoint is not substantiated by either the data we have presented or our interpretive assessment of their significance.

The successful sacred quest may best be viewed as a high point or peak experience set in a larger, ongoing matrix of supplication and ritual designed to bring spirit power to the individual (or group) in the form of what is usually translated as 'luck' or 'good fortune'; i.e., efficacy and success not only in the pursuit of wealth and prestige but also in hunting, fishing, gambling, warfare, curing, or religious endeavor.[30] In this respect it is clear that the Hupa, Yurok, Karok, and their tribal neighbors partake of a generic world view endemic to North America in which the individual is neither the sole master of his own fate nor can he attain that which is most valued simply by exercising his rational faculties. The sine qua non for accomplishment or achievement in virtually any area requires a sustained relationship to the supernatural, whether through offerings of incense or tobacco, prayer, song, supplication, sweating or smoking, weeping, self-abnegation, self-mutilation, enactment of a coercive ritual, recitation of an imitative magical formula, or a spontaneously-generated or arduously-induced trance experience with or without visions or a spirit helper.

## SIN, GUILT, AND SHAME

Goldschmidt, Kroeber, and Erikson all place stress on the so-called puritanism of the Hupa-Yurok character structure, moral code, and value system. As described previously, the cultural ideal calls for children to be carefully instructed in the rights and wrongs of their societal values, and exhorted to deport themselves in a manner befitting them and their family. Thus, it is argued, ideas of guilt and sin as well as of shame are inculcated early in life and affect many aspects of behavior. While Goldschmidt (1951:516) acknowledges the nebulousness of the internalization process with respect to a sense of guilt and sin, he invokes the practice of public confession to support the "individuation" of responsibility as do Kroeber and Erikson. To quote Kroeber on the Yurok: "Like puritans they feel sin as well as shame, expiating it by public confession on threat of loss by death of one of their loved ones—itself a puritan's ordeal of choice" (Spott and Kroeber 1942:158).

---

[30]Kroeber (1976:381n) mentions the Yurok word *koskololohkin* which he translates as "to wish for luck, to seek to be wealthy." It seems highly probable to us that this term refers to a much broader concept, one that encompasses the many and diverse manifestations of the quest phenomenon as we have described them.

The overall efficacy of confession in the treatment of certain illnesses where no other causative agent (e.g., object intrusion ['pains'], soul loss, or sorcery) can be found by the shaman is not at issue here. However, on the basis of our own data and other published accounts, any presumption of a one-to-one relationship between the practice of public confession and the experience of personal guilt must be seriously questioned.

There are instances reported in the literature where an individual typically is under intense pressure to save the life of a member of the family by revealing the prior commission of some 'sin' or wrongdoing, the withholding of which is the presumed or specified cause of the malady or morbid condition. Thus Spott and Kroeber (1942:201) relate the case of a Yurok woman whose confession years after the fact that she had boiled the scraped-up blood of a murdered kinsman together with the footprints of the enemy (Kerometsa Indians or their Karok friends) as part of a death curse resulted in the cure of her cousin's young son. In order to save an ailing granddaughter, a Yurok grandmother at the behest of two shamans who concurred in a diagnosis of *ohpok* poisoning admitted that she had once accidentally poisoned another granddaughter (the child of a different daughter) with this substance while intending to take the life of a girl from a family with whom she was feuding[31] (Kroeber 1976:419-420). Parenthetically and coincidentally, in both of these cases the 'cured' child died a few years later. When a Hupa man from one ranch (village) half-married[32] a girl from another with which there had been an ancient and bloody enmity, his kin, fearing that his residence at the other ranch might cause them harm, decided to get rid of him. A cousin arranged a hunting trip which provided him an opportunity to offer bread treated with strychnine to the intended victim, but at the last minute he had a change of heart. Years later when his own brother became seriously ill and the doctor said that a member of the family must have done something bad, the aborted attempt on the cousin's life was confessed (Wallace 1948:347-348). In each of these three cases there was a considerable lapse of time between the perpetration of the deed and its confession complex (Spott and Kroeber 1942:158). Notwithstanding the belated nature of such admissions, it seems reasonable to infer the harboring of some feelings of guilt or self-reproach. Even so, it should be noted that in two of the cases (and in the one to follow), the element of blood revenge was the prime motivating factor, while in the *ohpok* poisoning incident vindictive retaliation in the

---

[31]This was considered a killing even though the child's death occurred a year after the purported incident, since *ohpok* poison, generally concocted of such ingredients as dog flesh, rattlesnakes, frogs, salamander eggs, etc., and added to regular food, is expected to take effect after approximately such an interval of time and in the same season (cf. Kroeber 1925:67).

[32]If a man and his family were too poor to pay a full brideprice, the union was considered a half-marriage and residence was generally matrilocal (cf. Goddard 1903:56; Kroeber 1925:29).

context of an interfamily feud is implicit--all suggestive of socially-sanctioned and, to a certain degree, morally justifiable behavioral responses.[33]

Another element is sometimes added when not one but a series of potentially pertinent offenses is brought forth as in the episode cited by Goldschmidt (1951:517). The father of a sick boy confessed that years before he had committed an act with murderous intent. While visiting a household against whom his own family had had a long-standing and bitter grievance (killings having occurred on both sides), he had participated in the hunting of sea lions and had volunteered to prepare the bladders for grease storage bags. Lingering behind his hosts, he cut his leg with a mussel shell and put some of his blood in each bladder with the hope that this contaminant would prove lethal to the family. It was this revelation that was believed to have marked the turning point in the boy's return to health. However, prior to the establishment of the father's culpability, the mother confessed to having committed various infractions, none of which was deemed germane by the shaman who in her vision had seen the shadow of the father and blood dripping from something onto the boy (Spott and Kroeber 1942:188-189).

This latter type of confession, namely one in which more than one relative of the patient recites past misdeeds until the doctor at last singles out the relevant causative act, suggests not so much a strictly individualized moral responsibility as a more generalized sense of family obligation and commitment to the stricken person. This point is illustrated by another of Spott and Kroeber's (1942:157) narratives in which a man in his youth had secretly kept as a pet a *he'gwono'*, a legendary, supernatural, condor-like bird or being (apparently the equivalent of an *erl'erm*, a death omen--cf. Kroeber 1976:409). In time he married and had a son who, at one point in his childhood, became seriously ill. The outside shaman, called in after others had failed, saw in her trance states a huge bird flying across the ocean with the boy's life on its back. "'. . . It looks as if the bird came to your shadow [the father's]; perhaps you know what happened. Tell it and save the boy's life. He has no pain in him that I can suck out.' Then the boy's mother began to confess. She told everything wrong that her people had done for generations back. Then the father also began to confess a little something or other, and finally he told all about the *he'gwono'* he had kept. Then the doctor said, 'That is it. Now he will be well.'"

---

[33] It would appear that in native Northwest California law premeditated homicide per se was not necessarily a crime. In discussing an individual who "came close to the native ideal of a great man"--rich by inheritance, eminently successful in acquiring new wealth, generous, proud, brave, and headman of his village, Spott and Kroeber (1942:167-171) relate that "in all the killings in which he was involved he fought clean. If an enemy passed . . . on the trail . . . he would send word after him that the next time he would be attacked; but he disdained to attack him without warning." Perhaps in the confessions under discussion much of the culpability lies in the deviousness, secretiveness, or the conspiratorial nature of the act.

The role of ancestral behavior (or misbehavior), while not the crucial variable in the preceding example, is clearly pathogenic in the following two accounts.

A doctor called to treat a Hupa child whose mouth was always open determined that two dentalia were keeping it thus. She 'saw' an ancestor of the child's grandfather descend into a new grave and, on the pretext of kissing the deceased goodby, surreptitiously remove the two funerary dentalia from the septum[34] with his lips and hide them in his mouth while the grave was being filled. At this point the grandfather reportedly acknowledged that an ancestor of his had "risked this deed" (Kroeber 1925:42).

A Yurok girl failed to respond to attempts at treatment by several doctors until finally one shaman in a vision saw the form of a deer with the patient stretched across its antlers. She told the family that it seemed to be of stone rather than alive and that something from long ago had caused the illness, perhaps persons who had approached the stone deer while unclean from being with their wives, or who had not properly disposed of deer bones, or who had failed to wash their hands in the prescribed manner after eating venison. The father then related for the first time and in the presence of the required witness how the girl's great-great-grandfather on a lonely quest for supernatural power on a sacred summit had discovered and subsequently hidden a miniature stone deer with powerful magical attributes that over his lifetime had brought him great luck, wealth and, it is said, ten wives.[35] No one knew at what point in the family history the talisman had disappeared, although a residue of its power was said to linger still in its hiding place. Following this 'confession', the girl regained her health although it was never clear who had actually transgressed or in just what manner (Spott and Kroeber 1942:167-171). Here the role of guilt is rather amorphus, as Kroeber himself has noted. In discussing the determinants of this illness, he speculates that perhaps any object such as a talisman or magical charm which brings exceptional good fortune may, in itself, be dangerous to possess and that ultimately the owner or another in the family might have to pay the price, so to speak. Similarly for supernatural pets--e.g., *he'gwono*'s, water monsters, etc.--

---

[34]The Hupa and Yurok perforated the septum only after death; Karok and Tolowa men, however, wore a dentalium in the nose.

[35]This element of the story is, in all probability, apocryphal. For the Hupa, Karok, and Yurok the number ten has both sacred significance and magical efficacy, hence the ten-day cycles of the White Deerskin and Jumping dances, the ten days of seclusion and preparation by the formulist, the ten Boat Dance approaches to the shore, the ten-day puberty rite for the girl, the ten sticks laid out on each side of her representing the ten sons and ten daughters that she might bear, the ten sections of the fish dam at Kepel, the ritual ten days of sweating and gathering sweathouse wood, the good fortune that will attend the man who performs sexually ten times in one night, etc., etc.

"They bring luck for a time, but grief in the end" (Ibid.:158,171).[36]

In our view these cases with their origins in the distant past or those in which the confessed 'sin' was one of neither commission nor omission but rather a happenstance or circumstance which somehow or in some way brought misfortune down upon the house can hardly be said to support Goldschmidt's (1951:517) assumption of "the personalization of the moral act and the internalization of guilt."

A Hupa case will serve to illustrate one more variation on the theme of confession, one in which an unintentional breach of taboo is involved. One of our informants described a critical event in his life when at about the age of eleven he was treated by an Indian doctor for an excruciating and protracted headache. After hours of prayers, dances, songs, pipe smoking, several periods of trance and "talking to the spirits," she had a vision as dawn approached of a boy fishing at three different spots along the river gorge. The youth, near exhaustion, then acknowledged that he had, in fact, done this but had not realized that to set his net in more than one place was a grave violation of a sacred dictum. Nevertheless, this 'confession', following upon the shamanistic revelation and coupled with a promise to do right, brought about a rapid and lasting cure. Obviously in this instance it would be rather meaningless to attribute to the young patient any prior "puritanical preoccupation with sin" (Spott and Kroeber 1942:158) or "deep moral concern" (Goldschmidt 1951:517) vis-à-vis his unwitting wrongdoing.

Erikson (1943:261-262), as part of his study of a shaman's acquisition and use of her powers, touches upon the subject of confession and briefly cites typical examples of curing by this modality, including the recitation of ancestral improprieties. He suggests that the shaman "has a certain inventory of sins which . . . simply attaches, under ritualistic circumstances, one of a given number of explanations to a certain disturbance and makes people confess tendencies which, in view of the structure of the culture, can be predicted. . . . [She] is, of course, in possession of enough gossip to know her patients' weaknesses even before she sees them and is experienced enough to read her patients' faces while she goes about her magic business. If she, then, connects a feeling of guilt derived from secret aggression or perversion [on the part of a family member] with the child's [neurotic] symptoms, [these] usually disappear after [she] . . . has provoked a confession in public."

While the power of public confession in Erikson's analysis is directed to the reduction of ambivalence in the family and the remission of psychogenic symptoms in the individual, it can also be an effective agent for the renewal of public confidence, the reestablishment of trust

---

[36]While this is generally so, there are exceptions in which there is a reasonably satisfactory resolution including a continuation of the friendship or emotional bond and the extraordinary luck associated with such a pet (cf. Spott and Kroeber 1942:235-237; Kroeber 1976:64-65, 178-183).

in a leader, and the restoration of his luck as Snyder (1975:54) reports for the Skagit of Puget Sound. Citing the rationale that "the source of bad luck was invariably bad behavior," she describes the manner in which a Skagit headman, unable to sponsor a potlatch ceremonial because his fortunes were on the decline and his status was therefore in jeopardy, would make public confessions professing guilt and promising reform. The oratory, sometimes recited by a delegated spokesman, would be couched in vague generalities alluding to a violation of custom or some misdeed that might have already become known to the assemblage. We cite this datum here to indicate, first that the phenomenon of confession is by no means unique to California and, second, that here too neither pangs of conscience nor a sense of sin can be automatically presumed.

Returning to Northwest California, the ceremony of the White Deerskin Dance did constitute an institutionalized expiation and cleansing of individual and collective transgressions. Our own data also indicate, as reported in an earlier paper (Bushnell 1969:320-321), how disregard for or flouting of sacred tribal proscriptions may result in misfortune for specific individuals, for the entire tribe, or even for the area as a whole as was the case, for example, with the disastrous floods along the Trinity and Klamath rivers in 1956 and 1965 (with regard to which it was said retrospectively that the sacriligious behavior of the younger generation, the violation of an injunction against drinking water by the medicine woman, or the defilement of the ceremonial dance grounds by white mill owners must have provoked supernatural retribution).

Our interpretation of such phenomena as public confession and post-hoc blame attribution points more toward an inference of externalization or projection of guilt than to its characterologically regulated internalization. While our informants did give some inferential indications of possible feelings of unconscious guilt as suggested by self-defeating or self-destructive behavior, and while we certainly did hear occasional references to sin, usually in the context of Christian fundamentalism, there was relatively little or no clear-cut evidence to support the notion of burdensome feelings of personal guilt or a tortuous sense of sin, nor were there consciously expressed wishes for atonement or assuagement in the absence of compelling external circumstances. In fact, during the course of our studies of Hupa behavior, culture, and personality during the '40s, '50s, and '60s, we were never struck by an overriding concern with individual moral responsibility. We would concur with Wallace (1947:326) in his statement that "on the whole, the Hupa are tolerant of personality deviation because they believe that a man acts differently or wrongly because one of his ancestors did likewise and he really cannot help himself."[37] Of course, as he points out, such tolerance does not extend to situations that would threaten the

---

[37]Compare Erikson's (1943:289-290) comment that "if a [Yurok] child was not well-behaved . . . the explanation was simple. The child was neither inferior, nor sick, nor bad; but he had seen spirits of a special kind--bad ones, who had committed crimes in their time."

general welfare of the group, as with the ceremonials.

By way of concluding our consideration of guilt and sin in native Northwest California, we should like to add that these are conspicuous by their virtual absence in the myths, legends, and folktales of the region as are any clear-cut signs of contrition, compunction, repentance, and remorse.[38] This is all the more remarkable in the context of thematic motifs which include malice, murder, mayhem, incest, treachery, abandonment, rage, hatred, contempt, and the like. By contrast and, we feel, significantly, the recurrence in the oral literature of shame--an affective state quite different from guilt--is noteworthy.[39]

Hence in a Yurok story the earth has become dark because Coyote has killed the sun. A culture hero, Grown-in-a-Basket, effortlessly lifts and throws Sun back up into the sky with one hand although a hundred of the strongest men, working in unison, had been unable to move even one of his feet. These men, "in shame (at being so immeasurably surpassed), changed into rocks or bushes, or other things." Later, with Spider's help, the hero ascends to the sky and at first demurs but then accepts a challenge to play shinny, striking the ball to the farthest end of the sky and taking all that there was to win. In shameful defeat his opponents turn "into one thing, some, into another" (Kroeber 1976: 93-94; for a very different version, see p. 477). Another young man so thoroughly defeats his opponents at double-ball shinny, winning two sisters who were at stake, that one rival, Sandpiper, goes off to the hills in humiliation while another, Earthquake, who had never before experienced defeat, stops playing (quaking?) because he is so ashamed (Ibid.:234-235).

Not surprisingly, the ceremonial dances with their emphasis on display, splendor, status, and sacred power provide a setting not only for the experience of reverence, pride, and sentiment but also for the elicitation of latent envy and shame. A Yurok demi-god, after originating the sweathouse and acquiring by magico-religious means a great abundance of every kind of dance accoutrement, sets out with his sister to travel the world and institute dance festivals. Once, when they neared a coastal town, they drew back in shame at how clean and well-dressed the inhabitants appeared. But then the two, hiding behind bushes, put on their dance finery and proceeded. "As soon as the people saw them they did not look (at the young man and girl), being ashamed (at their splendor)." Upon learning that a Jumping Dance was being held across the river at Rekwoi, the hero confessed, "I was ashamed to go. I thought

---

[38]Frequent allusions in the mythology to loneliness, sadness, sorrow, pity, and self-pity seem to us to be of another genre and to reflect quite a different configuration involving infantile feelings of helplessness, abandonment, and deprivation, to be discussed later.

[39]That Kroeber was attuned to manifestations of shame is evident from his many footnotes and marginal notations on this point in the *Yurok Myths*. In his reflections on Yurok character (1971b) he describes a hypersensitivity to shame but guilt per se is nowhere mentioned.

I would stay on this side." However, he created the Boat Dance and, as they approached the far shore, those at the Jumping Dance could hear singing and dancing on the water. As the fog lifted, the headman came and looked about. "He saw his food turned to stone and some of it to ashes"--an indication of the depth of his mortification at being outdone. "They were poor at Rekwoi now, and ashamed." At the river's edge some of the women, too, turned into stone from shame upon seeing the sister--a woman!--in one of the leading boats (Ibid.:19-24).

In a somewhat similar vein, the people of Weitspus had never anticipated that a small village upriver could assemble sufficient costumes and dancers to outfit a dance party like other towns sending groups to the Weitspus Deerskin ceremonial. Then they heard from upstream the sounds of the approaching dance and in their consternation and shame hid indoors. Although they were told, "'It is a good dance. They have three white deerskins. It is a beautiful dance', . . . not one Weitspus person came out to look at the dance. All stayed in their houses" (Ibid.:37-38).

In two Yurok myths the pre-mortals felt ashamed that there was no Deerskin or Jumping Dance where they wanted them to be (rather than where events proved they were preordained to be). In one, there were four brothers--deities--who lived in a place where there was no Jumping Dance. The eldest was ashamed so he left the coast and went to an inland ridge where he set about making a redwood canoe. When it was completed, he and his three brothers crossed the western ocean beyond the perilous point where the sky rises and falls against the sea and returned in one night, their boat filled with woodpecker crests. Although the costumes they made were proper and beautiful, the dance did not go well there so henceforth it was held at the next town where it was right (Ibid.:163-164). In the other, a god, having had his proposed dance rejected by one town after another, came to a place along the coast where a Deerskin Dance was in progress. He cried to himself, saying, "'I tried and nobody wanted it. . . . That dance they shall not have here.'" In his humiliation and vexation he transformed the dancers into fir trees that can still be seen on the hillside. The sponsor of the ceremony, Widower-across-the-Ocean, "was ashamed that his dance had been stopped." His cane, a fir, is also there yet (Ibid.:163,196-198).

The occasion of the ceremonial dances provides a backdrop for (though not the cause of) two other episodes in which the principals experience intense shame. A young man of supernatural origin had come into being in Karok territory. He made many dances there and brought good luck to the people in gambling and games. After participating in Yurok dances and bringing gambling luck to them also, he heard of a Jumping Dance to be given in Hupa which he decided to attend. At Weitspus he learned that others had gone from there the day before. A man said to him, "I do not think you will be able to reach it. Many people from everywhere, some of them thinking that they (truly) were men, have been unable to arrive. Then, when they could not reach it, they were ashamed." Nevertheless he attempted it twice, each time reaching the Hupa Valley but then becoming disoriented and finding himself unable to proceed and even moving backwards. He was greatly ashamed, and at one point on his way back home wept so much that his tears created a spring which marks the spot now. On the night before the last dance he came downstream again to Weitspus, this time agreeing to go with one who could make the right 'medicine' for the journey. He confided, ". . . I am ashamed, my friend. Perhaps you know it; I tried twice to get there." The other replied, "Yes, I know it. Once, the first time you came back here by night" (to avoid the humiliation of being seen). "The other time you went by the trail over the mountain . . ." (because he was ashamed to return home through Weitspus). They arrived in the evening to see the final dance and "as they walked, [the] young man nearly fell when the Hupa people looked at him" (Ibid.:56-58).

A high-born Yurok woman who was disowned by her family after she took a lover of lowly status and bore him a son lived humbly and avoided the company of others. On the occasion of a dance being held upriver from her village, friends from downstream implored her to come with them until, feeling obligated, she attended on the final night with her young son. Experiencing both the shame of being ignored by the members of her family who were present and the awkwardness of being treated with unaccustomed respect and courtesy by the others, she left quietly before the dance was concluded. To avoid passing through the river settlements on her way home, she took a steep and circuitous mountain trail so that she alone would know her shame (T. Kroeber 1959:17-24).

When his sexual overtures met with success, a licentious Hupa creator-god was elated; when he was spurned he suffered mortification and chagrin. Bent on the conquest of women who struck his fancy, he went upriver on the Klamath and failing to entice two Karok girls out of their house, spoiled the lake he had just created for them. Far to the south along the Trinity, pursuing the same amatory objective, he created various features of the landscape in accordance with his strategy--for example, a dam with a waterfall so beautiful that even a new widow would sing love songs and then buttes to hide it since this would breach propriety--but sometimes destroyed his handiwork when he was frustrated and humiliated by a new failure (Goddard 1904:125-126).

In a Karok tale with a Yurok locale, two maidens who for some time had been teasing an attractive youth and coyly declining his advances, discovered with a shock that he had married another for whom he had paid a sumptuous brideprice. When next spoken to ". . . the young women did not answer. . . . They felt such fools they had slipped away and were never seen . . . again. Only their little round basket hats were left lying on the ground marking the place where the girls were last seen" (T. Kroeber 1959:101-104,115-116; see also Kroeber 1976:259 for a similar scene in a different tale).

Finally, in order to demonstrate that in the Yurok world even monsters were not immune to the pain of injured pride, we cite the case of Long One, a horned, serpent-like, supernatural creature. Discovered in a creek when it was very small and taken home by a young man who raised it as a pet, it thrived and grew on a diet of elk and deer meat which the youth was able to provide daily because of the magical 'luck' associated with Long One. In time his mother came to know about the pet which had, appropriately enough, grown to monstrous proportions! Increasingly she became exasperated with it since it ate vast quantities of meat. When she scolded, it would go away for a few days, and once she tried hitting it with a stick and failed. Finally she threw coals from the fire on the creature and it withdrew and disappeared. After a long and arduous search, the young man located his pet across the ocean in the sky. He pleaded with the monster to come back with him but Long One said, "'No, I am ashamed' . . . and told him what the old woman had done. Then the young man could not persuade it . . ." but at last the two agreed to start anew. Long One left his fellow monsters in the sky, the man removed his possessions from his house, and they went to live by a mountain lake (Kroeber 1976:65-68).

Kroeber (1976:18) has remarked that "a surprising proportion of [Yurok] traditional knowledge, myths as well as formulas, is nothing but a recital of their own customs thinly cloaked in narrative." We would extend this observation to include not only custom but also ethos, world view, cognitive orientation, character traits, emotional states, conscious desires, and repressed wishes. The shame experience that is projected so clearly into this body of literature reinforces one of our own subjective impressions of the Hupa and is consistent with Kroeber's (1971b:386) observation that the Yurok "are touchy to slight, sensitive to shaming, quickly angered." Also, "before other persons, pride often covers up their fear . . ." (Ibid.). In light of the foregoing, it seems feasible to postulate intense, underlying feelings of personal inadequacy or deficit, and deep-seated fears of rejection, abandonment, or loss. We shall have occasion shortly to explore this matter further.

THE PSYCHOANALYTIC QUEST

The issue of anality versus orality vis-à-vis the peoples of the Northwest California culture area is germane to the central themes under discussion, particularly so since these concepts have been invoked by Kroeber, Erikson, and Goldschmidt in an effort to understand the psychological determinants or constitutents of the wealth complex and the work ethic. Kroeber (1971b:390) was forthright on the matter: "I have long thought and still believe that the Yurok ["and their co-tribes of the same culture"--Kroeber 1948:618 ] adhere to the classical anal temperament. . . . My friend Erikson diagnoses rather an oral type of personality. . . . As for the oral constitutents, there is no doubt that the Yurok wealth-acquiring behavior connected with the sweat house strongly enacts infantile attitude and behavior. . . . I do not therefore see any quarrel between recognition of anal and oral components of Yurok personality; each is presumably true on its own level and degree." He goes on to say, "As for the type of neurotic behavior among ourselves which customary Yurok personality most suggests to me, it is compulsion" (Ibid.).

Erikson (1943:297,300-301) formulated an innovative hypothesis that de-emphasized the primacy of either the oral or the anal zone and instead focused on the alimentary canal as paradigmatic in the Yurok child's concept of body and world "in the sense of 'the tubular food-carrying passage extending from the mouth to the anus,' with a positive educational emphasis on the mouth." From this viewpoint cultural components can be recognized in the preoccupation with keeping channels open and uncontaminated: e.g., the river, the sweathouse (morphologically a tube with separate entrance and exit); and the avoidance of 'contaminating' cul-de-sacs: e.g., living house, vagina. Erikson (Ibid.:296-297) discerned in many of the Yurok a constellation of classical psychoanalytic anal characteristics--compulsiveness, suspiciousness, miserliness, and "a narcissistic holding on to the 'treasures' of the cloaca. . . . [The] 'pleasure of final evacuation and exhibition of stored up material' is most conspicuous at dances when, toward morning, the Yurok with a glowing face produces his fabulous treasures. . . ." Erikson continues: "However, the institutionalized obstinacy which allowed him to accumulate these treasures seems counteracted by the highly social experience of seeing his treasures enhance the prestige of the whole tribe. At least ceremonially, they belong to everybody."[40]

Notwithstanding his graphic symbolic anal imagery, Erikson was reluctant to assign the label "anal" to an entire people (personal communication) and, moreover, was unable to find confirmatory evidence in their child-rearing practices. "So far as we know now, the Yurok does not seem to focus any interest, pleasurable or phobic, on feces . . ." (Ibid.:297). Because of his failure to adhere to and account for an anal personality type for the Yurok, Erikson has been taken to task by some of his critics.

Goldschmidt (1951:522) stressed personality traits such as penuriousness, competitiveness, and compulsivity associated with an anal character structure which would be consistent with his conception of the native California approximation to the Protestant ethic. Regarding Erikson's position, Goldschmidt protested that he asserts "a requisite functional relationship (indeed, a causal one) between child training and personality traits but in the absence of methodology he compromises disconformity by finding the nearest loophole" (Ibid.:521).

---

[40]Posinsky (1957:9) claims that Erikson overlooks "the unconscious dynamics of the situation, the envy (and sometimes, violence) which the display of wealth touches off . . . and the decisive fact [!] that the Yurok lack a tribal sense and live in an amorphous and unorganized society where kinship . . . takes precedence over any communal or tribal loyalties. . . ." We have generally found that people can trace their antecedants back for some generations (stating, for example, that the mother's family line was Karok, or that they are 'full-blood' Hupa), usually with a sense of tribal pride and loyalty--even when this is necessarily divided (rather than amorphous or non-existent). Other data relevant to a purported lack of "tribal sense" would include such negative modes of identity reinforcement as the Hupa-Yurok war (Kroeber 1925: 50-52; Spott and Kroeber 1942:202-209; Wallace 1948:351-352), or the current protracted dispute concerning elegibility for the Hoopa Valley Reservation tribal roll and per capita payments.

Although Roheim (1950:272) accepted Erikson's alimentary orientation for the Yurok, he was convinced that the anal terminus is crucial in contradistinction to Erikson's oral-nutritional emphasis. Roheim was highly critical of Erikson's failure to recognize two factors which seemed to him to be of great importance, namely Yurok aggression and (defensive) reaction formation. His argument runs thus: it is inevitable that the child will react aggressively to the orally-frustrating narcissistic mother; since he is not permitted to rebel openly, he identifies with the maternal retentiveness, holding everything inside. "Sphincter morality," i.e., anal constriction, is extended in two directions, "backward to the oral and forward to the genital zone" (Ibid.:272), hence the restrictive controls imposed on eating and sexuality. As for reaction formation, "to distribute" (presumably food) contains the unconscious meaning "to retain" (Ibid.:287).

Posinsky (1957:15-16), following and often paraphrasing Roheim (who used concepts developed by M. Klein), posits for Yurok children a dual involvement with good and bad body contents, the dangers of both fullness and emptiness, and an ambivalent relationship with the sometimes gratifying, sometimes withholding, mother (see also Posinsky 1956:601-602). Posinsky (Ibid.:602) quotes Roheim (1950:275): "The men have to become *rich*, i.e., mothers full of '*good body contents*' (food, feces, embryo, etc.), because they have been frustrated by their own mothers. Hence their oral aggression is directed against the mother's body, and what follows is the corresponding talion anxiety. They will be 'scooped out', empty--i.e., poor. To be rich means to be full of *good body contents*, i.e., food stabilized into a fecal symbol. It also means to be magically and ambivalently identical, both with a *full*, i.e., gratifying, mother and with a bad, withholding mother" (italics in original).

Going beyond this formulation, Posinsky (1956:602) adds a phallic component to the equation, money (dentalium shells) = breast = feces so that "there is a synonymity of dentalium--breast--feces--penis, with anal retentivity the dominant theme." Just as dentalia epitomize good body contents, the positive introject, so do the illness-inducing 'pains' (*telogel* or *telogetl*) symbolize the bad body contents or negative introject, the former, then, being beneficent while the latter are maleficent.[41] These infantile introjects, i.e., the dentalium and the 'pain', Posinsky suggests, have "a remarkable if inverted similarity," the 'pain' being finger-like in shape and "suspiciously similar in appearance to dentalia . . ."[42] (Ibid.:598). Further, "the most powerful evidence

---

[41] In our opinion it would make better sense, both psychoanalytically and ethnographically, to conceptualize the 'pains' as malevolent or as negative introjects only when they function as illness-inducing agents, and as benevolent or as positive introjects when they are brought under control, that is, transformed and employed in a curing capacity.

[42] Few *telogetl* have actually been described in the literature.

about the phallic aspect of the dentalia comes from the stringent taboo on sexual intercourse within the 'living house'." However, ". . . the postulated flight of the shell money (which here refers to semen or penis), and the poverty which will result inevitably from intercourse in the living house and from a failure to bathe after coitus--these are patent rationalizations which spring from a deep-seated castration anxiety . . . and may be traced to the original trauma. Thus, to be poor means originally to be hungry or empty, but it also comes to mean *to be without a penis*" (Ibid.:602-603; italics in original). To recapitulate, "there is . . . a danger in emptiness (starvation, lack of love, poverty, castration, death), *and* a fear of fullness. The danger of fullness grows not only from the projection of oral aggressions onto the mother (and father) and the consequent fear of retaliation, but also from the ambivalence involved in fullness--which means both good and bad body contents. Thus, the fear of emptiness makes the Yurok greedy and retentive, while the fear of fullness makes them moderate eaters who must keep the

---

Some are "little things not bigger than a finger . . . usually longitudinal" (Spott and Kroeber 1942:156). Only one, insofar as we can ascertain, looked like a dentalium (Ibid.:160). A review of the available data reveals a considerable variety in color, shape, and character: one shaman's four largest pains were blue, red, yellow, and white (Kroeber 1925:65); another's pair of pains consisted of the dentalium-like one and ". . . a black *telogel* tipped red at the larger end" (Spott and Kroeber 1942:159); a shaman's pain looked like a salmon liver although when first ingested it appeared to be deer meat black with blood (Kroeber 1925:65); another vomited up something black, like a worm, also seen as "a clot of black blood [in] the form of a polliwog" (Erikson 1943:264); a Tolowa male shaman inhaled his first pain, a red obsidian arrowhead (Spott and Kroeber 1942:165n); a woman dancing to control her second pain took out a red-headed woodpecker, a replica of the first except that it was a deeper red (Ibid.:220-221). Kroeber (1925:68) reported the occurrence of specialists in the treatment of lunacy "who in the initial dream ate a snake, sucked snakes from their patients." It is not clear whether the internalized snake was regarded as a *telogetl*.

Posinsky (1956:616,624) has referred to most of these cases in one context or another (e.g., woodpeckers as wealth objects, venison, and salmon--antithetical since derived respectively from land and water) as a violation of taboo leading to "bad body contents" when eaten together. In any case, the striking discrepancy between such pains and Posinsky's arbitrary standard based on the alleged similarity to dentalia is scarcely accounted for. Instead, most of the discussion is discursive speculation: ". . . on the pre-Oedipal level, the 'pains' are visceral obstructions and parasites. Thus, the 'pains' always come in pairs, with the plurality suggesting breasts *and* dentalia . . ." (italics in original); ". . . the hallucinated oral gratification fails, both in infancy and in the wealth magic of the men; and it is only painfully realized in the wealth magic of the shamans, for dentalia and 'pains' are introjected at the same time" (Ibid.:616,629). However thought-provoking, these statements provide little, if any, support for the postulation of an inverse similarity between shell money and pains.

alimentary passage open . . ." (Ibid.:603-604).

Like Roheim, Posinsky (1956:599) sees Yurok culture as "patently anal," the people as "characteristically anal" (Posinsky 1957:5), and "the numerous avoidances and the heavy ritualization of daily life [as] akin to a compulsion neurosis" (Posinsky 1956:615; see also Posinsky 1957:18). Both Roheim (1950:287-288) and Posinsky (1957:15n) take strong exception to Erikson's (1943:274,283-284) position of cultural relativism and his view of the Yurok as well-adjusted and healthy.

While we do not subscribe to any of these psychoanalytic schemata in toto and will set forth some conceptualizations of our own shortly, we do feel that there is some validity, and we find support, for certain specifics within these theoretical strategies. From a consideration of the myths and tales of Northwest California it is readily apparent that, in psychosexual terms, the peoples of this area can, indeed, be characterized as having a number of pregenital features. Orality and anality are certainly foci of interest, and the indications of phallic concern are also clearly evident. However, beyond question the emphasis upon orality predominates.[43] For example, many of Erikson's previously-mentioned morality tales might just as well be called orality tales! Buzzard could not wait for the acorn soup to cool so that he could eat but plunged his whole head in; for this reason he is bald and must always wait for food that is not only cold but so old it stinks. Wolf sings: "I will eat the bones, too. I will eat the bones, too, whenever I kill the deer," reminding Yurok children to finish everything in their eating baskets. Blue Jay always stole and ate the acorn soup Deer was sending to Panther. When Panther finally had an opportunity to taste it, he always ate it all himself. Jealous Blue Jay learned the secret ingredient in Deer's soup and cracked open her own leg bone hoping, without success, to obtain marrow as Deer had done. Crow, wanting to be the prettiest of all birds (like a woodpecker), flew blindfolded and then found himself perched on a smokehole, and blackened. Thereafter he lived on excrement (coprophagy--orality fused with anality). Because she could not resist taking things, Mouse was banished from a land across the sea where she had introduced the Brush Dance. Unlike her well-behaved sister, Frog, who married and had a family, she was not liked by boys because of her uncontrollable "hunger for possessions" (orality combined with anal retentiveness, especially if Mouse refers to a California pack rat or wood rat).

---

[43]Dundes (1976:xxxv) in his commentary on Yurok mythology addresses himself to, among other topics, the question of anality, even suggesting examples of possible latent anal symbols (squeezing pebbles, or perhaps dentalia, from a live trout's belly; the "evacuation" sequence in which 'pains' are stolen and the only escape route from the sweathouse is through the exit hole; the connections among cleanliness, garbage [refuse, uncleanliness], and [dentalium] money). That he fails to take any notice whatsoever of the orality which is so manifestly evident in the corpus of literature under review is remarkable and attests to the singular tenacity of the anal-erotic hypothesis.

In rare instances there is a purely anal image in the native literature as when a Hupa creator-god defecates and his feces become the Yurok; at a later point, he wishes he had a dog for a companion and then proceeds to create one out of his own excrement (Goddard 1904:129,131). In the one other case of this type that has come to our attention Black Bear slipped down a steep rock slope along the Klamath and hit the bottom so hard that her excrement flew about. "One can see it now on the rocks" (Kroeber 1976:226).

In general, however, anal references appear only in the context of oral indulgence. Erikson (1943:286), in order to illustrate the tube configuration with emphasis upon unrestrained oral intake, cites the example of an always-hungry bear who sends his wife, the blue jay, for food. When she returns with but one acorn, he complains and she angrily throws it in the fire which causes it to explode, spreading acorn all around. The bear stuffs himself, becomes impacted,[44] and is finally relieved when Hummingbird whirrs through him from mouth to rectum which is "why the bear has such a big anus and can't hold his feces." In a variation recorded by Kroeber (1976:226-227), Duck Hawk's two wives, old woman Grizzly Bear and old woman Black Bear who accompany him on a war party to cook, swell from glutting themselves on acorn meal and are treated by Hummingbird in the same manner after she performs her doctoring dance.[45] In a Chilula legend a humanoid grizzly bear monster enters a dwelling, greedily consumes all the meat and even the untanned hides and is compelled to leave by the smokehole since his stomach is so big that he cannot get through the door. The house is nearly filled with his filth which then has to be taken out by the basketfull (Goddard 1914:352). In a simple Chilula animal fable (which certainly could not qualify as a morality tale) Skunk is able to take for himself all the baskets of edible wild bulbs, dug by a group of girls, through the tactic of expelling flatus in their midst, thus driving them all away (Ibid.:367). Coyote's grandmother, angry because he never brought food home, cooked for herself and ate only when he was away. Once while stone-boiling acorn soup, she heard him coming and quickly sat on the cooking basket, covering it with her dress. When he said that it sounded as if acorns were cooking, she dismissed this. Finally Coyote demanded, "What is the

---

[44]In Roheim's (1950:272) interpretation of this fable, he transposes wife into mother to show the relationship between the orally-frustrating mother (blue jay) and the anally-retentive child (bear) who imitates the maternal withholding since he dare not rebel openly.

[45]This same technique is employed, not for curing but for killing, in another tale. Pelicans, defiant and angry because of having been refused permission to fish by Duck Hawk who is grieving over the death of his children, plan to swallow him with their big mouths if he should attack. Duck Hawk, seeing their open bills, flies straight through each of them, killing them all (Kroeber 1976:224). The potential for a procedure, artifact, or other cultural or natural phenomenon to be employed either for good or for evil as exemplified here appears to be a basic duality in the native world view of Northwest California.

noise down there? What have you under your buttocks?" She replied, "I am just flatulating." Thereupon he pushed her aside and ran off with the basket of soup which he ate (Kroeber 1976:299).

Viewed from a psychoanalytic perspective, it can be seen that, in sharp contrast to the strongly reinforced cultural edicts for one to be clean, orderly, restrained, moderate, and temperate, the native oral traditions provide for the vicarious ego-alien gratification of forbidden contrary impulses such as gluttony, greed, filth, and untrammeled self-indulgence. Themes of orality with respect to excessive eating and drinking are evident in the story of the aforementioned Hupa creator god who by magic and cunning arranges to be left alone in a maiden's house so that he can devour "all the food of every kind," then seeks water for his enormous thirst, and finally finding a lake, drinks such a quantity that he cannot get off his back until Buzzard pecks his belly open (Goddard 1904:129-130). In the Chilula equivalent, the god becomes exceedingly thirsty after lying with a woman, finds a pond into which he falls, drinks up the contents including a floating log, and thinks that he is dead until pecked open by Raven the next morning (Goddard 1914:361). In Yurok and Karok stories with a similar motif, the protagonist is Coyote who, attempting to quench a desperate thirst (brought on by consuming something in violation of taboo), repeatedly chases elusive sources of water until, at last, he reaches a river or lake and while drinking slips in, drowns, and floats down to the ocean (Harrington 1930:141,146; Kroeber 1976:267,324).

Certain natural phenomena are explained by events that are oral in character. For instance, poisonous creatures such as rattlesnakes, ants, wasps, and yellow jackets obtained their stings by opening their mouths to receive chips and sparks of flaming flint that fell as a Yurok god made arrow points from the tenth and largest fiery arrowhead which he had tricked away from an evil one who had always killed out of jealousy whenever a man came near his wives (Kroeber 1976:277-278,320; see also pp. 215-216). The Hupa account for lunar eclipses (and phases of the moon?) with this story. The one who always travels at night and has ten wives in the east and ten wives in the west kills ten deer and then ten more and carries them to his place in the sky where his pets--(mountain) lions and rattlesnakes--hungrily devour them. Not satisfied, they jump on Moon and eat him, too. One wife, Frog, clubs them away but only blood remains. "He goes down in the west, nothing but blood. There his wives brush together the blood and he recovers" (Goddard 1904:196). The Yurok variant is embodied in a formula for healing wounds. Moon was attacked by animals as he traveled. "When they hurt him, the moonlight became dark. When they killed him, he was cut up: only his blood could be seen. . . . Those who killed him ate his flesh, his bones, everything." One of his two wives, Grizzly Bear, fought off the assailants, and the other, Frog, restored Moon to life with swordfern, madrone leaf, and efficacious ritual (Kroeber 1976:246-249).

As has been noted previously, supernatural pets rather frequently are the subject of myth and legend in Northwest California. Typically, thought not invariably, they grow to have voracious appetites, particularly so in the case of water monsters whose habit it is to lie atop the living house and by night to reach a long neck down through the smokehole, devouring most of the hanging meat. The 'luck' they bring enables their masters to kill large quantities of game (e.g., Kroeber 1976:165,410). Although pets never turn on their owners (with the exception of those in the Hupa moon myth), they tend to bring hardship and deprivation to the family both because of their enormous food intake and because of the obsessional, well-nigh consuming affectional ties that develop between a man and his pet. Parents, wives, and children may be decathected and neglected, with illness or even death a possible consequence; or the monster or other pet may depart in jealousy, humiliation, or out of regard for the welfare of the family (Spott and Kroeber 1942:235-237; Kroeber 1976:409,469-471).

From an analytic standpoint the pet phenomenon seems to us to have a number of psychodynamic connotations. The craving for oral supplies and the associated gratification can be viewed symbolically as reflecting a deep, perhaps insatiable, emotional hunger. The closeness and sometimes the inseparability of man and monster (or other pet) is indicative of the underlying loneliness which finds expression in many other ways in the Yurok mythology. For example, a young culture hero says to himself, ". . . I am always lonely. . . . I should like to have someone to talk to me always" (Kroeber 1976:19); another thinks, "Well, I had better take him [Coyote] along today. I am always lonely when I go there alone" (Ibid.:74); a deity, deserted by the other immortals, cries out to the earth, ". . . Pity me. I can find no one in the world" (Ibid.:311).

The serpentine water monster when considered as a phallic symbol suggests a narcissistic over-investment in one's self which no doubt stands for the whole as well as for the part; that is, the man as well as his manliness (phallus). Latent homosexual implications are, we feel, entirely consistent with our view of the pet as an alter ego, albeit desexualized. Allying oneself with a water monster, wood spirit, Thunder, rattlesnake, etc., may be viewed as somewhat akin to an identification with the aggressor in which the attributes and qualities of the otherwise potentially dangerous adversary are assumed or assimilated, and hence controlled or redirected. In a similar vein, outwitting or outlasting a marvelous supernatural creature, as in the tales of Sky Condor, may represent a means by which its inordinate powers (perhaps symbolic externalizations of pressing inner forces) may be tamed and harnessed.

Posinsky (1956:612) interprets an invincible, ascetic Yurok god as a personified superego and his repeated destruction of monster after monster as the struggle with his own instincts. This strikes us as being a reasonable hypothesis. However, Posinsky goes on to say, ". . . It becomes clear why he [the god] instituted (and/or drove women from) the sweat house" (Ibid.). Presumably, then, the instincts in question were sexual in nature. The fact is that these water monsters (ten of them in one version), "beings who had [always] sucked people in" whenever they attempted to cross the mouth of the Klamath, were finally obliterated, ironically, by their very own aggressive orality when they devoured the boat full of fire and hot stones paddled by the god who leaped to safety from the middle of the river. "The fire which they had swallowed with his boat had burned them [to death]" (Kroeber 1976:97; cf. pp. 212-213,273-274). Hence it seems that the dangerous, unacceptable impulses which are repressed and then projected on to monsters are chiefly oral incorporative or oral aggressive in character. Note also the similarity of imagery in the following: a man from Weitspus on a quest for strength and bravery subjected himself to the ordeals imposed by lake spirits (Thunders) who, among other means for toughening and testing his mettle, crammed a handful of red-hot stones down his throat (Ibid.:301); the pre-mortals before leaving the Yurok world attempted, though unsuccessfully, to do away with Adulterer, Hired Murderer, (evil) Salmon Wizard, and Uma'a (Indian devil or sorcerer) by shoving rocks down their throats (Ibid.:292-293); a monster in human form who went from village to village eating everyone and everything in his path was killed at last when a god, disguised as a kindred monster with wooden sticks for huge teeth, invited him indoors and tricked him into joining him in swallowing fiery hot stones from the hearth on the pretext that this would make them both impervious to destruction (Ibid.: 105).

In line with the concept of the conquest of culturally and personally unacceptable drives via the annihilation of monsters, there is one mythic tale which involves the attempted oral incorporation of such a creature, a salmon-like monster. In order to please his scheming mother-in-law, a young man at the risk of his life and with the aid of Kingfisher's medicine song, harpoons, clubs, and kills the monster. When the old woman, who had hoped that her son-in-law would be drowned in the water that always boiled up around the monster, began to cook it, the water again boiled up, filling the house and drowning her (Kroeber 1976:61,375; Spott and Kroeber 1942:238). This kind of attempted wholesale incorporation culminated, from the point of view of the law of talion, in a fitting demise for the perpetrator, probably not because the intended deed (i.e., the drowning of the man and/or the eating of the monster) represented a heinous aggression in itself but because its ulterior motive was purely selfish rather than constituting an eradication of evil for the public good as would customarily be the case in the slaying of a monster. In sum, while projection of oral aggressive impulses on to monsters who are then destroyed is a suitable means of curbing potentially destructive tendencies, their introjection or oral incorporation may be seen, metaphorically speaking, as a feeding of the monster in the self.

That the Hupa, Yurok, and, in all probability, their near neighbors did, indeed, have manifold unconscious oral incorporative and oral sadistic fantasies is abundantly clear from the manifest content of their mythology. A number of tales contain instances in which a protagonist or his adversary kills in order to gratify insatiable or gross oral cravings. However, the fact that these anti-heroes are virtually always cast as strange, evil persons or beings, as crafty or voracious animals, or even as carnivorous plants, attests to the need to distantiate intense oral strivings by rendering them ego-alien.

Coyote hoped that Owl, a clever hunter who drove deer into the river, rode across on their antlers, and killed them on the far bank, would have fresh venison. He learned from him, however, that a monster, Two-Neck, had on numerous occasions intercepted and made off with the catch. After several futile attempts Coyote finally killed the monster, and he and Owl carried the meat home to eat. Afterwards, while walking along he encountered Frog and killed her on the spot so that he could eat her dress which was made of deer fat. Coming to a house and entering, he found a group of boys who accused him of killing their mother, Frog, since her scent was still on him. When they attacked him, he pushed them repeatedly into the fire but to no avail until finally he learned from them that their hearts hung by the smokehole. Grabbing the hearts, he cast them into the fire, thus killing the boys after which he consumed the great quantity of venison stored in the house (Goddard 1904:167-168).

Owl, cunning and greedy, reappears in another story in which he feigns friendship with migrating geese in order to make them easy prey. He offers them lodging and once they are asleep, he feels for the fattest goose among those in the sweathouse and kills it. In the morning, pretending dismay, he cries, "I told you that I had enemies and that perhaps one of you would suffer [from indiscriminate revenge]." Having noticed belatedly that even fatter geese had slept in the living house, he offers to fly south with them and positions himself in the formation next to his intended victims after promising to sleep beside them when they make camp that night. Suddenly he grabs them, drops out of the flock, and flies home (Kroeber 1976:268).

A Hupa god on his travels through the world came upon a blazing fire with soap roots scattered about but no one in sight. Suddenly he felt himself pushed toward the fire but managed to jump over it. This pushing and jumping continued until he was nearly exhausted. Finally he threw the soaproots into the fire. "A-lo-lo-lo," he heard them cry. When he learned that they were accustomed to eating human beings, he said to them, "Become food. . . . There must not be those who eat people" (Goddard 1904:129). This brief segment taken from a lengthy narrative reveals the tip of the iceberg, so to speak, viz the frequent recurrence of cannibalism as a theme in the native lore of Northwest California, and is reminiscent of a similar, though more florid, cultural emphasis for the Northwest Coast, where it was epitomized in the rituals of the Kwakiutl Cannibal Society.

A stark and grisly tale recorded by Goddard (1904:172-173) for the Hupa is neither mythic nor legendary in setting or tone but rather suggests an event that might conceivably have taken place just beyond the memory of living men. Three sisters awoke one winter morning to find their aged father missing and blood spattered on the snow outside the door. The oldest said that they should cease their crying, dress themselves, and go in search of their father. They followed tracks to the river and then on the other side continued to a place where a fire was still burning and blood was scattered about. They knew then that someone had stopped to rearrange his load. They went on until they saw smoke coming from a house and heard talking. "Why do you sit there, why don't you cook a piece?" The oldest sister looked in and saw only an old man sitting alone cooking a human thigh over the fire. The sisters then rushed in, stabbed him in the throat, and fought with him until he was dead. They found the bones of their father who had already been eaten and gathered them up for burial the next day. They also took with them (perhaps as a self-awarded indemnity for the atrocity committed against their father) red obsidian blades, several valuable furs, and a quantity of dentalia which they found in the house.

In a Hupa fable told in an altogether different vein, a presumption of justifiable anthropophagy may be adduced wherein the intended punishment neatly fits the crime. A younger brother who, despite previous warnings, breaks a taboo against roasting and eating the short ribs of the deer is taken away to the world above by the immortals. There they hang him in a bag over a fire and begin to roast him for his human short ribs. His older brother, Rough-nose (File-nose in a version collected by us), gathers together animal helpers and with a rope made by Spider and a trail made by Caterpillar ascends to the sky and rescues Younger Brother. Rough-nose, disguised as an old woman, substitutes Woodrat for his brother and the escape succeeds thanks to Mouse who chewed the bowstrings and nibbled holes in the canoes, to Frog who put out the fires, and to Louse who tied the hair of the gods together (Ibid.: 154-156). In our variant the informant concluded with the oral moral, "He shouldn't have eaten that piece of meat."

There are a number of texts recorded for the region in which a principal deity engaged in eradicating evil from the land uses himself as a decoy to entrap or destroy cannibals. One of the Hupa myths contains a sequence in which a series of old blind men endeavor by various devious strategies to catch a creator god in order to kill and eat him as is their custom with their victims. One, for example, attempted to snare him with a long hook; a second tried to cut him to pieces on a seemingly harmless see-saw device, actually made of sharp obsidian; another, intending to crush him in the cleft of a partly-split log, placed a basket-pot underneath in which to catch the blood. In each instance the god escapes at the last moment, and the cannibal is typically destroyed by his own contrivance and the world thus rid of cannibalism (Ibid.:127-129). The Yurok have an equivalent divinity who, when confronted by similar, sometimes identical, treacherous attempts to kill and devour him, escapes by using ingenious, often magical, tactics that foil the wicked beings, sometimes killing them, sometimes transforming them into, for example, a maggot, bird, or star (Kroeber 1976:96-105).

A place notorious for the practice of cannibalism was the village of Segwu, the center of the Karok universe, from which noxious winds blew downstream sickening the inhabitants of other villages even at a great distance. When a world-improver god arrived there, he accepted and ate the food that was offered. "They fed me with dead person's bones. Then with dead snake. And then with old women's flesh." Later he made a fire and burned a token portion of this poison food, thereby ending the scourge. One by one the cannibal people disappeared, taking their houses with them underground, until finally there remained only an old and lonely head man whose heart was magically replaced by the god with a (sacred?) white oak gall. Thus Segwu was purified and as good people repopulated the town, they had four important dances left to them by the god (Ibid.:155-161). In a Chilula story a two-headed monster killed three brothers by running them to death. He and his family who lived by eating human beings also caught them in nets and had devoured so many that "the hillside below the house was white with the bones of people" (Goddard 1914:364-366). Comparable imagery also appears with some frequency in Yurok lore: "He looked about outside the town and thought, 'Many bones are lying here.' He knew they were people's bones" (Kroeber 1976:102); "He also saw many human bones lying about" (Ibid.: 211); ". . . The ground looked white [with human bones]" (Ibid.:225); blind cannibal women armed with sharp-pointed (human?) bones were grinding a white substance into an acorn-like flour, inferentially pulverized human bones (Ibid.:99).

At this point we may pose the question, what is the nature of the unconscious fantasies embodied in these cannibalistic stories? From a psychoanalytic frame of reference, it seems likely that they represent a highly complex admixture of projective and introjective mechanisms directed toward coping with over-valent oral sadistic and oral incorporative drives. An infantile fear of being eaten (that is, swallowed up, engulfed, overwhelmed) by others, originally by parental--especially maternal--figures upon whom intense oral cravings may have been projected, is probably condensed with an equally-powerful unconscious wish to be eaten (that is, taken in, absorbed, merged with the projected, idealized parental object) in order that all needs might be met magically, as it were, by this primitive projective identification. The cannibals, then, might stand either for the frustrated, hostilely voracious child, or the primary mothering figure perceived as devouring and predatory, or both. Thus the infantile archaic ego (person) had best be wary lest it be cruelly consumed by the 'bad' mother (cannibal). However, there is some comfort in the mythic prescience and providence of the gods (good mother/father figures) who maintain vigilence over destructive beings or forces (psychodynamically, impulses of the individual whether introjected, projected, or re-introjected).

These formulations appear to lend at least partial support to the hypotheses set forth by Roheim and Posinsky with respect to early oral trauma[46] and the infantile fantasies of attacking and devouring the

---

[46]Oral trauma here does not necessarily refer to literal maternal deprivation either in the nutritional or the emotional sense but rather to the child's experience of oral frustration over felt withholding whether or not this represents a significant distortion. It may be noted, however, that in Hupa and Yurok texts there are a number of examples of the rejection or abandonment of small children by mothers and occasionally fathers; e.g., a mother pounding acorns repeatedly pushed away her hungry baby who tried to crawl up on her until finally when she looked

mother's body as well as the talion anxiety regarding punishment in kind. 'Bad body contents' as opposed to 'good' are consistent, at least theoretically, with the poison-eating at Segwu, symbolically the ingestion of sour, tainted, or poisonous mother's milk. Rich, nourishing milk, on the other hand, may be equated at the ethnographic level with the magical heart transplant, the purification of the village, the return to traditional food, and the privilege of performing the sacred dances--in short, with an array of 'good body contents' vastly broader in scope than the symbol of the shell money espoused by Posinsky.

An auto-cannibalistic motif provides the basis for a Yurok tale in which a young man seems to have become increasingly obsessed with his quest for 'luck', constantly fasting and going for sweathouse wood. On one occasion while resting half-way up the mountain on a sacred stone seat, he decided to gash himself. As he watched the blood flow, "he liked it. . . . Then he thought, 'Let me try to eat this blood.' And then he ate it." Thereafter he ate only his own blood, thinking, "'I will do this because I shall have good luck,' for it is thus with *tsekseyil* [ceremonial use of the sacred stone seat and, by implication, ritual self-laceration]. So it was with him, this young man." When the geese were beginning to fly, he lay near the river, watching them and wishing intensely that one would throw him a woodpecker crest. "Then it was thrown there where he was lying, a woodpecker crest was thrown." After that, he ceased eating his own blood, and then he died[47] (Ibid.: 380-381).

---

around, it was gone (Goddard 1904:187-188). A mother gave birth to her second child, a boy, whom she hated and never took care of. One day "she dropped the boy, baby-basket and all, down a steep bank by the trail," after which a sister rescued and cared for him (Ibid.:193). A young woman, unable to resist warnings never to gather a double-stemmed bulb, dug one up. A boy baby emerged and calling her "mother," followed her when she ran to the house. Although in the manner of a god he grew almost immediately to manhood, he never forgave his mother because she had not wanted him and had never accepted him as a son (Kroeber 1976:293-295; see also Goddard 1904:146; Kroeber 1976:55-56). While we are wary of extrapolating from such thematic material to the actual mother-child relationship, it does provide some support for our assumption of an unconscious oral preoccupation. For a comprehensive review and appraisal of research and theory regarding developmental aspects of the early formative years with respect to attachment and separation including the work of Freud, Klein, Fairbairn, Winnicott, Erikson, Spitz, Mahler, Bowlby, etc., see Bowlby 1969, 1973.

[47]The passion for drinking one's own blood is vividly depicted in a Maidu account of the Cannibal Head. A man who has received an accidental wound first wipes away the blood, then licks it, and liking the taste, starts tearing at his flesh and eating himself until only his

169

This narrative is illuminating both because it epitomizes the culturally-sanctioned self-punitive ritual of *ki-pehpego*, carrying it, however, to grotesque proportions, and because it exemplifies another fate, so to speak, of the oral aggressive impulses. Here they are turned entirely inward against the self so that oral masochism rather than oral sadism is uppermost. Although the young man's eating (drinking) of his blood takes on the character of a sanctified act as an extension of the self-inflicted flesh-wounding, the oral gratification is only thinly masked. Speculatively, this might be seen in psychoanalytic terms as the regressive withdrawal from and denial of dependency upon others for need satisfaction with the important exception of the supernaturals who control the power to dispense good fortune: i.e., narcissistic 'oral' supplies including love, security, and self-esteem. Meanwhile, the young man's blood has become isomorphic with the properties of mother's milk—instantly available, warm, nutritive, and wholly sufficient in and of itself. As he weakens, seeming to spend more and more time in hypnogogic states, there is that poignant hope that, just once, the idealized 'other' might give him one small token of its largesse for which he has sacrificed so much of himself. Death following the granting of his fervent wish brings the ultimate union, or reunion, with the infinite symbolized by his return to mother earth.

No consideration of orality for Northwest California tribes would be complete without a closer look at the dentalium, that small univalve which has been of such value to Indians and of such interest to anthropologists and psychoanalysts. Whether the shell if perceived as phallic, as nipple-like or, for that matter, as suggestive of the alimentary canal, depending upon one's theoretical persuasion or personal preference, the fact (at least the mythic fact) remains that as an animal, the dentalium is unquestionably oral. Not only does it suck, drool, spit, and feed hungrily on such delicacies as the vine maple, the yellow pine, the Douglas fir, buck brush, and angelica, stripping them bare in the process as we have described in some detail earlier, but in the native tradition it is actually a predator.

From the mythology of the region we have pieced together the links of a quasi-ecological food chain, so to speak, in which the gods

---

head and shoulders remain. The head rolls and bounces about, killing and eating people and terrorizing the countryside (Gifford and Block 1930: 198). In a Yana version a man (actually a personified wildcat) dismembers himself piece by piece until only a skull is left. It sees its new baby, abandoned by the terrified wife, swallows it up, and rolls around killing as it goes (Ibid.:198-200). The Shasta have a similar tale in which a cannibalistic human head, unearthed by girls digging bulbs, menaces children and is finally killed by Coyote who pronounces that "when they are dead they shall be dead forever. Heads shall not follow people" (Ibid.:201-203). In his Yurok collection Kroeber (1976:123) did record one scant reference to a deadly rolling head along the Klamath but lamented that his narrator had failed to develop this theme, widespread among North American Indians, more fully.

feed on dentalia[48] (dentalium soup, money's meat--Goddard 1904:148,212), and dentalia, in turn, feed on people! (Kroeber 1976:191). Indeed, human flesh seems to be the favorite food of the sacred mollusks and for this reason it is used as bait by the immortals whenever they fish for dentalia (Ibid.:225). Thus the myths tell of legendary fishing grounds where a river bank or an ocean beach is strewn with the bones of people who have been killed for their flesh. One of the major dilemmas sometimes posed for culture heroes turns on the matter of how to escape such a fate (Ibid.:191-192,255-257). The rapacious appetite of dentalia is depicted in the course of a story in which a young man on a quest for supernatural power found himself trapped inside a cavernous ocean rock. "Then he saw the water boiling up and he saw many . . . dentalia. And they fastened on his body. . . ." When finally rescued "he had no flesh left on him, only bones; those dentalia had eaten his flesh off." Following a recovery in which deer marrow was employed as an unguent to restore his body, he became an important man with extraordinary and invincible luck at gambling that brought him great wealth--all because he had dared to enter that rock and "because the money had eaten his flesh" (Ibid.: 391-393).

A very different aspect of the dentalium's primal orality lies in its monumental power as encapsulated in the following two brief tales. When the one who said that it was time for the gods to leave the world heard that Dentalium did not wish to go, he asked, "What shall you be able to do? You are very small." Dentalium explained that he would remain so that the people who were coming would live well (i.e., have 'money' as a basis for social institutions and social control). "Then he began to (suck in and) swallow the sky (to show his power) and ate most of it. Then that one said, 'Stop!' So Dentalium remained . . ." (Ibid.: 438). Small Money told Thunder, who was raging about and ruining the world in grief over the death of his son, that he knew who had killed him. But Thunder would not listen. Then Small Money became angry too and "began to swallow this world [or sky?--*Wes'ona* translates 'This sky together with its flooring of landscape, constitutes "our world"'--Waterman 1920: 191, as cited by Kroeber]. He swallowed half of it. Now Thunder said, 'Stop! Let it be! [And] I will let it be.'" So Small Money stopped (Ibid.:445). This mighty flexing of the gastropodic muscle can be seen

---

[48]According to Kroeber (1925:22-23), the Yurok "speak in their traditions of the shells living at the downstream and upstream ends of the world, where strange but enviable peoples [immortals] live who suck the flesh of the univalves." (It is this reference that Posinsky [1956: 611] draws upon to support her assertion that dentalia have a breast-like aspect in addition to their phallic character.) Although Kroeber (1925:22) states that no California Indians seem to have taken dentalia alive, and that the Yurok apparently were not aware of their presence in the off-shore deep waters, dentalia were occasionally found on the beach in the wake of a heavy storm (Pilling and Pilling 1970:101). Whether the Yurok knew of their anatomical features and functions from first-hand observation or via diffused oral traditions is uncertain although we tend to favor the former possibility.

analytically as a reflection in the indigenous folklore of a subliminal wish to restore the state of infantile grandiosity and omnipotence experienced prior to what Erikson (1943:295), writing on Yurok childhood, has succinctly described as the "expulsion from oral paradise."

The dentalium, a soft, miniscule marine creature encased in a hard protective shell and lacking great significance in the natural scheme of things, has nevertheless, as we have seen, come to be of major symbolic importance in a localized pantheon of gods and a correspondingly small world of men. Its vulnerability is signified by the fact that in a fraction of a moment it can be sucked out--and snuffed out--but only, according to mythological custom, by the divinities who alone may relish these delicate morsels. That which remains, the aesthetically pleasing shell, has come to be the most highly prized of items--sought after, fought over, earned or won at no small cost, and destined to be cherished in perpetuity.

The enigma of dentalia, portrayed on the one hand as gluttonous, predacious, and omnivorous and, on the other, as magical, sacred, and treasured, may perhaps be better understood if we postulate an equation between Indian and dentalium. In fact, it may not be beyond the bounds of psychoanalytic or even ethnographic credulity to posit an unconscious identification of the former with the latter.[49] In the wholesale orality of the dentalia, we see a condensation of all the oral sadistic, oral incorporative, and grandiose fantasies which, it seems to us, characterize the unconscious strivings of the Northwest California indigenous peoples. At the same time there is also reflected a deep sense of insecurity and vulnerability. The vicissitudes of the psycho-dynamics delineated

---

[49]Cf. Erikson's (1943:278n) comment that "the more one thinks about a possible identification of the Yurok with the salmon, the more do certain comparisons become suggestive. . . . He certainly shares its 'high degree of homing' and its disinclination to 'stray from the parent stream'. Furthermore, the Yurok so far favored intercourse in summer (when the salmon spawns) that most of their babies were born in the spring (when the salmon eggs hatch)." He also noted the opposition between "strong salmon [running upstream]--no food--little sex" and "weak salmon [while spawning]--hungry (prolonged [phallic?] snout)--strong sex," wondering whether "this observation may have participated in the Yurok's decision that in order to be as strong as his prey he had better abstain from sex and have no breakfast before he should begin to build on the [Kepel] dam, or, for that matter, begin any ordinary day's fishing."

While we are somewhat skeptical regarding the origin of and rationale for these food and sex taboos, we would, in general, be favorably disposed to Erikson's postulated Yurok/salmon equation which, we feel, in no way contravenes an unconscious identification with the dentalium. In fact, it is most probable that the Indians of Northwest California identified to one degree or another with any or all of their mythic figures or personifications--e.g., gods, culture heroes, monsters, deer, woodpecker, Coyote, etc.

previously for the earliest phases of development in the young child, and
the relationship to the 'good'/'bad' mother are emphatically recapitulated
in the metaphor of the dentalia nibbling at human bait or affixing themselves to a person and sucking out the vital fluids (indeed, stripping
the flesh down to the bone). The oral attack against human beings (unconsciously, the parental body) is both savagely retaliatory and para-
doxically sustaining. In turn, to be eaten by the gods (idealized
parentified surrogates) may be at one and the same time, from a dentalium's eye-view, both a terrifying and a gratifying prospect--representing
annihilation on the one hand and a pathway to immortality on the other.

Extending our analogue one step further, the prototypic Hupa,
Yurok, or Karok, like the dentalium, could be perceived as having a
tender inner core surrounded by a hardened, narcissistically enhanced exterior or shell. This image is consistent with a number of the features
of Yurok national character as described by Kroeber (1971b:386): ". . .
an inwardly fearful people cautious and placatory," and, as previously
noted, ". . . pride often covers up their fear. . . . They are touchy to
slight, sensitive to shaming, quickly angered." Again, "they scarcely
know forgiveness; their pride is too great. If unlimited acting-out of
hostility is unfeasible, they take refuge in the negation of blotting out
an opponent's existence by complete nonintercourse within which they continue to nurse their hurt." Erikson (1943:280,283) speaks of "the re-
sistive and suspicious temperament of the Yurok as a group," and in describing a man who epitomizes our construct of the 'hard shell' of
character defenses reports that "both the pride and the restrained
cruelty expressed by this informant were extraordinary indeed. . . . He
was the only Yurok, he would repeat over and over [protesting too much?],
who never cried. Even should his wife die, he would . . . not shed one
tear." However, "institutionalized crying . . . can be provoked in
Yurok individuals as well as in groups at any time by the mention of a
beloved dead person.[50] . . . A deliberate activation of infantile crying,
it is, like all regressions, full of ambivalence . . ." (Ibid.:281).

---

[50]Compare the following from Kroeber (1976:312): "In the sunny
afternoon [a Yurok pre-mortal] is sorry for the human beings who are to
be--a sort of nostalgia in reverse, much as the Yurok think of and pity
their older kinsmen who are gone. The finer the day, the more splendid
the dance, the greater the sorrow." Kroeber also drew upon his personal
experience in describing how the Yurok dwell upon sadness and sorrow:
"More than once, when recording a song or story, I have been asked to
remember the teller when he was gone; and once was literally entreated
with tears to weep at least a little when I should hear of his death.
This last was from a rich man noted for his sharp bargaining. There is
no doubt that myths and songs contain to the Yurok an intense association
of personality and its perishing. They evince a similar emotion in weeping at the climax of certain dances; and while this is said to be for
their dead relatives who used to witness the same scene, it may be suspected that they mingle with their grief some anticipated sorrow for
their own end" (Ibid.:65).

Like Wallace (1947b), we have been struck by the wide range of personality variation among the Hupa. Nevertheless there seems to be a basic pattern common to many individuals in which a protective exterior or public image shields a sensitive, private interior. Thus the responses of one Hupa man to a psychological test measuring social maturity reflected "in an exaggerated manner the tendencies of the group as a whole to be characterologically rigid, punitively moralistic, . . . intolerant of inner feelings, absolutistic vis-à-vis good and evil, and defensively projective of unacceptable impulses." According to his adjective check list he was a fearful child, and his stories for the Thematic Apperception Test were strongly disaster-oriented. His human figure drawings captured such "central themes as passivity, victimization, deprivation, and fruitless longing for what might have been . . ." (Bushnell 1970: 792-793). Another man's test scores suggest "moodiness, brooding, and restlessness, in combination with a distrust for, or dislike of, sharing confidences and seeking help from others. In this light his tough, taciturn, stolid, and self-sufficient posture may be seen as a defense against a great deal of underlying agitation, frustration, and despair . . ." (Ibid.:795). For yet another, the personality assessment concludes: "It seems probable that his unusual degree of intellectual, artistic, and aesthetic interest and his sensitive, intuitive, mystical bent (which stand in contrast to his authoritative, hard, invulnerable public image) represent the conscious manifestations of latent facets of personality that have evolved out of his unique early experiences" (Ibid.:799).

As for the narcissistic enhancement which we have included in the dentalium shell/core simile, we have in mind the ceremonial embellishment of native life and personal experience as embodied in the possession and display of the sacred treasures of the Northwest California Indian world, and the rich store of symbolism, belief, lore, tradition and custom with which they are intertwined. In a simple but captivating Yurok myth, the shells themselves are ceremonially enhanced (although the requisite adornment and accoutrement are left to the imagination) as they perform the Boat Dance down the Klamath on their way to the ocean. They passed, two boats abreast, in a long double line with additional boats joining the procession at every village along the way. The shell dancers "did not paddle, but stood up in the boats, each holding the shoulders of the one next in front, singing and making the boat go by their dancing. . . . In front went dentalia. . . . Next were the small dentalia, . . . then the dentalium beads. . . . Behind these were the haliotis . . ." and half a dozen others including clamshells and snail shells, like those sewn on women's dresses, and so on through the smallest and poorest of them all. It was the period of the change-over from pre-human to human times, and the shell immortals who had once all dwelt upstream were going to live in the ocean, some to the north, some to the south, some near, and some far (which explains their present-day distribution). Each sang a special song and dentalium's was "Dentalium, dancing in a boat, I go far, to the north, to capsize." At Dentalium Home they tipped their boats over but they knew they would return from time to time. "That is why they will use my shells there" (Spott and Kroeber 1942:249-250).

To Kroeber this was an idyllic tale, light in tone and with a touch of humor but lacking the note of sadness and regret which typically characterizes the departure of the gods. To us, in addition, it is rich with symbolism and sentiment. The dentalia are transparently Indian, with ambivalences resolved, drives sublimated, identity secure, and status defined. The transition from the epoch of the pre-humans to that of the humans, the riverine route between land and sea, the spectacular pageantry of the departing flotilla--all convey a sense of pleasure in the present, promise for the future, and continuity with the past. The dugouts, the dances, the songs, the sacred articles--in short, the many aspects of the ceremonial complex as depicted in this myth--may be regarded as symbolic bonds (or, in psychoanalytic terms, as transitional objects--cf. Winnicott 1953; Greenacre 1970; Volkan 1976) linking men to their money, mortals to their gods, Indians to their land, dentalia to their home and, by transposition, children to their mothers, or parents. Just as that which we have called narcissistic embellishment is directed to enhancing feelings of value and self-worth, so the use of the transitional object is aimed at meeting deeply-rooted early and persisting needs for security, belonging, and attachment. The clinging to or searching for a transitional object, whether it be a security blanket or a cherished cultural symbol, is both derivative and expressive of basic oral longings.

From all that has been said with respect to the dentalium--its primitive orality, its psychodynamic equation with people, its magico-sacred properties, its function as a transitional object--there is, in our view, little doubt that the so-called acquisitiveness and hoarding of 'money' as well as of other treasure is far more oral than anal although, along with Kroeber (and, for that matter, Erikson, Roheim, and Posinsky), we do not see that they are of necessity mutually exclusive.

Recognition of a basic oral substratum in the personality gives us additional insight into the meaning of stories which have phallic or genital themes but nevertheless are essentially oral in character. For example, an episode in a Yurok origin myth concerning Arrowhead might be interpreted as having latent phallic-intrusive significance, but such symbolism is overshadowed by the manifest orality. Since war had become a permanent feature of human existence, Arrowhead was permitted to continue in the world notwithstanding his destructive power, one that he himself described in graphic oral imagery: "I eat persons. I like to catch persons. When I enter person's flesh, I live. Arrowhead, that is who I am" (Kroeber 1976:53). The origin of the sex act is interwoven with orality and incest in a brief Yurok tale. A young woman became pregnant even though she had never slept with a man. She gave birth to a son who cried endlessly and inconsolably until the mother at last said, "Maybe you want female genitalia, maybe that is what you want to eat, that is what you are crying for." Whereupon the baby stood up (symbolically became erect) and had intercourse with her. "Then he sang, 'That is the kind I like to eat, woman's genitalia.'" He was grown up now and his name was Meihkwet or Penis (Ibid.:296).

In a Yurok story with a Chilula locale indexed by Kroeber under "Incest" and which, indeed, involves a mother's attempt to have sexual relations with her daughter (thus rendering the incest homosexual in nature), the genital theme seems to us to be an obfuscation of a more basic underlying oral orientation. A mother who remained in a sleeping position all the time required her daughter to bring her mushrooms constantly since this was the only food she would eat. Now and again she would ask the daughter to turn her over and on one such occasion she directed her to straddle her. "As the girl took hold, her mother seized her and tried to cohabit with her with a penis that had grown on her,"[51] which, Kroeber noted astutely, had 'grown mushroomlike, no doubt, from her exclusive fare" (Ibid.:269). Not only is the emphasis upon eating in this story obviously oral, but more importantly, the mother has regressed to an infantile level of oral dependency forcing a role reversal on the daughter and insisting in the manner of a spoiled child that her every whim be satisfied. The attempted sexual assault reflects a characteristic oral-impulsive inability to defer gratification and it also suggests an oral aggressive demand for admiration, love, and esteem disguised as a show of phallic potency (seen clinically in the pseudogenitality of the Don Juan syndrome and well illustrated in Yurok mythology by the child-like impetuous promiscuity of Widower-across-the-Ocean).

The Yurok story of the ubiquitous vagina dentata (Ibid.:278-281) need not be retold here in detail. Suffice it to say that the castrating obsidian teeth of the murderous woman represent oral sadism cast in a genital mold. Parenthetically, Kroeber seems to have been disappointed with the performance of the ascetic god-hero, feeling that he was miscast in the role and did not measure up in terms of masculinity to others in versions found elsewhere who break out the teeth with a stone pestle. In the Yurok case the device of surreptitiously using hollow alder sticks to protect the penis during intercourse (ten times in one night in keeping with the mythico-cultural ideal), and of having the god's mother destroy the woman by telling her to straddle the smokehole so that a burst of steam would shatter the teeth and scatter them up and down the river (thus accounting for the distribution of red and black obsidian) are elements that, in our opinion, are entirely consistent with Yurok narrative tradition.

---

[51]Posinsky (1956:618,621,630) states that the shaman (who, like a man, can sleep in the sweathouse, gather sweathouse wood, smoke a pipe, and who "introjects," that is, takes in or earns the "phallic" dentalia) is the epitome of the phallic mother. Erikson (1943:269) interprets Bluejay's tearing out of her clitoris and placing it on top of her head as a manifestation of "masculine protest" of which penis envy is obviously a part. While we feel that both of these viewpoints may well have some validity, we see the central issue as one of oral rather than phallic strivings as witness the sucking, ingesting-egesting modality of the shaman; also Bluejay's overriding desire to be fed (acorn soup) and her oral envy of Panther (the man-child who is constantly fed) and of Deer (the nurturing mother-feeder).

Apropos of oral, anal, phallic, and/or genital symbolism in the native world view, Snyder (1975:154-161) in her discussion of the potlatch delineates an intriguing set of relationships that involve the equating of natural body functions and modalities with man's impure, imperfect, and profane state. Drawing upon compelling linguistic evidence she shows how the Skagit word for food and digested products, with its plural form also meaning reproductive processes and sexuality, is closely related to the word that denotes spoiled, unclean, impure—and, in addition, the conditions of menstruation and pregnancy—all in contradistinction to an opposite term encompassing the concepts of purity, perfection, and sexlessness. She develops the further thesis that since man must live by ingesting food, with eating obviously being closely associated with both oral and anal functions, and since he must reproduce himself (as is also true for his essential foodstuffs, the plants and animals), then sexual contact becomes an unavoidable and unfortunate dimension of man's condition. Nature, man, animal, and plant life, and all the life-sustaining and procreative processes are abhorrent and antithetical to the spirits, immortals, and related manifestations of the supernatural which, by contrast, are perfect, potent, and pure. Since humans must appeal to the spirit powers to provide and restore abundant supplies of that which is repugnant to and incompatible with the higher order of things, they seek to appease and cajole by striving for that which is the opposite of what they are asking, that is, by purification through fasting, sexual abstinence, and the avoidance of unclean persons or states. Once the ambivalent wishes have been granted, it is incumbent upon men and women to disavow all that which would suggest greed, gluttony, or excess, hence the ritual giving away of food as proof of their ability to withstand temptation and to rise above impure nature.

Snyder points to parallels between the Skagit view of man, nature, and the universe, and the world view of the Yurok as described by Erikson. Emptying of the alimentary canal, purification where defilement has occurred, and a need to control orifices through the practices of restraint and self-denial characteristic for Northwest California are, she feels, consistent with similar concerns for Puget Sound (Ibid.:159-160).

While we find her postulates illuminating and possessed of considerable explanatory power, we feel that they do not sufficiently account for the oral-anal-phallic preoccupations of the Hupa, Yurok, Karok, *et al.* as reflected in the native lore. Furthermore, the supernatural figures associated with these tribes have been created in a very human image, as we have seen, possessing, it is true, greater potency than mortal man but being far from fully omnipotent as, for example, when the Hupa Creator-God, despite repeated attempts, failed to secure everlasting life for the Indians who were about to come into being (Goddard 1904:132,224; see also Kroeber 1976:330-331). Like mortals, these pre-mortals experienced pangs of hunger and thirst, glutted themselves, were tempted from their path or purpose by seductive women, could be competitive, hostile, and aggressive, engaged in trickery and deceit, grieved over their losses, wept in self-pity, and had to prove their own power and worthiness by ordeal, self-laceration, and ritual purification.

It appears then that in contrast to the Skagit, both the earthly Indian world of the tribes of Northwest California and the deified supernatural realm pertaining to it were characterized by dichotomies of purity and impurity, sanctity and defilement, virtue and villainy, restraint and excess, good and bad 'luck'.

## CONCLUSION

In our consideration of the symbolic significance of wealth and of work among the Hupa, Yurok, Karok, and adjacent northern California tribes of virtually identical cultural configuration; cognitive orientation; and, from what we can ascertain, character traits, we have returned repeatedly to the theme of the quest for spiritual power and sacred purpose, motifs which, not surprisingly, ramify beyond the various aspects of the wealth complex and the somewhat ineptly dubbed 'work ethic'. To perceive the valuation placed on dentalia as primarily a thirst for riches, power, status, and personal advantage, or to view the investment of time, energy, and care lavished on the acquisition, preparation, and display of the artifacts and articles fashioned of rare obsidian, feathers, furs, and skins, or to see the unflagging dedication to the gathering of special firewood for the sweathouse, or the zeal manifested in the performance of other ritual duties as evidence of an overall passion for work or a compulsion to labor productively as a moral end is, we are convinced, to miss the very essence of the ethos and eidos of this cultural efflorescence. It is also to overlook, or at least to give insufficient recognition to, the many obvious parallels to the tribes of the Northwest Coast proper. Indeed, we feel that the phenomena we have discussed are entirely consistent with and intrinsic to the essential religiosity of North American Indians generally rather than a unique, localized, aberrant development.

Once having, we believe, restored what we may somewhat whimsically call treasure and travail to their rightful and culturally-congruent positions in the native California Weltanschaaung, we then asked whether there might be some deeper meaning or rationale inherent in the sacred quest--some psychological symbolism perhaps, and we turned to the derivative signification of the mythology, the formulas, and the deeply-ingrained traditional belief system for at least an approximation to an answer. Through the medium of what we hope has been judicious psychoanalytic interpretation, we have reconstructed inferentially a life-long, personal quest for significance, security, and belonging with unconscious roots in early, predominantly oral, infantile experience. The infant's-eye-view of the world that we have sketched does not refer to a clinical concept of developmental arrest, to a pre-genital fixation of pathological proportions, or to a primitive ego structure but, rather, it suggests that period in the lives of all of us when, in order to receive the love and bounty of our mothers, we wailed and raged, even banged our heads self-punitively, until, if we persisted in our rituals, we magically brought her and breast or bottle back to us and so were sated and secure again for a time. The more insecure our earliest world was, or if our nurturing and mothering were less than optimal--and whose, we sometimes wonder, was not?--the more we were likely to believe in and to practice our magical supplications or later to seek solace in our lonely vigils. And when as adults we are at times overtaken by feelings of anxiety, frustration, or existential despair, we may take some transitory comfort in regression to archaic patterns or in clinging to our personal or tribal transitional objects--the amulets and talismans, the sacrosanct relics and cherished memories which bind us to our heritage, renew our hope, and validate our identity once more.

    The Hupa, Yurok, and Karok lived in a world characterized by imminent and potential disaster, not to mention the inevitability of decline and death, the fate of those mortals who dwelt in 'the center of the world'. Understandably they cast their lot with the gods and demigods who exercised control, albeit capriciously and less than perfectly at times, over them and their domain. In a universe where pestilence might spread like a cloud, where the land can tilt and slip, where the valleys and mountains may quake, where floods have been known to wash over the earth, and where, indeed, by a single wrong act the world might be 'spoiled', it becomes not only a matter of prudence and wisdom but even a sacred commitment to see that the world is renewed from time to time and that the harmony and balance of man, nature, and that which is beyond nature be maintained or restored. From this perspective it is clearly incumbent upon religious leaders and families of means to sponsor and underwrite the tribal ceremonials, lending the authority, prestige, and accoutrements essential for their performance. At the same time, for those with little in the way of material wealth, it is possible to make a contribution of considerable incorporeal worth; for example, the immeasurably valuable knowledge of the formulist or the medicine woman, a sacred song inherited in the family line or personally received from a supernatural, and certainly the participation of the dancers, rich and poor alike, whose stamping feet are intended literally, as well as figuratively, to tamp the earth firmly in place.[52]

    Surely this view of the ceremonial performance is a far cry from the erroneous notion, perpetuated for the past fifty years, that the participants "were little more than manikins exhibiting the treasures" (Kroeber 1971a:468; see also Gould 1966:86) and that "the regalia are of forms strictly standardized by custom but are wholly unsymbolical and in no sense regarded as sacred" (Kroeber 1925:54). Or again, "not one of the ornaments worn or carried in either of the two ceremonies [White Deerskin and Jumping dances] appears to have the least mythological or ritualistic significance" (Ibid.:56). Gifford (Gifford and Block 1930:39) reinforced this characterization: "Although gaudy paraphernalia were worn in the two principal dances of this [renewal] cult . . . these

---

[52]An indication of the power of dancing is found in a variant of the myth of the fallen sun in which two Raccoons by singing and stamping their feet raise Sun a little at a time until he is in the sky at last and it is light once again (Kroeber 1976:477).

were not sacred and might be touched or worn by anyone. They were simply profane objects of wealth, the treasure of the wealthy men of the tribe. The really sacred thing about the renewal ceremonies was the formula or fiat murmured by the priest. . . ." Garbarino (1976:178) in her text on American Indians paraphrases Kroeber (alas!): "The dance outfits, songs, and steps were standardized by custom, and were neither symbolic nor sacred."

That the contrary is, in fact, the case should be abundantly clear by now. Not only are the esoteric prayers, offerings, and incantations of the formulist and medicine woman sacrosanct and symbolically meaningful, but so also are the many features of the esoteric, non-secret ritualistic dances, songs, costumes, and associated paraphernalia. We have repeatedly observed that the participants—cermonialists, dancers, and spectators alike—maintain a devout and reverential attitude. Wallace (1965:239) makes essentially the same point, adding that such an outlook on the part of all concerned is essential for the success of the tribal ceremonies. Although Goldschmidt and Driver (1940:121) discerned (erroneously, we believe) "no clear evidence that the actions or materials of the performance have any ritualistic associations," they also state that the dance "expresses the supernatural sentiments of the people in their most poignant form," a characterization with which we fully concur.

Finally, Posinsky (1956:612-613), in a rather incongruous admixture of largely factual ethnographic fragments and usually internally consistent psychoanalytic theorizing, writes, "The Wealth Display dances, marking an aggressive display of inherited and borrowed wealth, frequently result in brawls.[53] . . . Since the aggressive display of wealth takes place in the context of feasting, it would then seem that the exhibitionism is made possible only by the oral abundance and reassurance. In a sense, the exhibitors will not be eaten (or castrated) if they themselves eat modestly and stuff their guests with food. . . . [These festivities mark] a victory of anal and phallic aggressiveness over genital drives. . . ." However interesting, well-intentioned, and well-constructed, such interpretive forays do slight justice to the sacred nature of the world renewal cult system, and considerable violence to its integral place in the lifeway of a people. A basic psychoanalytic tenet, that of overdetermination, frequently invoked by Posinsky, has been, we feel, applied in such a manner as to narrow and distort our perception rather than to broaden and illuminate it.[54] Thus the

---

[53]While minor disputes, rivalries, and residual grudges sometimes mar the preparations for the ceremonies, the eruption of actual violence is probably rare, is highly disapproved of, and would not be permitted to impinge directly upon the rituals. However, drinking and rowdiness may occur on the periphery of any public gathering, sacred or secular, since alcoholism continues to be a chronic problem on the reservation.

[54]Wälder (1936), writing on the occasion of Freud's eightieth

postulated unconscious determinants and inferred latent meanings seem to have acquired a reductionistic verity in their own right, so to speak, rather than being more appropriately seen as but one possible dimension of a dynamic interplay among multiple vectors that include the conscious and manifest emotional, experiential, symbolic, and traditional components of these cultural phenomena.

From the myths and from the people it is clear that the ceremonials were to be performed in perpetuity. As Obsidian said to the young man who found him, "I shall endure as long as human beings dance," meaning, as Kroeber (1976:47) noted, as long as the world shall last. While today the dances tend to be held sporadically[55] and while participation is not actually mandatory, the performances are usually well attended, perhaps in part because it is believed that to be absent might bring ill luck. In any case, the ceremonials have a strong attraction and a deep emotional significance for many, perhaps most, of the contemporary Indian people. They know that the dances are loaned to them by the gods and caution their children that "He-Who-Became-Lost [the creator god] is watching behind you." And no one stands behind the line of dancers because to do so would obstruct the view of the deity (or deities) witnessing the ceremony in order to see that it is conducted properly (Bushnell 1969:320,324). Goddard (1903:83) reported that on the occasion of the White Deerskin Dance the immortals ceased their own dances in the World-beyond-the-Sky so that they might observe the performance of the mortals. Goldschmidt and Driver (1940:121) cite the

---

birthday, presented a respectful critique of the concept of overdetermination, proposing as an alternative the principle of multiple functions. Although encumbered by certain now somewhat outmoded psychoanalytic assumptions, his proposal nonetheless has the virtue of conceptualizing instinctual aims, superego demands, and other intrapsychic attributes as interrelated, conjointly functioning properties of the organism acting as a whole. His thinking clearly embraced the sociocultural level. "The principle of multiple function . . . implies the consideration of typically social phenomena . . . (adjustment to the outer world or overcoming the outer world) with allowance for instinctual gratification, collective ideals, etc." Also, ". . . man in his experience steps beyond himself and looks at himself as the object--be it in a way aggressively penalizing, tenderly cherishing, or dispassionately neutral--as, for instance, in the case of self-observation and the ability of abstracting one's self from one's own point of view. Here belongs the ability to see a garden as a garden . . . [and a ceremonial as a ceremonial!]" (Ibid.:58,61).

[55]That the dances are sometimes delayed or even omitted entirely, usually because of unreconciled disagreements, is not a recent phenomenon. Cf. Kroeber's (1976:236) description of problems besetting the 1910 Deerskin Dance at Weitspus, and Goddard's (1903:82-83) pessimistic commentary on the fate of this ceremony among the Hupa: "Until 1897 it had been held for some time biennially. It has now been discontinued and may never be celebrated again."

belief that the "spirits dance at Bald Hill during the night after the last dance and brave Indians are said to go there sometimes to watch (or rather hear) them dancing." Whether it is thought that the gods resume dancing in their own abode or in the haze that shrouds the nearby hills, the ritual return of the dance to its supernatural owners until its esoteric recall another year, marks the essential sacred conclusion of any major dance cycle. Although Kroeber's (1976:25) statement that "the great dances are at once the capstone of human life on earth and the buttress of the physical world" would obviously require some modification in order to bring it into closer correspondence with the actual present (as contrasted to the ethnographic present to which Kroeber was referring), it can, we feel, still be said that any form of respectful or reverential commitment or involvement in the ceremonies not only contributes to their sacred symbolic purpose but also renews and enhances feelings of inner strength or spiritual power for both group and individual and, perhaps most important of all, reinforces the bonds of Indian heritage and tribal identity.

# References

Bahr, Donald, Juan Gregorio, David Lopez, and Albert Alvarez
   1974    *Piman Shamanism and Staying Sickness (Kaicim Mumkidag)*. Tucson: University of Arizona Press.

Beals, Ralph L.
   1933    Ethnology of the Nisenan. *University of California Publications in American Archaeology and Ethnology*, Vol. 31, pp. 335-410. Berkeley: University of California Press.

Bean, Lowell J.
   1972    Introduction. In *Aboriginal Society in Southern California*, William D. Strong, pp. xi-xxiv. Banning: Malki Museum Press.

   1975    Power and its Application in Native California. *Journal of California Anthropology*, Vol. 2, No. 1, pp. 25-33.

Bean, Lowell J. and Thomas C. Blackburn
   1976    *Native Californians: A Theoretical Retrospective*. Ramona: Ballena Press.

Bean, Lowell J. and Thomas F. King (editors)
   1974    *ʔAntap: California Indian Political and Economic Organization*. Ramona: Ballena Press.

Benedict, Ruth
   1926    Serrano Tales. *Journal of American Folklore*, Vol. 31, pp. 1-17.

Blackburn, Thomas C.
   1975    *December's Child*. Los Angeles: University of California Press.

Bloom, L. B.
   1931    A Campaign Against the Moqui Pueblos. *New Mexico Historical Review*, Vol. 10, pp. 242-248.

Bowlby, John
   1969    *Attachment*. New York: Basic Books.

   1973    *Separation: Anxiety and Anger*. New York: Basic Books.

Brandt, Elizabeth A.
   1975    Unpublished Taos field notes.

   1976    Unpublished Taos field notes.

Bushnell, John
1968 From American Indian to Indian American: the Changing Identity of the Hupa. *American Anthropologist*, Vol. 70, pp. 1108-1116.

1969 Hupa Reaction to the Trinity River Floods: Post-hoc Recourse to Aboriginal Belief. *Anthropological Quarterly*, Vol. 42, pp. 316-324.

1970 Lives in Profile: A Longitudinal Study of Contemporary Hupa Men from Young Adulthood to the Middle Years. *Transactions of the New York Academy of Sciences*, Series II, Vol. 32, pp. 787-801.

Cappannari, Stephen C.
1947-49 Unpublished field notes.

Curtis, Natalie (editor)
1907 *The Indians' Book*. New York: Harper & Row.

Cushing, Frank
1965 *The Nation of the Willows*. Flagstaff: Northland Press.

Davis, Edward H.
1921 Early Cremation Ceremonies of the Luiseño and Diegueño Indians of Southern California. *Indian Notes and Monographs*, Vol. 7, No. 3. New York: Heye Foundation.

Devereux, George
1937 Mohave Soul Concepts. *American Anthropologist*, Vol. 39, No. 3, pp. 417-422.

1961 Mohave Ethnopsychiatry and Suicide: The Psychiatric Knowledge and the Psychic Disturbances of an Indian Tribe. *Bulletins of the Bureau of American Ethnology*, Vol. 175, pp. 1-586. Washington, D.C.

Dixon, Roland B.
1905 The Northern Maidu. *Bulletin of the American Museum of Natural History*, Vol. 17, pp. 119-346. New York.

1907 The Shasta. *Bulletin of the American Museum of Natural History*, Vol. 17, No. 5, pp. 381-498. New York.

Dozier, Edward P.
1961 Rio Grande Pueblos. In *Perspectives in American Indian Culture Change*, Edward H. Spicer (editor). Chicago: University of Chicago Press.

Driver, Harold E.
1936 Wappo Ethnography. *University of California Publications in American Archaeology and Ethnology*, Vol. 36, pp. 179-220. Berkeley: University of California Press.

Driver, Harold E.
   1937    Culture Element Distributions: VI, Southern Sierra Nevada. *Anthropological Records*, Vol. 1, pp. 53-154. Berkeley: University of California Press.

   1939    Culture Element Distribution: X, Northwest California. *Anthropological Records*, Vol. 1, No. 6, pp. 297-433. Berkeley: University of California Press.

   1969    *Indians of North America*. 2nd edition. Chicago: University of Chicago Press.

Drucker, Philip
   1937    Culture Element Distributions: V, Southern California. *Anthropological Records*, Vol. 1, pp. 1-52. Berkeley: University of California Press.

   1965    *Cultures of the North Pacific Coast*. Scranton: Chandler.

Drucker, Philip and Robert F. Heizer
   1967    *To Make My Name Good: A Reexamination of the Southern Kwakiutl Potlatch*. Berkeley: University of California Press.

Du Bois, Constance G.
   1901    Mythology of the Diegueño. *Journal of American Folklore*, Vol. 14, pp. 181-185.

   1906    Mythology of the Mission Indians. *Journal of American Folklore*, Vol. 19, pp. 52-60, 145-164.

   1908    Ceremonies and Traditions of the Diegueño Indians. *Journal of American Folklore*, Vol. 21, pp. 228-236.

Du Bois, Cora
   1935    Wintu Ethnography. *University of California Publications in American Archaeology and Ethnology*, Vol. 36, No. 1. Berkeley: University of California Press.

   1936    The Wealth Concept as an Integrative Factor in Tolowa-Tututni Culture. In *Essays in Anthropology Presented to A. L. Kroeber*, R. H. Lowie (editor), pp. 49-65. Berkeley: University of California Press.

Dumarest, Noel
   1919    Notes on Cochiti, New Mexico. *American Anthropological Association Memoirs*, Vol. VI, No. 3.

Dundes, Alan
   1976    Folkloristic Commentary. In *Yurok Myths*, A. L. Kroeber, pp. xxxi-xxxvi. Berkeley: University of California Press.

Erikson, Erik H.
   1943    Observations on the Yurok: Childhood and World Image. *University of California Publications in American Archaeology and Ethnology*, Vol. 35, No. 10. Berkeley: University of California Press.

Forde, Daryll
   1931    Ethnography of the Yuma Indians. *University of California Publications in American Archaeology and Ethnology*, Vol. 28. Berkeley: University of California Press.

Foster, George M.
   1944    A Summary of Yuki Culture. *Anthropological Records*, Vol. 5, pp. 155-244. Berkeley: University of California Press.

Garbarino, Merwyn S.
   1976    *Native American Heritage*. Boston: Little, Brown.

Garth, Thomas R.
   1953    Atsugewi Ethnography. *Anthropological Records*, Vol. 14, pp. 129-212. Berkeley: University of California Press.

Gayton, Anna H.
   1935    The Orpheus Myth in North America. *Journal of American Folklore*, Vol. 48, pp. 263-293.

   1948    Yokuts and Western Mono Ethnography. *Anthropological Records*, Vol. 10, Nos. 1 and 2, pp. 1-290. Berkeley: University of California Press.

Gayton, Anna H. and Stanley S. Newman
   1940    Yokuts and Western Mono Myths. *Anthropological Records*, Vol. 5, No. 1, pp. 1-109. Berkeley: University of California Press.

Gifford, Edward W.
   1931    The Kamia of Imperial Valley. *Bulletins of the Bureau of American Ethnology*, Vol. 97, pp. 1-94. Washington, D.C.

   1933    Northeastern and Western Yavapai Myths. *Journal of American Folklore*, Vol. 46, pp. 347-415.

   1934    The Southeastern Yavapai. *University of California Publications in American Archaeology and Ethnology*, Vol. 29, pp. 117-252. Berkeley: University of California Press.

   1936    The Northeastern and Western Yavapai. *University of California Publications in American Archaeology and Ethnology*, Vol. 34, pp. 247-354. Berkeley: University of California Press.

Gifford, Edward W. and Gwendoline H. Block
   1930    *Californian Indian Nights Entertainments*. Glendale: The Arthur H. Clark Co.

Gifford, Edward W. and A. L. Kroeber
   1937    Culture Element Distributions: IV, Pomo. *University of California Publications in American Archaeology and Ethnology*, Vol. 37, pp. 117-254. Berkeley: University of California Press.

Goddard, Pliny E.
   1903    Life and Culture of the Hupa. *University of California Publications in American Archaeology and Ethnology*, Vol. 1, pp. 1-88. Berkeley: University of California Press.

   1904    Hupa Texts. *University of California Publications in American Archaeology and Ethnology*, Vol. 1, No. 2. Berkeley: University of California Press.

   1914    Chilula Texts. *University of California Publications in American Archaeology and Ethnology*, Vol. 10, No. 7. Berkeley: University of California Press.

Goldschmidt, Walter R.
   1951    Ethics and the Structure of Society: an Ethnological Contribution to the Sociology of Knowledge. *American Anthropologist*, Vol. 53, pp. 506-524.

Goldschmidt, Walter R. and Harold E. Driver
   1940    The Hupa White Deerskin Dance. *University of California Publications in American Archaeology and Ethnology*, Vol. 35, No. 8. Berkeley: University of California Press.

Gould, M. K.
   1921    Two Legends of the Mohave Apache. *Journal of American Folklore*, Vol. 34, pp. 319-320.

Gould, Richard A.
   1966    The Wealth Quest among the Tolowa Indians of Northwestern California. *Proceedings of the American Philosophical Society*, Vol. 110, pp. 67-89. Philadelphia: American Philosophical Society.

   1975    Ecology and Adaptive Response among the Tolowa Indians of Northwestern California. *Journal of California Anthropology*, Vol. 2, pp. 148-170.

Greenacre, Phyllis
   1970    The Transitional Object and the Fetish: With Special Reference to the Role of Illusion. *International Journal of Psychoanalysis*, Vol. 51, pp. 447-456.

Harrington, John P.
   1930    Karuk Texts. *International Journal of American Linguistics*, Vol. 6, pp. 121-154.

Harrington, John P.
   1942     Cultural Element Distributions: XIV, Central California Coast. *Anthropological Records*, Vol. 7, No. 1. Berkeley: University of California Press.

   n.d.     Ethnographic and Linguistic Notes on File at the Smithsonian Institution, Washington, D.C., and with the Department of Linguistics, University of California, Berkeley.

Heizer, Robert F. and M. A. Whipple
   1971     *The California Indians: A Sourcebook*. 2nd edition. Berkeley: University of California Press.

Hooper, Lucile
   1920     The Cahuilla Indians. *University of California Publications in American Archaeology and Ethnology*, Vol. 16, pp. 316-380. Berkeley: University of California Press. (Reprint: 1972, Ballena Press.)

Hudson, J. W.
   1902     An Indian Myth of the San Joaquin Basin. *Journal of American Folklore*, Vol. 15, pp. 104-106.

Hultkrantz, Ake
   1953     Conceptions of the Soul among the North American Indians. *Ethnographical Museum of Sweden, Monograph Series*, No. 1. Stockholm: Ethnographical Museum of Sweden.

Klein, Melanie
   1934     *The Psychoanalysis of Children*. London: Hogarth Press.

Kroeber, Alfred L.
   1906a    Religion of the Indians of California. *University of California Publications in American Archaeology and Ethnology*, Vol. 4. Berkeley: University of California Press.

   1906b    Two Myths of the Mission Indians of California. *Journal of American Folklore*, Vol. 19, pp. 309-321.

   1907     Myths of South Central California. *University of California Publications in American Archaeology and Ethnology*, Vol. 4. Berkeley: University of California Press.

   1925     *Handbook of the Indians of California*. Washington, D.C.: Bureau of American Ethnology.

   1935     Walapai Ethnography. *Memoirs of the American Anthropological Association*, No. 42. Menasha.

   1948     *Anthropology*. New York: Harcourt, Brace.

   1953     *Handbook of the Indians of California*. Berkeley: California Book Company.

Kroeber, Alfred L.
   1963    Seven Mohave Myths. *University of California Publications in American Archaeology and Ethnology*, Vol. 11, No. 1. Berkeley: University of California Press.

   1971a   The World Renewal Cult of Northwest California. In *The California Indians*, R. F. Heizer and M. A. Whipple (editors), pp. 464-471. (Pp. 1-5 of A. L. Kroeber and E. W. Gifford, World Renewal: A Cult System of Native Northwest California. *University of California Publications in American Archaeology and Ethnology*, Vol. 13, No. 1, 1949.)

   1971b   Yurok National Character. In *The California Indians*, R. F. Heizer and M. A. Whipple (editors), pp. 385-390. (Pp. 236-240 of A. L. Kroeber, Ethnographic Interpretations, *University of California Publications in American Archaeology and Ethnology*, Vol. 47, No. 7, 1959.)

   1972    More Mohave Myths. *Anthropological Records*, Vol. 27. Berkeley: University of California Press.

   1976    *Yurok Myths*. Berkeley: University of California Press.

Kreober, Theodora
   1959    *The Inland Whale*. Bloomington: University of Indiana Press.

Loeb, Edwin M.
   1926a   The Creator Concept among the Indians of North Central California. *American Anthropologist*, Vol. 28, pp. 467-493.

   1926b   Pomo Folkways. *University of California Publications in American Archaeology and Ethnology*, Vol. 29, pp. 149-405. Berkeley: University of California Press.

   1932    The Western Kuksu Cult. *University of California Publications in American Archaeology and Ethnology*, Vol. 33, pp. 1-137. Berkeley: University of California Press.

Lowie, Robert H.
   1939    Ethnographic Notes on the Washo. *University of California Publications in American Archaeology and Ethnology*, Vol. 36, pp. 301-352. Berkeley: University of California Press.

McCown, Theodore D.
   1929    Unpublished field notes.

McFeat, Tom
   1974    *Small-Group Cultures*. New York: Pergamon Press.

Meigs, Peveril
   1939    The Kiliwa Indians of Lower California. *Ibero-Americana*, Vol. 15, pp. 1-114. Berkeley: University of California Press.

Nequatewa, E.
  1936    Truth of a Hopi. M R. F. Colton (editor). *Museum of Northern Arizona Bulletin*, No. 8. Flagstaff.

Nomland, Gladys A.
  1938    Bear River Ethnography. *Anthropological Records*, Vol. 2, pp. 91-124. Berkeley: University of California Press.

Ortiz, Alfonso
  1965    Dual Organization as an Operational Concept in the Pueblo. *Southwest Ethnology*, Vol. 4, pp. 389-396.

  1969    *The Tewa World: Space, Time, Being and Becoming in Pueblo Society*. Chicago: University of Chicago Press.

Parsons, Elsie C.
  1939    *Pueblo Indian Religion*, 2 vols. Chicago: University of Chicago Press.

  1940    Taos Tales. *American Folklore Society Memoirs*, No. 34. New York.

  1962    Isleta Paintings. Ester S. Goldfrank (editor). *Bulletins of the Bureau of American Ethnology*, No. 181. Washington, D.C.

Piddocke, Stuart
  1965    The Potlatch System of the Southern Kwakiutl: A New Perspective. *Southwestern Journal of Anthropology*, Vol. 21, pp. 244-264.

Pilling, Arnold R. and Patricia L. Pilling
  1970    Cloth, Clothes, and Bows: Nonsedentary Merchants among the Indians of Northwestern California. In *Migration and Anthropology*, R. F. Spencer (editor), pp. 97-119. Seattle: University of Washington Press.

Posinsky, S. H.
  1956    Yurok Shell Money and "Pains": A Freudian Interpretation. *The Psychiatric Quarterly*, Vol. 30, pp. 598-632.

  1957    The Problem of Yurok Anality. *American Imago*, Vol. 14, pp. 3-31.

Powers, Bob
  1971    *South Fork Country*. Los Angeles: Westernlore Press.

Powers, Stephen
  1877    Tribes of California. *Contributions to North American Ethnology*, Vol. III. Washington, D.C.: U.S. Government Printing Office.

Ray, Verne F.
   1963   *Primitive Pragmatists*. Seattle: University of Washington Press.

Roheim, Geza
   1950   *Psychoanalysis and Anthropology*. New York: International Universities Press.

Russell, Frank
   1908   The Pima Indians. *Twenty-sixth Annual Report of the Bureau of American Ethnology*. (Reissued: 1974, University of Arizona Press.)

Sapir, Edward
   1930-31 The Southern Paiute Language. *Proceedings of the American Academy of Arts and Sciences*, Vol. 65, pp. 1-730.

   n.d.   Hupa Myths, Formulae, and Ethnologic Narratives. Unpublished Ms.

Sapir, Edward and Leslie Spier
   1943   Notes on the Culture of the Yana. *Anthropological Records*, Vol. 3, No. 3, pp. 239-297.

Scholes, Frances V.
   1942   Troublous Times in New Mexico, 1659-1670. *Historical Society of New Mexico Publications in History*, Vol. 2.

Smith, M. Estellie
   1969   Governing at Taos Pueblo. *Eastern New Mexico Contributions in Anthropology*, Vol. 2, No. 1.

   1970   Notes on Ethnolinguistic Study of Governing. In *Studies in Linguistics in Honor of George L. Trager*, M. Estellie Smith (editor). The Hague: Mouton.

   1974   Tourism as a Force for Tradition and Change in an American Indian Community. Paper presented at the XLI International Congress of Americanists, Mexico City.

Smithson, Carma L. and Robert Euler
   1964   Havasupai Religion and Mythology. *University of Utah Anthropological Papers*, No. 68. Salt Lake City: Department of Anthropology, University of Utah.

Snyder, Sally
   1975   Quest for the Sacred in Northern Puget Sound: An Interpretation of Potlatch. *Ethnology*, Vol. 14, pp. 149-161.

Sparkman, Philip Stedman
   1908   The Culture of the Luiseño Indians. *University of California Publications in American Archaeology and Ethnology*, Vol. 8, pp. 197-234. Berkeley: University of California Press. (Reprint: 1972, Ballena Press.)

Spicer, Edward H.
1962    *Cycles of Conquest.* Tucson: University of Arizona Press.

Spier, Leslie
1928    Havasupai Ethnography. *American Museum of Natural History Anthropological Papers*, No. 29, pp. 83-392. New York: American Museum of Natural History.

1933    *Yuman Tribes of the Gila River.* Chicago: University of Chicago Press.

1936    Cultural Relations of the Gila River and Lower Colorado Tribes. *Yale University Publications in Anthropology*, Vol. 3.

Spott, Robert and Alfred L. Kroeber
1942    Yurok Narratives. *University of California Publications in American Archaeology and Ethnology*, Vol. 35, No. 9. Berkeley: University of California Press.

Stephen, Alexander M.
1936    Hopi Journal. *Columbia University Contributions to Anthropology*, Vol. XXIII. New York.

Steward, Julian H.
1933    Ethnography of the Owens Valley Paiute. *University of California Publications in American Archaeology and Ethnology*, Vol. 33, pp. 223-350. Berkeley: University of California Press.

1934    Two Paiute Autobiographies. *University of California Publications in American Archaeology and Ethnology*, Vol. 33, No. 5, pp. 423-438. Berkeley: University of California Press.

Strong, William D.
1929    Aboriginal Society in Southern California. *University of California Publications in American Archaeology and Ethnology*, Vol. 26, pp. 1-358. Berkeley: University of California Press. (Reprint: 1972, Malki Museum Press, Banning, California.)

Suttles, Wayne
1960    Affinal Ties, Subsistence, and Prestige among the Coast Salish. *American Anthropologist*, Vol. 62, pp. 296-305.

Trager, Felicia H. and William L. Leap
1968    Vocabulary Acculturation in Two Rio Grande Pueblos. Paper presented at the annual meeting of the American Association for the Advancement of Science, Dallas.

Underhill, Ruth
1946    *Papago Indian Religion.* New York: Columbia University Press.

Voegelin, Erminie W.
   1938    Tübatulabal Ethnography. *Anthropological Records*, Vol. 2, No. 1. Berkeley: University of California Press.

   1942    Culture Element Distribution: XX, Northeast California. *Anthropological Records*, Vol. 7, pp. 1-251. Berkeley: University of California Press.

Volkan, Vamik D.
   1976    *Primitive Internalized Object Relations*. International Universities Press.

Wälder, Robert
   1936    The Principle of Multiple Function: Observations on Over-Determination. *Psychoanalytic Quarterly*, Vol. 5, pp. 45-62.

Wallace, William J.
   1947a    Hupa Child-training--A Study in Primitive Education. *Educational Administration and Supervision*, Vol. 33, pp. 13-25.

   1947b    Personality Variation in a Primitive Society. *Journal of Personality*, Vol. 15, pp. 321-328.

   1948    Hupa Narrative Tales. *Journal of American Folklore*, Vol. 35, pp. 345-355.

   1949    Hupa Warfare. *Southwest Museum Leaflets*, No. 23. Los Angeles: Southwest Museum.

   1965    The Hupa. In *The Native Americans*, R. F. Spencer, J. D. Jennings, *et al.*, pp. 232-243. New York: Harper and Row.

Waterman, Thomas T.
   1910    The Religious Practices of the Diegueño Indians. *University of California Publications in American Archaeology and Ethnology*, Vol. 8, pp. 271-358. Berkeley: University of California Press.

   1920    Yurok Geography. *University of California Publications in American Archaeology and Ethnology*, Vol. 16, No. 5. Berkeley: University of California Press.

White, Leslie A.
   1932    The Pueblo of San Felipe. *American Anthropological Association Memoirs*, Vol. XXXVIII. Lancaster.

   1935    The Pueblo of Santo Domingo, New Mexico. *American Anthropological Association Memoirs*, Vol. XLIII. Lancaster.

   n.d.    Supplementary Data on Acoma, New Mexico. Ms.

Winnicott, D. W.
   1953    Transitional Objects and Transitional Phenomena. *International Journal of Psycho-analysis*, Vol. 34, pp. 89-97.

Zigmond, Maurice L.
   1941    *Ethnobotanical Studies among California and Great Basin Shoshoneans*. Ph.D. dissertation on file at Yale University.

   n.d.a   *Kawaiisu Dictionary*. Ms.

   n.d.b   *Kawaiisu Ethnobotany*. Ms.

Zigmond, Maurice L. and Stephen C. Cappannari
   n.d.    *Kawaiisu Mythology*. Ms.